STO

ALLEN COUNTY PUBLIC LIBRARY

ACPL ITEM

DISCARDED

S0-BWT-689

10-14-75

The U.S. Merchant Marine

John G. Kilgour

The Praeger Special Studies program—utilizing the most modern and efficient book production techniques and a selective worldwide distribution network—makes available to the academic, government, and business communities significant, timely research in U.S. and international economic, social, and political development.

The U.S. Merchant Marine
National Maritime Policy
and Industrial Relations

PRAEGER SPECIAL STUDIES IN U.S. ECONOMIC, SOCIAL, AND POLITICAL ISSUES

Praeger Publishers   New York   Washington   London

Library of Congress Cataloging in Publication Data

Kilgour, John G
   The U. S. Merchant Marine.

   (Praeger special studies in U. S. economic, social,
and political issues)
   Bibliography: p.
   Includes index.
   1. Merchant marine—United States. 2. Industrial
relations—United States—Case studies. 3. Trade-unions
—Merchant seamen—United States. I. Title.
HE745. K48   387. 5'0973   74-31506
ISBN 0-275-05930-8

PRAEGER PUBLISHERS
111 Fourth Avenue, New York, N.Y. 10003, U.S.A.

Published in the United States of America in 1975
by Praeger Publishers, Inc.

All rights reserved

© 1975 by Praeger Publishers, Inc.

Printed in the United States of America

1882996

To May

ACKNOWLEDGMENTS

Research for this study was supported in part by a fellowship and grants from the New York State School of Industrial and Labor Relations at Cornell University and by a grant from California State University, Hayward.

I am indebted to Professors George W. Brooks, Robert L. Aronson, and John G. B. Hutchins of Cornell University for their guidance and help. I acknowledge a special intellectual debt to Dr. Hutchins. The central thesis of the present study is an extension of his treatment of the subject for the period 1789-1914.

I am grateful to the numerous people in labor, industry, and government who provided valuable information and comment and to Pat Jaskot for her excellent clerical assistance.

Finally, a word of tribute to the many older seamen and waterfront characters who, over coffee and beer on twenty-five ships and in a hundred ports, gave the author the great benefit of their personal observations. A few names that come to mind are Jake Shuller, Blackie Vaughn, Sandy Zwicker, and Joe Marr.

CONTENTS

Page

ACKNOWLEDGMENTS   vii

LIST OF TABLES   xii

ABBREVIATIONS   xiv

Chapter

1   INTRODUCTION   1

         The Problem   1
         Purpose and Description of the Study   2
         Scope of the Study   3
         The International Ocean Shipping Industry   4
         The U. S. Ocean Shipping Industry   7
         Shipping Companies   11
         Industry Sectors   14
         Should the United States Have a Merchant Marine?   15
         How Should the Shipping Industry Be Maintained?   17
         Are Subsidies and Protection Justifiable?   18
         Subsidies versus Foreign Building   20
         Summary   21
         Notes   22

     PART I: NATIONAL MARITIME POLICY AND CHANGE

2   NATIONAL MARITIME POLICY, 1850-1936   27

         Technological Change in Shipping   27
         The Importance of National Maritime Policy   28
         U.S. Maritime Policy and the First Technological
             Revolution   29
         The Second Revolution in Marine Technology   32
         Summary   35
         Notes   36

3   UNITED STATES MARITIME POLICY, 1936-70   37

         Introduction   37

Chapter   Page

          The Labor-Cost Disadvantage   38
          Elements of Recent U.S. Maritime Policy   41
          Summary   49
          Notes   50

4   THE THIRD MARITIME REVOLUTION   53

          Introduction   53
          Technological Changes   55
          The Demand for Sea Transport   66
          Political and Institutional Developments in
              World Shipping   69
          Summary   73
          Notes   73

5   PERFORMANCE OF U.S. MARITIME POLICY, 1936-70   77

          Introduction   77
          The Merchant Marine Act of 1936 and the
              Liner Sector   78
          Cargo Preference and the U.S.-Flag Tramps   91
          The Cabotage Laws and the Domestic Fleet   94
          Summary   98
          Notes   99

          PART II: LABOR-MANAGEMENT RELATIONS

6   MARITIME UNION RIVALRY   103

          Introduction   103
          The Importance of Jobs   104
          Origins of Maritime Union Rivalry   105
          Consolidation   111
          Depoliticization   113
          Notes   117

7   THE EXPANDED UNION RIVALRY   119

          Expansion of the Rivalry to the Officers' Unions   119
          American Coal Shipping   121
          Co-optation of the MEBA   123
          The New Alignment and the Strike of 1961   124
          The Expanded Rivalry   126
          Maritime Strikes   129
          Summary   131
          Notes   132

Chapter   Page

   8   INTERSECTORAL RIVALRY   133

            Introduction   133
            The SIU-AMA Camp   139
            The Labor-Management Alliance in the
               Subsidized Sector   141
            The West Coast   144
            Summary   147
            Notes   149

        PART III: THE DEBATE ON NATIONAL MARITIME POLICY

   9   THE ISSUES   153

            Introduction   153
            The Maritime Advisory Committee and the
               IMTF Report   154
            The MAC Report   156
            Impact of the IMTF Report   157
            The Public Campaign   161
            The Industry Campaign   163
            Summary   164
            Notes   165

  10   THE DEBATE   167

            Introduction   167
            The New Boyd Proposals of 1967   168
            Foreign Building Reconsidered   172
            Cargo Preference   176
            Other Issues   178
            Summary   180
            Notes   181

  11   COMPROMISE AND RESOLUTION   183

            Introduction   183
            The Nixon Maritime Proposal   184
            Foreign Building   185
            Cargo Preference   189
            Reserve Funds   192
            Summary   193
            Notes   194

Chapter   Page

  12   THE U.S. MERCHANT MARINE IN THE 1970s   197

          The Merchant Marine Act of 1970   197
          Maritime Industrial Relations   203
          The Decline   204
          Evaluation   207
          Conclusion   208
          Notes   210

BIBLIOGRAPHY   215

INDEX   225

ABOUT THE AUTHOR   232

LIST OF TABLES

Table		Page
1.1	World and U.S.-Flag Merchant Fleets, 1955-71	8
1.2	Merchant Fleets of Selected Countries, 1956 and 1970	9
2.1	U.S. Participation in the Oceanborne Foreign Trade of the United States, 1921-40	34
3.1	Relative Earnings of U.S. Able-Bodied Seamen and Production Workers in Manufacturing, 1925-68	40
3.2	Capital and Special Reserve Funds of U.S. Subsidized Operators, 1955-70	44
3.3	Federal Ship Mortgage and Loan Insurance Program (Title XI), 1958-70	45
3.4	Nonmilitary Preference Cargo Carried by U.S.-Flag Ships, 1955-69	48
4.1	Merchant Fleets of World War II Belligerent Maritime Powers, 1939 and 1949	54
5.1	Containership Capacity of U.S. Subsidized Operators, 1970	79
5.2	U.S. Nonsubsidized Companies with Important Operations in the Foreign Trades, 1970	80
5.3	Full Containerships Operated by Subsidized and Nonsubsidized U.S.-Flag Companies, June 30, 1970	82
5.4	Characteristics of Full Containerships Operated by Selected Countries, June 30, 1970	83
5.5	Tonnage and Value of Commercial Cargo Carried in U.S. Oceanborne Foreign Trade, Calendar Year 1970	86
5.6	U.S. Maritime Subsidy Expenditures, 1936-70	88
5.7	Cost of CDS, 1956-70	90
5.8	Characteristics of U.S. Domestic Dry-Cargo Fleet, as of December 31, 1968	95

Table   Page

7. 1   Companies and Ships Under Contract to the
       NMU, SIU, and SUP as of June 30, 1970   125

8. 1   Experience of the U.S. Merchant Marine, 1950-70   134

8. 2   The Ship Exchange Program, 1961-70   137

8. 3   Pacific Maritime Association Companies and Ships,
       1970   146

12. 1 Operating-Differential Subsidy, 1960-71   199

12. 2 The Impact of General Agency Agreement Ships on
       the U.S. Merchant Marine, 1960-71   206

LIST OF ABBREVIATIONS

ACFN	American Committee for Flags of Necessity
ACS	American Coal Shipping
AEIL	American Export-Isbrandtsen Lines
AFL	American Federation of Labor
AFL-CIO	American Federation of Labor-Congress of Industrial Organizations
AID	Agency for International Development
AIMS	American Institute of Merchant Shipping
AMA	American Maritime Association
AMMI	American Merchant Marine Institute
AMO	Associated Maritime Officers
ARA	American Radio Association
ASOA	American Steamship Owners' Association
AUL	American Unsubsidized Lines
BME	Brotherhood of Marine Engineers
BMO	Brotherhood of Marine Officers
CASL	Committee of American Steamship Lines
CATO	Committee of American Tanker Owners
CDS	Construction-differential subsidy
CIO	Congress of (Committee for) Industrial Organizations
CMU	Canadian Maritime Union
CMX	Competitive Merchant Ship, Project
dwt	Deadweight tons
EUSC	Effective United States control
FCC	Federal Communications Commission
FIRST	Fleet in Ready Status Today (plan)
FMC	Federal Maritime Commission
GAA	General Agency Agreement
ICC	Interstate Commerce Commission
ILA	International Longshoremen's Association

ILWU	International Longshoremen's and Warehousemen's Union
IMTF	Interagency Maritime Task Force
ISU	International Seamen's Union
IWW	Industrial Workers of the World
LASH	Lighter aboard ship
LMMC	Labor-Management Maritime Committee
MAC	Maritime Advisory Committee
MARAD	Maritime Administration
MCS	Marine Cooks and Stewards
MEBA	Marine Engineers' Beneficial Association
MEC	Maritime Evaluation Committee
MFOW	Marine Firemen, Oilers, Watertenders, and Wipers
MFP	Maritime Federation of the Pacific
MFU	Marine Firemen's Union
MLRO	Maritime Labor Relations Organization
MMP	Masters, Mates, and Pilots
MSB	Maritime Subsidy Board
MSC	Maritime Service Committee
MSTS	Military Sea Transport Service
MTD	Maritime Trades Department (AFL-CIO)
MWIU	Maritime Workers' International Union
NCMB	National Committee for Maritime Bargaining
NDRF	National Defense Reserve Fleet
NIRA	National Industrial Recovery Act
NLRB	National Labor Relations Board
NMEBA	National Marine Engineers' Beneficial Association
NMU	National Maritime Union
NMU-CASL	National Maritime Union-Committee of American Steamship Lines
NUMCS	National Union of Marine Cooks and Stewards
ODS	Operating-differential subsidy

PASSA	Pacific American Steam Ship Association
PFEL	Pacific Far East Lines
PMA	Pacific Maritime Association
RDS	Reconstruction-differential subsidy
ROU	Radio Officers' Union
SCA	Shipbuilders' Council of America
SIU	Seafarers' International Union
SIU-AMA	Seafarers' International Union-American Maritime Association
SUP	Sailors' Union of the Pacific
TSC	Tanker Service Committee
UMW	United Mine Workers
USL	United States Lines
WSA	War Shipping Administration

The U.S. Merchant Marine

THE PROBLEM

The U. S. merchant marine has been generally unable to compete in international shipping and in chronic decline since the latter part of the 19th century. The only exceptions have been the years of World Wars I and II. Had it not been for direct and indirect government support and protection, the industry would have disappeared. The U. S. government has been determined to maintain a sizable U. S. presence in international shipping; but despite considerable effort and large sums of money spent in support of the industry, the result has been disappointing.

During World Wars I and II and, to a lesser extent, the Korean and Vietnam wars, the U. S. -flag fleet expanded considerably. When peace returned, the industry resumed its chronic decline— but from the height of its war-induced expansion. Thus the contractions and the problems associated with a declining industry have been especially severe.

On the eve of the passage of the Merchant Marine Act of 1970, [1] the U. S. ocean shipping industry stood at the edge of disaster. It carried only 5.6 percent of the nation's oceanborne foreign trade by volume and 20.6 percent by value. [2] There were 819 ships in the active fleet, two-thirds of which were 25 years or older and at the end of their normal economic life. [3] Only 383 of these ships were engaged in the foreign trade. Actually, 362 were employed in the overseas foreign trade, only 19 of which were tankers. [4] As will be developed in Chapter 5, even these figures exaggerate the performance of the U. S. -flag fleet. The degree to which the flag was engaged in truly competitive international shipping was negligible. To make matters worse, there was no realistic means of replacing most of this aging tonnage and a large part of the industry was about to disappear.

The failure of the U. S. merchant marine occurred despite decades of governmental effort to support and protect the industry and the

expenditure of billions of dollars in direct and indirect subsidy. Moreover, it occurred against a background of enormous expansion in
international trade, impressive growth in the fleets of other nations,
and a technological revolution that should have been to the relative
advantage of a high-wage country such as the United States.

PURPOSE AND DESCRIPTION OF THE STUDY

The purpose of this study is to explain the chronic failure of the
U. S. merchant marine. Its main theme is that the industry has been
rendered non-competitive by a misdirected national maritime policy.

U. S. maritime policy operates on two levels. The fundamental
problem is an effective requirement that its factors of production (ships
and labor) be purchased in high-cost domestic markets. * The effect
of this requirement has been to burden the industry with extremely high
equipment and operating costs and to prevent it from adopting the
latest and most efficient technology.

The resulting inability of the flag to compete required programs
of support and protection if the United States was to have a merchant
marine. As the costs associated with employing domestically built
ships and American-citizen labor increased over the years, the secondary elements of maritime policy needed to offset them also grew. The
modest level of protection and preference that had developed before
World War I was expanded somewhat during the interwar period and
was supplemented by an elaborate system of construction and operating
subsidies. During the period since World War II, the cost of the
subsidy program has grown considerably. In addition, the modest
prewar protection and preference afforded U. S.-flag ships has mushroomed into an elaborate and costly system of indirect subsidies.

The second-level elements of U. S. maritime policy may be
classified as subsidy, cargo preference, and cabotage (protected
domestic trades). The operation of these elements fractured the shipping industry into competing segments that owe their existence to
different aspects of the maritime program. At the same time, the
accidents of history have produced a system of labor-management
relations that reinforce this segmentation.

By the 1960s much of the U. S.-flag ocean shipping industry was
about to disappear. An attempt was made to correct the underlying
problems of U. S. maritime policy by the Johnson administration. By
then, however, the operation of the various programs of support and

_____

*High-cost relative to international standards. The cost of
American-built ships and seagoing labor is not out of line with comparable American industries or labor.

an institutionalized interunion rivalry had transformed the industry into two opposing camps. The proposals to alter the fundamentals of national maritime policy would have destroyed one of these groups, and it successfully fought the change. The outcome was the Merchant Marine Act of 1970.

This study is divided into three parts. Part I will first identify the origins and development of the underlying problems of the U.S. maritime policy. It will then describe the structure of secondary policy elements designed to offset the basic problems and will evaluate their effectiveness.

Part II will examine the development of industrial relations in ocean shipping. It will trace the evolution of a bitter interunion rivalry from its beginning in the 1930s between two large crew unions to its expansion to the officers' unions during the 1950s and finally to the employers during the 1960s. The main objective of the union disputants was the control of jobs by their respective hiring halls. The goal of their contract companies was ships and cargoes to fill them. They are largely the same thing viewed from different angles.

As the conflict evolved, it went from the waterfront to the courts and finally to the Congressional committee hearing room and the press. It culminated in a complex debate on national maritime policy between the two opposing camps in the 1960s that is the subject of Part III.

SCOPE OF THE STUDY

The subject of this study is the U.S.-flag commercial ocean-shipping industry. This does not include shipbuilding, longshoring, or shipping on the Great Lakes or inland waterways. It occasionally will be necessary to go beyond the limits of ocean shipping as defined. The longshore unions sometimes play an important part in shipping industry disputes. Shipbuilding is related to shipping both as a supplier of its capital equipment and through the intricacies of the politics surrounding national maritime policy. However, such excursions will be limited. Longshoring and shipbuilding are separate industries. To the extent possible, they will be treated as such.

The eventual focus of this study is the debate on national maritime policy that took place between 1965 and 1970. However, first it will be necessary to trace the development of U.S. maritime policy from its origins in the 19th century. It also will be necessary to describe the parties and their positions in the debate from its beginning in the 1930s.

In discussing recent developments in the industry, data and information for fiscal year 1970 will be used whenever possible. This is desirable for two reasons. First, the years 1965-68 saw an artificial expansion of the U.S. merchant marine due to the Vietnam conflict. Although the war continued, the number of ships and the level

3

of employment had returned to general pre-1965 levels by 1969. The industry has continued to decline since then. [5]

In addition to avoiding the distortions associated with the war-induced expansion, the year 1970 should not reflect the uncertainties caused by the debate on national maritime policy. The critical issues in the debate were resolved by 1969, and the end of fiscal 1970 occurred prior to the passage of the Merchant Marine Act of 1970. Data after 1970 reflect the impact of the new legislation and will be called upon only as an early evaluation of that law in the concluding chapter.

THE INTERNATIONAL OCEAN SHIPPING INDUSTRY

The world ocean shipping industry is fragmented, with the product or service market divided into several sectors. The most important division is between the operation of liners, tramps, and tankships. These sectors, however, may be further broken down. Liners may be either passenger ships, freighters, or a combination of passenger and freight. A tramp ship may be either a conventional freighter or a bulk carrier. And a tankship may be a proprietary tanker or an independent, depending on ownership.

The difference between a liner and a tramp is in the mode of operation rather than in the type of ship employed. A liner is operated on a more or less fixed schedule over an established trade route. It is a common carrier and stands ready to transport the public's goods at published rates. A tramp, on the other hand, is a contract carrier and is chartered for a period of time or for a number of voyages. It usually carries a full load of one or a few commodities between whatever ports and under whatever conditions are agreed upon in the contract.

A liner, or berth liner, may be either a conventional breakbulk freighter, a containership, or even a barge-carrying vessel. The only condition is that it operate on a schedule as a common carrier. A tankship may be only a tanker— or it may be a supertanker, depending on size. But a 35,000-ton supertanker of the 1950s is just a tanker in comparison with the 200,000- and 300,000-tonners of today. *

Proprietary tankships are owned and operated by the large oil companies as an integral part of their producing and refining operations. Independent tankers, in contrast, usually are owned by companies that specialize in this type of shipping. They generally charter their ships to the oil companies at competitively established rates that may fluctuate violently. [6]

---

*In recent years the terms "very large crude carrier" (VLCC) and "ultra large crude carrier" (ULCC) have been used to refer to tankships of over 100,000 and 400,000 deadweight tons, respectively. The term "supertanker" will be employed throughout this work.

These distinctions are far from absolute. Liner companies regularly bid on tramp or bulk-type cargoes, which they carry as "bottom cargo." Liner companies charter tramp ships and use them as liners when the demand for shipping is temporarily high. When demand is low, they may use their excess liner capacity as tramps rather than place it in lay-up. When the demand for tankship capacity is weak, owners may employ their vessels in the carriage of bulk grain rather than put them in lay-up. Furthermore, the distinction between proprietary and independent tankers is blurred by long-term charters that may run for 10 or 15 years.

The various markets for sea transport service are highly competitive among flags when not restricted or distorted by the actions and policies of countries seeking to promote or protect their national-flag shipping industries. Ships go anywhere in the world. After unloading a cargo in a port, a ship is naturally in position to carry cargo out of that port, regardless of its flag. In fact, an efficient international transportation system requires that all ships have access to the cargoes of other countries. When this is not the case, ships spend more time in ballast and rates are commensurately higher.

The demand for shipping service in the aggregate is derived from the demand for the numerous products transported. Thus it may be inferred that the demand for shipping service in total is quite inelastic. That is, if the general level of rates went up or down within reasonable limits, it would have little effect on the volume of goods transported.

In contrast, the demand for the transportation of a particular good between two ports may be highly elastic. This is especially so when the demand for the good itself is elastic, when an alternative supply exists, and/or when transportation costs are relatively high compared with the value of the good. An increase in the cost of transporting a commodity from one source to a given market will favor competing sources. Most important, from the point of view of this study, is the fact that the demand for the shipping service supplied by a particular flag is, in the absence of national restriction or preference, infinitely elastic. That is, the demand curve for the shipping service supplied by any country would be horizontal if it were not for market restrictions and distortions. This follows from the fact that transportation of a good between two points under specified conditions by a ship of one flag is perfectly substitutable with that of any other flag. The flag of registry adds nothing to the value of the commodity transported.

The important implication of the infinitely elastic demand curve faced by the shipping industry of an individual flag is that, in the absence of noneconomic forces, rates will be set by the low-cost flags. A country with costs higher than those of others logically should be forced out of the trade.

If pure competition prevailed in ocean transportation, all shipping would be done by those flags that could match the rates published by the lowest-cost flag. Since the factors of production may usually be obtained anywhere in the world without extra cost, national dis-economies of scale are not important. However, if the factor markets were completely free of restrictions, costs would be the same to all flags. In practice, an approximation of this condition prevails among most important shipping flags.

Ships may usually be bought anywhere in the world for documen-tation under any flag. Likewise, in the absence of nationally imposed requirements, crews may be hired and stores, insurance, repairs, and whatever else is needed to maintain a national-flag fleet may be bought where the price is best.

Costs in international shipping are inherently equal to all flags. All cost inequality between flags is fundamentally the product of national policies. It is possible for any flag, including that of the United States, to match the costs of the lowest-cost flags. All that need be done is to allow shipowners to buy their vessels from whom-ever they wish, crew them wherever they think best, and exempt the industry from all taxation and regulation. The result would be identical to that now prevailing under the flags of Liberia and Panama.

At first glance it might appear that none of the established mari-time flags have chosen this course. In fact, though, most countries allow their nationals to build or purchase ships where they can get the best price. Likewise, most countries allow the employment of foreign seamen on their national-flag ships. The fact that most European ships are manned largely by citizens of the ship's registry indicates that the cost of employing a largely Norwegian crew on a Norwegian ship is competitive with employing Greeks, despite the lower wages of the latter.

For most countries engaged in international sea transport, factor costs are similar. Ships are bought where the price and delivery date appear most favorable. Crews usually may be hired where it is con-sidered most advantageous, although there is a tendency to hire nation-al crews. Undoubtedly there are economies in employing trained and disciplined seamen that speak the same language. Even Liberian- and Panamanian-registered ships usually sail with crews from relatively high-wage European countries. Similarly, other factor costs, such as insurance, are usually incurred in the country where their costs are the lowest.

The tendency for most shipping flags to face roughly comparable cost structures is reinforced by the considerable international mobility of the factors themselves. Shipping capital moves easily across national boundries, although it moves more easily between certain countries than between others. The flow from the United States to Liberia today, and to Britain in the past, are examples. Merchant seamen are also quite mobile internationally. Again the movement is selective. It is usually from lower- to higher-wage countries or between countries with the same or similar language and customs.

THE U.S. OCEAN SHIPPING INDUSTRY

On June 30, 1970, the U.S. merchant fleet consisted of 1,780 ships of 23,280,000 deadweight tons (dwt). Of the 928 owned by the government (8,325,000 dwt), 898 (8,045,000 dwt) were in the National Defense Reserve Fleet (NDRF). The more relevant number of privately owned U.S.-flag ships stood at 852 (14,955,000 dwt).[7] The number of ships in active operation was 798, and they supplied 37,580 shipboard jobs.[8]

These figures tell little. The industry was in the midst of a major contraction. Two years earlier, on June 30, 1968, there were 1,080 active ships and 54,150 shipboard jobs.[9] Three years later, on June 1, 1973, there were only 574 active ships in the privately owned fleet and 25,514 jobs.[10]

The experience of the U.S.-flag shipping industry stands in contrast with international shipping in general. The world fleet has grown impressively throughout the post-war period. Table 1.1 shows that the stagnation of the U.S. fleet has been overwhelmed by the expansion of the world fleet. Consequently, the share of the world fleet flying the American flag has declined significantly throughout the period 1955-71.

The experience of the U.S.-flag merchant marine measured against world shipping in general is disappointing. When it is compared with certain of the more successful flags of registry, such as Japan, Russia, Norway, and Liberia, it is even more so. Table 1.2 illustrates this fact.

The relative and absolute decline of the U.S. merchant marine in the face of impressive world and individual flag growth is striking. However, it is not the only feature that distinguishes U.S.-flag shipping from world shipping in general. In fact, the American shipping industry is not really a part of international shipping in any important sense.

U.S. liner companies may receive considerable direct subsidy from the government and be subject to a number of controls and regulations not found in other business situations. Other liner companies are unsubsidized. The nonsubsidized liner companies, as well as other segments of the merchant marine, receive considerable aid from other elements of U.S. maritime policy.

International tramp shipping is highly competitive between flags, and the low-cost operator has the best chance of survival and profit. During the period under study, the U.S. flag did not participate in this carriage. The 100 or so U.S.-flag ships usually referred to as tramp ships operate in an insulated market created by the various programs of cargo preference and protection in which only U.S.-flag ships may compete. Thus, the term "tramp" has a different meaning in the American-flag context.

TABLE 1.1

World and U.S.-Flag Merchant Fleets, 1955-71

(million deadweight tons)

Year	World Fleet	U.S. Fleet Total	U.S. Fleet Privately Owned	U.S. Private Fleet as Percent of World Fleet
1955	130.0	34.7	13.6	10.5
1956	136.9	33.7	13.5	9.9
1957	147.3	33.3	13.1	8.9
1958	158.0	33.7	13.4	8.5
1959	166.0	33.3	14.0	8.5
1960	171.9	32.6	14.1	8.2
1961	177.3	31.0	14.1	8.0
1962	185.8	31.1	14.6	7.9
1963	194.3	30.5	14.6	7.5
1964	204.2	29.6	14.7	7.2
1965	217.2	28.3	14.7	6.8
1966	232.2	27.2	15.0	6.5
1967	250.4	26.1	15.1	6.0
1968	273.2	25.5	15.3	5.6
1969	283.9	25.1	15.5	5.5
1970	309.6	23.3	15.0	4.8
1971	327.0	21.3	14.4	4.4

Note: For 1955-1969 inclusive, year ends December 31. For 1970 and 1971, June 30.

Sources: U.S. Department of Commerce, Maritime Administration, "World Merchant Fleet," unpublished table and chart (211.01) dated June 30, 1969; MARAD 1970, Year of Transition, annual report of the Maritime Administration for fiscal year 1970 (Washington: U.S. Government Printing Office, 1971), Appendix II, p. 62.

TABLE 1.2

Merchant Fleets of Selected Countries, 1956 and 1970

Country		1956	1970
United States			
Total	number	3,108	1,780
	dwt	33,674	23,280
Privately owned	number	1,059	852
	dwt	13,537	14,955
Greece	number	230	1,137
	dwt	1,983	16,500
Japan	number	651	1,996
	dwt	5,443	35,327
Liberia	number	655	1,754
	dwt	10,365	56,668
Norway	number	1,145	1,164
	dwt	11,530	29,941
U.S.S.R.	number	716	1,766
	dwt	3,439	13,272

Sources: U.S. Department of Commerce, Maritime Administration, The Handbook of Merchant Shipping Statistics Through 1958 (Washington: U.S. Government Printing Office, 1959), pp. 44-45; MARAD 1970, Year of Transition, annual report of the Maritime Administration for Fiscal Year 1970 (Washington: U.S. Government Printing Office, 1971, Appendix II, pp. 62-64.

Most U.S.-flag tankers also are dependent upon protection and preference. Occasionally one is in position to pick up a true foreign-trade cargo and, when rates go high enough, a few of the larger ones enter internationally competitive trades. Essentially, however, the U.S. tanker fleet is dependent upon the cabotage laws that restrict the domestic trades to vessels of U.S. registry and construction. A curiosity is the tanker transporting grain rather than oil. However, that type of movement and that portion of the tanker fleet that it supports are more related to the cargo preference program and the bulk-tramp fleet, respectively.

No part of the U.S. merchant marine is internationally competitive in a strict sense of the term. All, including the subsidized liners, are largely or entirely supported by the government's reservation of certain trades for U.S.-flag ships. Competition for such cargo is among American-flag ships only. Although merchant shipping is usually thought of as an inherently international industry, the U.S. merchant marine is to a very large degree a domestic industry serving predominantly one customer, the federal government.

The factor market faced by the U.S. shipping industry also is different. Unlike operators in other maritime countries, those in the United States are (with a few exceptions) statutorily or effectively required to purchase their capital equipment within the United States. No other American industry is subject to this requirement and, ironically, no other industry has been as ill-served by the producers of its capital equipment. Until recently the cost of a ship built in the United States was double that of a ship built abroad. [11] The result was that few ships for foreign-trade operation were built under the American flag without subsidy. And when a subsidy is paid, it includes a host of regulations and restrictions that add to the cost of operation and lend a rigidity not suffered by foreign competitors.

Similarly, American shipowners may (with minor exceptions) employ only U.S. citizens as seamen. Few other shipping countries have such a requirement. Significantly, the wages of U.S. seamen are by far the highest in the world. The relative wage costs of an able-bodied seaman for the United States and various foreign flags, as of January 1, 1970, are shown below. The able seaman's wage is widely accepted as representative of seagoing wages in general.

Country	Cost
United States	$16,900
Norway	6,450
Japan	6,000
Italy	6,000
Greece	3,300
Hong Kong	2,400

Source: Letter to the author from Charles C. Mollard, Transportation Institute, Washington, D.C., November 24, 1971.

The wages of U.S. seamen are several times higher than those of other flags. However, this is only part of the story. The employment of U.S. seamen carries with it the requirements of U.S. labor law and policy. As will be shown, the industry is fully organized in a complex pattern of competing and often feuding unions that has resulted in an unsuccessful and costly system of industrial relations.

The important competition in international shipping takes place among flags, not companies. All companies operating under a given registry face similar cost structures. This follows from the fact that all cost inequality among countries is solely the product of their respective national maritime policies. These policies naturally apply equally to all operators of a given flag.

The convenience flags (mainly Liberia and Panama) apparently enjoy the lowest operating costs in the world, despite the general use of relatively expensive European labor. The established shipping flags of Europe face cost levels that are approximately equal to each other. There are of course differences in the cost of operating under different European flags but they are modest when compared with the convenience flags, the United States, or the developing countries.

The major advantage of Liberian or other convenience registry to European shipping capital is the virtual absence of taxation and regulation. Ship costs and labor costs are roughly equal. In fact, convenience-flag ships usually pay wages slightly higher than those prevailing in the countries in which they hire crews. Most shipping countries grant their shipowners tax concessions or other benefits in one form or another. Since many national flags do compete successfully in international carriage with the convenience flags, it may be assumed that the tax breaks and whatever other advantages are available to national-flag operation are sufficient to match the advantage of convenience registry. Other benefits of national-flag documentation include access to what is known as "establishment traffic, " an established diplomatic and consular service, and perhaps a stronger position in the capital markets of the world.

Some countries have chosen not to compete in international shipping. They have done this by subjecting their national flags to requirements and restrictions that result in higher costs than would prevail in their absence. The most glaring example of this among the more advanced countries is the United States.

SHIPPING COMPANIES

With a few exceptions, the operating companies that make up the U.S. shipping industry are small. In 1970 there were 13 liner companies receiving operating-differential subsidies (ODS) from the Maritime Administration for the operation of 247 vessels. They ranged in size from 55 to 4 ships each. There were 207 nonsubsidized liner, tramp, and tanker companies. The largest was a nonsubsidized liner company with over 40 ships; 153 other companies operated only one ship. Another 38 companies operated 2 or 3 ships each. [12]

Many nominally independent or operating companies are interrelated through common parent organizations. At the margin, ships and operating companies enter and leave the active industry with surprising ease. Ships go in and out of lay-up as the market demands. Companies that cease active ship operation may continue in legal existence indefinitely for some business or tax purpose. Unless otherwise stated, the companies referred to in this study are operating companies with ships in service on a particular date, usually June 30, 1970.

Because shipping companies vary widely in size, organization, and their relationships to other organizations, it is difficult to

11

generalize about them. At one end of the scale are the large liner companies. Some, such as United States Lines, Sea-Land Service, and Lykes Brothers, are components of larger conglomerate organizations. Others are independent and relatively closely held organizations. Compared with the rest of the industry, however, liner companies are elaborate organizations with considerable sunken investment in offices, land, piers, and equipment. This shoreside investment has expanded greatly in recent years. The introduction of containerization has required massive investment in thousands of containers and chassis and the facilities and equipment to store, handle, and keep track of them.

Liner operation has very high fixed cost relative to total cost. Most investment is in ships, which are financed by debt rather than equity. The cost of servicing ship mortgages and other debt is fixed and must be paid regardless of the level of operation. Moreover, once a liner is on berth (schedule), almost all of its costs become relatively fixed, in the sense that they will be incurred whether the ship sails "full and down" or empty. Thus a reduction in revenue due to a decrease in rates, a work stoppage, or a shortage of cargo may quickly result in a crisis to the company.

The liner companies have developed institutions and programs to deal with this problem. They have joined with foreign and other American operators to form cartellike organizations known as shipping conferences that establish and maintain fixed rates based on value-of-service criteria. The conferences also restrict entry to a trade and may allocate sailings or cargo shares among their members. Thus price competition among conference members is controlled in the short run.

It must be emphasized that liner shipping remains inherently competitive between flags. There are sometimes nonconference ships in the trade. More important, there is always a potential for entry into a trade that becomes too lucrative. Conference rate levels must be kept below the long-run total cost of nonconference companies or potential companies. In addition, the low-cost flags or companies within a conference prefer relatively low rates, at least to the extent that demand for their service is elastic. The high-cost flags resist this and press for higher rates. In such a contest the low-cost flags are the stronger party, since they can always withdraw from the conference and set their rates where they want. Of course this would start a rate war that would hurt everyone, but it would hurt the high-cost operators more.

The conferences stablize rates at a level that prevents the chaos of rate wars. Competition takes place at conference negotiations, when a new company attempts to enter a trade, and among conference members in terms of costs. The last is most relevant to this study. When U. S. -flag costs advance more rapidly than conference rates, ships are laid up and companies go out of business (or enter tramp

12

shipping). Competition between companies that receive identical prices for their product or service but face different factor cost levels is not basically different from price competition.

The rate stabilizing function of the conference is extremely important. Because of the high fixed costs of liner operation, the cost of carrying a marginal unit of cargo is close to zero. Thus there is a strong inducement to the company to cut rates on marginal shipments, providing they pay even a small part of the ship's fixed cost. Once competitive bidding begins among liner companies, it tends to get out of hand and result in marginal cost pricing or cutthroat competition. The conference system prevents this.

Interruption of service due to a work stoppage is most costly to the company when its immediate competition remains in service. To minimize this problem most American-flag liner companies have joined together in employer associations that negotiate and administer coast-wide collective bargaining agreements with the various maritime unions.

The most dependable source of cargo to U. S. -flag operators throughout the post-World War II period has been the U. S. government. To promote and protect their access to this government traffic, the liner and other ship operators have formed multicompany political or lobbying institutions that are either a part of their industrial relations organizations or separate.

At the other end of the scale from the large, usually subsidized, liner operator is the one-ship independent tramp or independent tanker company. If it operates a fully depreciated war-built ship, its costs are almost all variable, since it has few shoreside expenses. As a contract carrier the ship operates under voyage or time charter rather than on a schedule over an established trade route. Unrealistically assuming the ship free of all debt, such an operator would have prac-tically no fixed costs. Rate reductions, work stoppages, or a lack of cargo would leave it relatively unaffected, since its variable costs would be near zero during lay-up.

In practice all ships carry some debt and all companies have some fixed costs. Therefore a reduction in revenues, from whatever source, presents the company with a problem. The tramp and indepen-dent tanker companies have organized with the nonsubsidized liner companies for industrial relations and lobbying purposes.

Most of the industry lies between the large liner company, with its high fixed costs, and the one-ship tramp company. In general, fixed costs in the shipping industry are fairly high. This has led most firms to organize along multicompany lines in order to fix prices, min-imize the cost of work stoppages, and insure their access to a steady flow of government cargo.

Subsidy, cargo preference, and cabotage are political instruments. Each has produced a client sector dependent upon it for its survival. The subsidized liners are primarily dependent upon the direct subsidy program. The non-subsidized liners and tramps (including bulk carriers and tankers carrying grain) are supported mainly by the various elements of the cargo preference program. American-flag tanker operation is overwhelmingly a product of the cabotage restrictions. *

These divisions are not absolute. The grain tanker phenomenon has been mentioned, and subsidized liners carry large amounts of preference and military cargo. The nonsubsidized liners carry some internationally competitive cargo and operate extensively in the domestic trades. All sectors charter ships to the Military Sea Transport Service (MSTS)† which is an important aspect of the requirement that military shipments be carried in U. S. -flag ships.

The companies that operate in each sector have an established interest in the continuation and expansion of the relevant programs. A feature of maritime industrial relations is that the two large rival crew unions have their main source of jobs in different sectors. Thus the unions, as well as the companies, identify their interests with specific sectors and the part of national maritime policy that supports them rather than with the industry as a whole.

The political nature of the programs that support the shipping industry has resulted in a peculiar situation. The U. S. -flag shipping industry does not compete internationally to any significant degree, and the small amount that does occur is made possible by the subsidy program. There is little price (or cost) competition between American companies within each sector. There are some 20 liner companies, but only a few operate on each trade route. Proprietary tankers are owned by the large oil companies and do not compete directly. There is some market competition among tramps and independent tankers, although not as much as one would think at first glance. Many of the large number of nominally independent operating companies are interrelated by common ownership. There may be a degree of price leadership within the tramp and independent tanker sectors.

The important competition in the U. S. shipping industry is among groupings of companies (and unions) operating in a sector and owing their survival to a particular program of support. The competition is

---

*These divisions have begun to break down under the operation of the Merchant Marine Act of 1970. See Chapter 12.

†MSTS was renamed Military Sealift Command (MSC) effective August 1, 1970. It will be referred to as MSTS throughout this study.

over the privilege of operating in certain trades. Since such a privilege is the result of political decisions, the competition takes place mainly in Washington, in the form of lobbying, rather than in the market place.

The political function of the companies and unions that constitute the shipping industry is more important than their economic or market operations. Both management and labor are highly organized in an array of organizations designed primarily to influence the formation and operation of national maritime policy. The various associations are highly interrelated within each major sector of the industry. The member companies may belong to more than one association, and a union may project its views through various union or labor-management organizations. Different organizations often are represented by the same spokesman at Congressional hearings, or a person may speak on behalf of one association at one time and a different association at another.

There is, however, a basic logic to the intercompany, interunion, and labor-management organizations: they reflect the structure of the industry. The companies and unions that identify their interests with the nonsubsidized sector are associated through a number of groups. However, they seldom overlap with the organizations of labor and management that are dependent primarily upon the direct subsidy program. Two opposing positions, reflecting the interests of the subsidized and nonsubsidized dry-cargo sectors, usually can be identified on important matters.

Although they benefit primarily from the cabotage laws, the proprietary tanker operators generally have found it in their interest to side with the subsidized liner operators. The independent tanker operators, in contrast, are closely allied with the unsubsidized liners and tramps, with whom they share many common interests. With the exception of Matson Navigation Company, the important dry-cargo operators in the domestic trades also are heavily involved in the carriage of preference and military cargoes. Matson occupies a unique position in this division and usually identifies with the subsidized sector.

The importance of the cabotage restrictions is largely canceled out in terms of political interest. The main division is between the subsidized and nonsubsidized sectors, with other segments of the industry endorsing one side or the other. This division became most pronounced during the debate over national maritime policy in the 1960s. Each sector pursued a course that, if implemented, would have destroyed or greatly injured the other.

SHOULD THE UNITED STATES HAVE A MERCHANT MARINE?

The question of whether the United States should or should not engage in international shipping is generally confused with the question of whether such shipping should be supported with subsidies and other forms of aid and protection. Given the history of the industry, it is understandable that the two issues are often confused. Most people, including many within the industry, assume that the history of government involvement proves that the industry cannot stand on its own feet. This quickly leads those who are against subsidy and in favor of free competition and international specialization to conclude that the United States should leave its shipping to others.

The United States has throughout its history had the potential to engage successfully in international sea transport. The only thing, or at least the major thing, that has prevented it from doing so has been a dysfunctional national maritime policy. The major defect in that policy has been the effective requirement that American operators build their ships in domestic yards. The shipping industry has been burdened with the task of supporting the domestic ship-yards since the 19th century. U. S. operators have been effectively required to pay prohibitively high prices for their ships. Consequently, they did not build as many as they should have, when they should have. Nor did they incorporate technological advances at a pace that would have kept the industry competitive.

Chapter 4 describes the technological and institutional revolution now sweeping world shipping. If allowed to, it would operate to the relative favor of the U. S. flag, as would have earlier "maritime revolutions." This has been prevented by a continuation of the fundamental elements of an erroneous maritime policy.

The high costs faced by the U. S. -flag shipping industry lead to a second level question. Should the United States maintain a subsidized merchant marine? It is on this level that the issue is usually discussed. Shipping and shipbuilding labor and management and their friends argue in the affirmative. A few economists argue against. [13] To date the forces in favor of a U. S. shipping industry have consistently won the debate, and they will continue to do so. The question is essentially political. The most convincing argument has little effect unless it is translated into political clout. The forces in favor of supporting a U. S. -flag presence in international shipping are well-organized and united on this basic issue, if on nothing else.

It must be emphasized that the topic under discussion is the U. S. -flag merchant marine. It may be argued that this is only part of the U. S. -controlled shipping industry. Massive sums of American capital have flowed into the shipping industries of other countries in recent years, Liberia and Panama being the most visible examples.

In the context of this study, a Liberian-flag ship is a foreign-flag ship. It may or may not be owned by an American company. It may or may not be considered to be under "effective United States control." This is not to ignore the importance of U. S. capital in international shipping under other than American flags or to deny that the great majority of these ships would be available to the United States during a national emergency. However, the political realities are such that the goal of U. S. maritime policy must be assumed to be U. S.-flag ships. Everyone interested in the question who has the ability to influence the outcome agrees that the country must maintain a sizable merchant fleet documented under U. S. law and manned with American seamen. Many think the ships should be built in the United States as well.

A large part of this study deals with an intraindustry dispute over the spoils of U. S. maritime policy. The apparent disunity should not be thought to extend to the fundamental question of whether the United States should have a shipping industry. When the combined political forces of the important parties are brought to bear on that simple question, the overwhelming response is in the affirmative. A study of the national maritime policy of the United States must begin with the premise that a U. S. merchant marine is here to stay. The relevant question is how it can best be maintained.

HOW SHOULD THE SHIPPING INDUSTRY BE MAINTAINED?

The position developed throughout this study is that U. S. ship operators should be allowed to buy and build in foreign countries without penalty. This would immediately allow the industry to equate its capital equipment costs with those of its competitors under other flags. It also would encourage the employment of the latest and most efficient developments in marine technology, which would go a long way toward offsetting the higher wage costs of the United States. Even if they were not completely offset, the difference could be made up by the favorable tax treatment practiced by most other shipping countries or by some other minor form of aid. With the ship-cost and labor-cost disadvantages nullified, there is no reason why the U. S. merchant marine cannot compete internationally.

Such an approach would leave two problems. The first is the disruptive effect of introducing cheaper and more efficient foreign-built tonnage into the protected markets in which U. S.-flag ships operate. There would admittedly be a major transitional problem that cannot be ignored. However, it would be a short-lived affair of limited cost that could be coped with. It should not be allowed to stand in the way of a sensible maritime policy.

The second remaining problem would be the shipyards. Less than 20 percent of their business is in the captive market created by the effective requirement that U. S. ships be built in domestic yards. The remainder is in naval orders. [14] Again the problem is limited. The loss of the modest amount of merchant ship construction would not deprive the nation of a shipbuilding industry. And if the resulting reduction in shipbuilding capacity is considered prohibitive for national security or other reasons, it would be far better to subsidize the yards directly to the extent necessary. All recent proposals to allow foreign building have included a provision that a number of ships be built in domestic yards with subsidy.

It is patently ridiculous to support a domestic shipbuilding industry by effectively prohibiting the shipping industry from building abroad. The result has been that, in the absence of subsidy, few ships are built. The shipping industry suffers and the shipbuilding industry is no better off.

Unfortunately, the die has been cast for the immediate future in favor of domestic construction. When the issue of foreign building was seriously debated during the 1960s, a combination of the part of the shipping industry that would suffer most from a transition to foreign building and a shipyard industry afraid of losing its captive market defeated the proposal.

If foreign building is ruled out, the question of how to maintain a merchant shipping capacity boils down to subsidies and/or protection. There is little difference. It would be more accurate to say direct subsidy and/or indirect subsidy. Cargo preference and cabotage operate to subsidize parts of the merchant marine just as much as the subsidy program. The battle over cargo preference discussed in Part III really involved a question of which industry group would enjoy the bounty of the taxpayer rather than the abstract merits of direct or indirect subsidy. Nevertheless, this study will refer to that part of the industry dependent upon cargo preference and cabotage as the nonsubsidized sector. The term "subsidized sector" will be applied only to that part of the industry receiving direct construction and operating-differential subsidies under provisions of the Merchant Marine Act of 1936. [15]

ARE SUBSIDIES AND PROTECTION JUSTIFIABLE?

It has been decided that the United States will have a merchant marine. It will be required to operate only expensive or inefficient tonnage, and its consequent high ship and labor costs will be offset by some form of government support. This has been basically a political decision. It is possible to devise an array of economic or commercial arguments based on the existence of economies of scale in the industry (infant industry), that shipping produces a public good by providing established service on the trade routes essential to the United States, or that it contributes to the balance of payments as justification for government support. None is overly convincing. The most compelling justification of a government-supported merchant marine is its position as a military auxiliary. Although this can be challenged on several grounds, the experience of two World Wars and Vietnam has convinced many observers, including the present writer, of the military value of a merchant marine.

18

A second tenable justification of government support that has been overlooked may be based on the fact that the inability of the flag to compete is due to the national maritime policy. If the government so burdens a legal enterprise with additional costs, it is only reasonable that it offset those costs in some way.

Domestic industries have similar costs imposed on them by the state, such as the payment of duty on imports, immigration restrictions, and taxes. However, they are imposed equally upon all competitors and may thus be passed forward to the domestic consumer. When an industry sells its product or service in competition with the industries of other countries, this is not possible. A competitive market does not allow a producer to pass forward costs not shared by all or most of its competitors.

If an American industry is to compete internationally, it must somehow offset the additional costs associated with operating within the U.S. economy. The usual way of doing this is to employ more capital, thus offsetting high wage costs. This usually means the use of the latest, most efficient technology as well.

If capital or technological superiority is unavailable to an American industry in competition with lower-cost or more efficient foreign competitors, and it is considered necessary or desirable to maintain that industry, some form of government subvention will be required. If the market is within the country, this usually takes the form of tariff protection or quota on certain commodities.

Cargo preference and the cabotage restrictions are similar to quota protection. Foreign shipping service is generally excluded from these trades. The restricted supply maintains prices at levels high enough to keep U.S.-flag operators in business.

If a market does not lend itself to the exclusion of foreign- or third-flag competitors and it is considered necessary to maintain a national presence in that market, the only remaining solution is to subsidize the industry.

Thus, if government support is necessary for military reasons or to offset a cost disadvantage imposed by the government, the only way of doing the job for liner operation is the direct subsidy. Until 1970 that was the only area in which it has been used.* The less politically objectionable methods of cargo preference and cabotage have been employed in other sectors. Which approach is better is debatable, and will be discussed in Chapter 5.

---

*The Merchant Marine Act of 1970 calls for the payment of direct subsidies to bulk carriers (including liquid bulk carriers or tankers).

SUBSIDIES VERSUS FOREIGN BUILDING

Construction subsidies theoretically equate the cost of foreign and domestic building to the shipowner. If properly administered, they could be an adequate substitute for foreign building, provided four conditions are met. The first is that there be unlimited funding of the program. If operators cannot build the number and type of ships they need within the limits of their resources, they are at a severe disadvantage with competitors who can.

A second condition necessary for a fully successful construction-subsidy program is that operators have access to a ready market for used tonnage, regardless of age. Ideally this would mean that they could sell abroad or at home without restriction. A provision whereby the government stood ready to purchase used ships at world prices would be a workable substitute. If operators do not have this right, they are again at a competitive disadvantage with their foreign counterparts. In addition, they would be inhibited from fully employing the unlimited funding of the first condition because of an inability to rid themselves of existing investment without undue loss.

The third condition of a successful construction-subsidy program is that it apply to the whole industry. All sectors must have access to the program. If this is not allowed, the industry that results will not be in balance with the shipping needs of the country, as determined by the changing patterns of foreign trade. In addition, firms new to the industry must have access to the subsidy program. Otherwise, entry will be restricted and the new ideas and managerial talent it affords will be denied to the industry. This would place the flag at a disadvantage with other shipping countries that do not prevent entry.

Finally, shipbuilding capacity in domestic yards must be large enough or expandable enough for quick response to an increase in demand for merchant tonnage, for if American operators must wait significantly longer for delivery of a ship than their foreign competitors, they are, again, at a disadvantage.

Needless to say, none of these conditions prevails in the United States. Funding of the subsidy program has always been meager relative to the needs of the industry. Given the political institutions of the United States, a general economic philosophy that frowns on subsidies, and the rising costs of U.S.-flag operation in recent decades, this was to have been expected. Since all of these things continue, there is little likelihood in the foreseeable future of an increase in subsidy appropriations large enough to offset the effective prohibition on foreign building, let alone unlimited funding.

Given the military orientation of current U.S. maritime policy and the political importance of job-conscious seamen's unions, it is unlikely that the United States would allow its shipowners to sell used ships built with subsidy on the world market without restriction,

20

regardless of age. It also is unlikely that it would use limited funding to purchase those ships at world prices, regardless of age. This problem would be immediate only if unlimited funding was available for construction subsidies (or foreign building was allowed). Finally, shipyards do not have unlimited capacity. The current "success" of the Merchant Marine Act of 1970 has resulted in a backlog of about 90 ships, or over 6 million deadweight tons, in U.S. shipyards (1974). This means a wait of three or more years for a ship. Naturally this is a cost of considerable magnitude.

As will be seen, the subsidy program in operation from 1936 to 1970 applied only to part of the liner sector (passenger and cargo liners). As passenger transport was captured by the airlines and the oceanborne foreign commerce of the United States shifted heavily in the direction of bulk commodities throughout the period, the subsidy program became increasingly less effective. This problem was corrected in principle by the legislation of 1970.

SUMMARY

United States maritime policy has effectively kept the U.S. shipping industry from employing the most economical factors of production, a situation that has made it impossible for the industry to remain or become competitive internationally. To prevent this essential national security asset from disappearing, a number of programs have been enacted or allowed to evolve that were designed to offset the basic cost disadvantage. These programs can be classified as subsidy, cargo preference, and cabotage.

The operation of the various secondary elements of national maritime policy have divided the industry into segments that tend to group around two major camps that may be roughly identified as the subsidized and the nonsubsidized. The accidents of history have caused different crew unions and their allies to be dependent upon each sector. When an attempt was made in the 1960s to correct the underlying problems of national maritime policy, a coalition of labor and management in the sector with the most to lose from the changes, and the shipbuilding industry, were able to prevent its passage.

During the period 1965-70 the U.S. shipping industry rapidly approached disaster. Much of it was destined to disappear with the end of the Vietnam buildup. A new maritime program was urgently needed, yet the parties to the debate on national policy were intractable on the basic issues.

The eventual compromise was the Merchant Marine Act of 1970. Although it carries forward the seeds of its own failure by continuing the effective prohibition on foreign building, it is an improvement on the stalemate that had preceded it.

This work attempts to broach two usually separate fields of study: industrial relations and transportation (especially maritime economics and policy). It draws upon the literature of both. This is a necessary approach. Indeed, the subject matter demands it. Industrial relations in an industry owing its existence and structure to national policy cannot be interpreted from a collective bargaining perspective. Likewise, the debate on national maritime policy and its outcome is not fully intelligible without an understanding of the labor-management relationships that so greatly shaped them.

No attempt will be made to state concrete objectives for the national maritime policy recommended in this study. The Interagency Maritime Task Force (IMTF) report recommended a fleet of 1,000 ships of specific size and appointment in 1965. Other observers base their goals on the percentage of U.S. oceanborne foreign trade carried in U.S. ships. In this regard the word "substantial" in the Declaration of Policy of the Merchant Marine Act of 1936[16] has usually been read to mean either 30 or 50 percent. Such statements raise more questions than they answer.

NOTES

1. Public Law 91-469 (October 21, 1970), 84 Stat. 1018 (1970), 46 U.S.C.A. 1101 (1972).

2. U.S. Maritime Administration, MARAD 1970, Year of Transition, annual report of the Maritime Administration for fiscal year 1970 (Washington: U.S. Government Printing Office, 1971), Chart I, p. 12. Hereafter cited as MARAD 1970.

3. Ibid., p. 1.

4. Ibid., App. I, p. 61.

5. U.S. Department of Commerce, Maritime Administration, "Seafaring Employment, Oceangoing Commercial Ships, 1000 Gross Tons and Over," unpublished table dated Apr. 5, 1970.

6. For an excellent treatment of tanker rates, see Zenon S. Zannetos, The Theory of Oil Tankship Rates, An Economic Analysis of Tankship Operation (Cambridge, Massachusetts and London: Massachusetts Institute of Technology Press, 1966).

7. MARAD 1970, App. II, p. 62.

8. U.S. Department of Commerce, Maritime Administration, "Seafaring Employment, Oceangoing Commercial Ships, 1000 Gross Tons and Over," unpublished table dated Apr. 5, 1971.

9. Ibid.

10. U.S. Department of Commerce, Maritime Administration, "Merchant Marine Data Sheet," June 1, 1973.

11. Committee of American Steamship Lines survey, cited in Traffic World, July 7, 1962, p. 21.

12. U. S. Department of Commerce, Maritime Administration, Vessel Inventory Report, United States Flag Dry Cargo and Tanker Fleets 1000 Gross Tons and Over As of June 30, 1970, report no. Mar-560-19 (Washington: Maritime Administration, 1971).

13. See Allen R. Ferguson et al., The Economic Value of the United States Merchant Marine (Evanston, Illinois: Transportation Center, Northwestern University, 1961).

14. Leonard A. Rapping, "Overhauling the Nation's Maritime Policy," Challenge 14, no. 4 (Mar./Apr. 1966): 14, 15; U. S. Congress, Senate, Committee on Commerce, Subcommittee on Merchant Marine and Fisheries, Hearings on U. S. Maritime Policy, 90th Cong., 1st sess. (Washington: U. S. Government Printing Office, 1967), table XII, pp. 23, 28. Cited hereafter as Senate, Hearings on U. S. Maritime Policy, 1967.

15. 49 Stat. 1985 (1936), 46 U. S. C. A. 1101 (1958).

16. 49 Stat. 1985 (1936), 46 U. S. C. A. 1101 (1958).

PART

I

**NATIONAL
MARITIME POLICY
AND CHANGE**

2

TECHNOLOGICAL CHANGE IN SHIPPING

Marine technology is extremely international. Not only do ideas move freely across national boundaries, as in other industries, but the whole industrial plant, the ship itself, usually can be bought and sold in the free international market. The United States is the only major maritime country that is an exception to this rule. [1]

Shipping is highly competitive between flags of registry, more so than between companies. When the costs of operating under a particular flag change relative to other flags, they affect all shipping firms of that nation in roughly the same way. The cost differences between companies are minor compared with those between flags. And, when the costs of a flag of registry rise above the amount that can be supported by internationally determined rates, all the companies of that flag will be driven from the trade.

A flag that does not avail itself of the latest and most efficient technology (or cannot offset not doing so with low labor costs) quickly finds itself at a competitive disadvantage. This is recognized by shipowners, and new developments in marine technology spread quickly when not interfered with by institutional barriers.

When the technological base of an internationally competitive industry changes markedly, it alters the relative advantage of the competing countries, just as the relative positions of different companies would change in a domestic industry. In a free economy it is expected that a company that fails to keep pace with technological change will go out of business. The business that is surrendered by the unsuccessful firm is acquired by the more successful ones. In shipping, if a flag fails to compete effectively and is driven out of business, that country is left without a shipping industry because the surrendered business is won by the ships of other countries. In economic theory this presents no problem; it is only another step in international specialization,

which is to the advantage of everyone. In reality, however, the failure
to maintain ships under one's own flag may be a real or imagined
disaster.

THE IMPORTANCE OF NATIONAL MARITIME POLICY

The essentiality of the merchant marine to the military is an
important distinction between the shipping industry and other industries.
There are others, though. A flag's ability to compete is entirely dependent upon the policies pursued by the government. Sovereign states
are free to adopt policies and take actions to aid (or hinder) their national-flag fleets. Unlike competitors in domestic industries, the
parties in international shipping do not have "equal protection under
the law." The range of policy alternatives goes from considerable
direct and indirect support and protection through laissez-faire or in-
difference to a program that actually renders the national flag noncompetitive. The United States has historically followed the last approach.
    The national maritime policy of the United States has for over
100 years prevented the flag from employing the latest technology.
Even the recent partial exception of containerization has occurred out-
side of and in spite of that policy. As will be seen, this is the result
of effectively requiring U.S. operators to purchase only domestically
built tonnage. This policy alone has been enough to doom the American
marine to failure. However, it is not the only burden the industry has
had to carry. It has paid very high labor costs relative to those of
other flags since World War II. Moreover, the U.S. merchant marine
has had, by far, the most complex, costly, and unsuccessful industrial
relations system of any shipping flag. (These points will be discussed
in Part II.)
    It is important to recognize that relative factor costs (including
the hidden labor costs of a dysfunctional industrial relations system)
and national maritime policy are interrelated. The lower the cost of
building and operating ships to a flag, the less need its fleet has of
state support or protection and the more effective is a given level of
such support. The fleet of a high-cost flag competing in the same
market will be in more need of a positive maritime policy and will
suffer more from an inept one.
    During a period of rapid advancement in marine technology, it
is essential that a nation's maritime policy allow it to stay in step
with the times. This is especially important for a high-cost flag. It
may require fundamental changes in orientation from time to time,
which often will conflict with vested interests. This may be difficult.
However, the failure of a maritime nation to adjust its policies in time
can quickly lead to the destruction of its shipping industry, as the
history of the American merchant marine testifies.

U.S. MARITIME POLICY AND THE FIRST
TECHNOLOGICAL REVOLUTION

The second half of the 19th century saw a complete transformation in ocean shipping. Wood and canvas gave way to steel and steam. There were such technological developments as the iron and then the steel hull, the triple expansion steam engine, and a host of other advances in naval architecture and marine engineering. Their combined effect was to drastically alter the requirements of the best ship for a given trade.

The expanded capital requirements of the new ships demanded that they be kept in operation full time. This necessitated a break between trade and shipping organizations. The merchant-owned ship, operated as an adjunct of a company's trading activities, was replaced by the independent shipping company operating as a common carrier on schedule or as contract carriers in the tramp trades. [2]

The new type of shipping firm and the existence of high fixed costs made international shipping very competitive. This was especially so in liner operation, where the maintenance of a schedule makes practically all costs fixed. To offset the effects of cutthroat competition and the absence of any possible governmental regulation, the steamship lines formed conferences to effectively limit price competition and entry. The conferences were formed mainly between 1875 and 1895. [3]

The shipping industry that emerged around the turn of the century was totally different from that of 40 years earlier. The United States had been the world leader in the production of wooden ships, because of the availability of excellent ship timber. However, as the forests were cut down, the costs of production of wooden ships in the United States rose. Great Britain, meanwhile, captured the lead in the production of iron and steel ships. As the new technology developed, the British yards experienced large economies of scale. By 1860 the British could market an efficient vessel constructed entirely of iron. [4] By the end of the century they were the undisputed masters in shipbuilding.

The United States was slow to get into the business of building metal ships. The new ship technology drew its skilled labor chiefly from the iron, steel, and engineering industries. In the United States these industries were protected by tariffs and their wages were relatively high. Thus, it was these shoreside industries that effectively set the wage levels in the American shipyards. [5]

This development in itself need not have destroyed the American merchant marine. The impact of new technology and high wage levels in U.S. shipyards was to place the shipyards at a competitive disadvantage with their British counterparts. The logical course for the United States to follow would have been to allow its operators to purchase the cheaper and better British ships and then support the domestic yards to the extent necessary to maintain the shipbuilding capacity desired above that supported by the market and naval demand.

The response of the United States, however, was to protect its shipyards at the expense of the shipping industry. This was done by continuing to adhere to a law passed in 1817 that prevented the purchase of foreign-built ships. [6] This requirement originated under industrial conditions totally different from those prevailing after the advent of steel and steam. Initially the requirement did not penalize American operators, since the U. S. shipyards were more efficient than those of any other country. After the 1860s or 1870s, however, the requirement to build in high-cost domestic yards made no sense for the shipping industry, and very little for the shipyards. True, the U. S. yards had a captive market, but that market quickly shrank to insignificance as the U. S. operators found it impossible to compete while using more costly tonnage.

The protection of the domestic shipyards from British competition raised the price of ships to U. S. operators by 40 to 50 percent. [7] No flag can afford such a surcharge and long survive in international shipping. The response of the U. S. shipping industry was to attempt to compete while using the old technology. In consequence the U. S. fleet engaged in foreign trade was overwhelmingly a fleet of sailing vessels as late as 1890. [8]

The decline of the U. S. merchant marine must properly be blamed on the failure of the political system to respond adequately to the new situation rather than on the technological revolution itself. Had the country adopted a free ship policy, as many were advocating, and a sensible program of direct support to the shipyards, the technological changes could have worked to the advantage of the U. S. flag. Instead, the fates of the shipping and shipbuilding industries were tied together, to the disadvantage of both. They remain together to this day.

It is essential that a nation's maritime policy distinguish between the shipping and the shipbuilding industries. They are quite separate; and what benefits one, need not benefit the other. Indeed, as customer and supplier, their interests are, to a large degree, naturally in conflict. For some reason, however, the U. S. Congress has historically considered them interdependent. The reason may lie in the peculiarities of the election system for Congress. The single-member, simple-majority principle amplifies the influences of concentrated votes and contributions. Ships are built in a relatively small number of states and in only a few Congressional districts within those states. But shipyards employ large numbers of workers and are important to the local economy. A Congressman from a shipbuilding district must naturally consider the needs of the many shipyard workers, their unions, and the management organizations associated with the yards.

Although ports also are concentrated in a relatively small number of states and districts, their prosperity is not dependent upon the success of the U. S.-flag shipping industry. Shipping service can be supplied to the port just as well by any other flag. Furthermore, many seamen move from port to port and seldom vote in political elections. Others that regularly ship through one port live some distance away. Thus, there is no concentration of voting strength and political influence associated with the shipping industry, as there is with the shipbuilding industry. This has been somewhat offset in recent years by the political contributions of some of the seamen's unions.

Maritime policy seems to be shaped in the relevant Congressional committees. Of course, the major pieces of legislation usually are submitted by the Administration. However, the main forum within which the issues are debated is the committee hearing room. The issues often are complex and technical, and the list of witnesses long. This sort of debate does not find its way to the House or Senate floor because it takes a degree of expertise to understand the discussions. As in many areas, the Congress relies on the recommendation of its committees.

The committee report is usually hammered out by a subcommittee. Both the Senate Commerce Committee and the House Committee on Merchant Marine and Fisheries rely heavily on the Subcommittee on Merchant Marine and Fisheries and the Subcommittee on Merchant Marine, respectively. These subcommittees are to a large extent made up of Congressmen from coastal and shipbuilding districts. * This is not absolute, of course, but the members who remain on these commitees year after year and who take an active part in their work are almost always from shipbuilding districts. The consistency with which U.S. maritime policy has been designed to protect and promote shipbuilding rather than shipping supports this argument.

An attempt was made to offset the ship-cost disadvantage of the U.S.-flag shipping industry with ocean mail subsidies in 1891. It had little effect, and the industry continued to decline.

In 1912 an amendment to the Panama Canal Act allowed the purchase of foreign-built ships for the foreign trade fleet. However, no ships were registered under it and the law was soon superseded by the Ship Registry Act of 1914 and World War I. [9]

---

*The most active members of the Senate Commerce Committee and its Merchant Marine and Fisheries Subcommittee during the period 1965-70 were Warren G. Magnuson (D-Wash.), E. L. Bartlett (D-Alaska) (died Dec. 11, 1968), and Daniel B. Brewster (D-Md.). The House Merchant Marine and Fisheries Committee and its Merchant Marine Subcommittee have been strongly chaired by Edward A. Garmatz (D-Md.) since 1966. Other active and knowledgeable members are Alton Lennon (D-N.C.), Thomas N. Downing (D-Va.), William S. Mailliard (R-Calif.), and Thomas M. Pelly (R-Wash.). All are from coastal and shipbuilding districts, as are numerous other less active members of the committees. U.S. Congress, Joint Committee on Printing, Congressional Directory (Washington: U.S. Government Printing Office, 1965-70).

The decline of the United States merchant marine came to an abrupt reversal with the massive shipbuilding program of World War I. Suddenly the United States was again a major maritime power. However, with the return of peace the market was glutted with war-built tonnage and the flag was in trouble again. The bubble burst about 1921, which coincided with the beginning of a second period of revolutionary change in marine technology.

THE SECOND REVOLUTION IN MARINE TECHNOLOGY

Although less dramatic than the nineteenth century development, the interwar period, especially the 1920s, witnessed a second technological revolution. Its basis was the development of the marine diesel engine, the high pressure turbine, the oil fired boiler, the expanded use of the tankship and many other lesser developments.

World War I, like World War II, punctuated what would have been a more gradual development of marine technology with profound results for the various shipping countries. The impact of modern war on international shipping operates in several stages. First it rids the world of its older tonnage. The increased demand for shipping capacity presses many older ships from relatively quiet domestic duty into operation overseas, where much of it is destroyed. Others are sacrificed— for instance, they may be sunk to effect immediate breakwaters or to block channels. Perhaps most important is the fact that the technical developments adopted during the war render the older ships non-competitive in the postwar period. There was very little prewar tonnage in operation after either World War.

Second, the belligerents, especially the United States, began massive shipbuilding programs during both World Wars. These programs were very complex and required a long lead time before full operation was attained. At the end of each war the shipbuilding program was going full force, with the result that when the demand for shipping capacity returned to peacetime levels, the market was flooded with excess tonnage. This brought shipbuilding to a halt for a few years and, in the case of the United States, for many years.

Third, a modern war creates a plateau in marine technology. This is due in part to the adoption of the latest developments by the wartime building programs, but mostly to the massive numbers of ships built. When new construction is resumed, the postwar developments in marine technology appear as a revolution compared with the static mass of war-built tonnage.

As in the 19th-century development, the effect of the rapid developments in marine technology during the 1920s was to alter the relative positions of the maritime nations. As ships became more specialized and more expensive to build, the ship-cost disadvantage of the American flag increased. As the government rid itself of its large fleet of war-built ships under the provisions of the Merchant Marine Act of 1920, [10] the American-flag position deteriorated.

Again, as in the case of the first maritime revolution, the logical course for the United States would have been to employ the latest, most efficient, and most capital-intensive technology available. Instead, it sold or leased its war-built ships to its citizens at favorable prices. The impact of this was to make the operation of older ships more profitable than it otherwise would have been, thus lessening the economic incentive to build new ships at home or abroad.

U.S. operators in the foreign trades were technically free to build in foreign yards after 1912—or, more realistically, after World War I. However, the existence of the large number of war-built ships in operation, usually under lease from the government at favorable terms, made this competitively impossible throughout the 1920s. Once the depression began in 1929, there was so much excess shipping capacity available and the outlook was so uncertain that very little shipbuilding was done by anyone. During this period it was the more efficient postwar fleets, employing the latest technology, that set the rates and dominated the trade routes. The U.S. fleet was not among them.

The Merchant Marine Act of 1920 directed the Shipping Board to establish a system of trade routes and steamship lines to be sold or leased to American citizens. [11] It also required that all U.S. mail be carried in ships built and documented in the United States. [12] Further, it restricted preferential import-export railroad rates to goods carried in American bottoms. [13]

Despite these and other aids, the U.S. fleet carried the seeds of its own destruction. There was no effective provision or inducement for the replacement of the war-built ships. Since most of the ships under the U.S. flag had been built during World War I, the whole fleet aged as one. This was recognized, and in 1928 another Merchant Marine Act was passed to correct it. [14]

The Merchant Marine Act of 1928 expressly recognized the need to replace vessels under the U.S. flag. [15] Title IV strengthened the provision that U.S. mails were to be transported only in U.S.-built and -registered vessels, and established a subsidy system based on mail contracts. The rationale was that mail rates would be generous enough to allow the contracting companies to replace their fleets. [16] Although a number of ships were built under the provisions of the 1928 legislation, the system was ineffective in overcoming the more fundamental problems in U.S. maritime policy.

The failure of the U.S. merchant marine during the interwar period was a failure to replace the fleet. The decline never reached the crisis state that the industry now faces. The Merchant Marine Act of 1936 and, more important, World War II prevented that. As can be seen in Table 2.1, the percentage of U.S. foreign trade by volume carried in

TABLE 2.1

U.S. Participation in the Oceanborne Foreign Trade
of the United States, 1921-40

	Total Cargo		Percent U.S.	Foreign Flag
	Total Tons	U.S. Tons		
1921	70,554	34,390	48.7	36,164
1922	75,450	36,394	48.2	39,056
1923	79,096	31,813	40.2	47,283
1924	80,234	32,542	40.6	47,692
1925	80,610	29,477	36.6	51,133
1926	100,206	31,743	31.7	68,463
1927	84,072	31,794	37.8	52,233
1928	87,799	33,434	38.1	54,365
1929	92,764	35,486	38.3	57,278
1930	81,734	30,864	37.8	50,870
1931	65,328	23,552	36.1	41,776
1932	52,123	18,367	35.2	33,765
1933	50,750	16,851	33.2	33,899
1934	56,337	18,555	32.9	37,782
1935	60,875	19,697	32.4	41,178
1936	64,808	19,283	29.7	45,585
1937	82,970	22,012	26.5	60,958
1938	74,597	19,446	26.1	55,151
1939	77,991	17,426	22.3	60,565
1940	75,962	23,204	30.5	52,758

Note: Tonnage in 1,000 long tons.

Source: U.S. Department of Commerce, Maritime Administration, The Handbook of Merchant Shipping Statistics Through 1958 (Washington: U.S. Government Printing Office, 1959), p. 163.

U. S. bottoms reached a low of 22. 3 in 1939. Otherwise it remained above 26 percent throughout the interwar period. By present standards this is quite respectable.

Table 2.1, however, does present evidence of a declining industry, although the decline had not yet threatened to deprive the United States of its shipping capacity. The share of total tonnage carried fell generally throughout the 20 years and reached its low at the end of the period. Even though the sharp drop between 1938 and 1939 of four percent is probably explainable by the operation of the Neutrality Laws, the general movement of the industry throughout the period is downward. Undoubtedly, the recovery in 1940 reflects the growing war in Europe.

During the first technological revolution, the flag was prohibited by statute from adopting the new technology by a requirement that it build only in domestic yards. During the interwar period, that requirement had been lifted. Operators were technically able to build abroad. However, the availability of cheap war-built tonnage purchased or leased from the government, plus a few added encouragements, made this alternative unprofitable.

One of the added encouragements, the ocean mail contract system of the Merchant Marine Acts of 1920 and 1928, has been mentioned. Another was the restriction of the domestic trades to U. S. -built ships, begun in 1817. [17] The Merchant Marine Act of 1920 extended this protection to what is called the noncontiguous trades (Alaska, Hawaii, Puerto Rico). [18] In addition, a law passed in 1904 reserved all military cargo for U. S. -built ships. [19] These requirements and protections were not nearly as important during the interwar period as they are today. However, they undoubtedly had some impact for all U. S. operators and probably were determining for some.

SUMMARY

The effect of U. S. maritime policy during the interwar period was to prevent the flag from replacing its tonnage to the extent necessary to remain modern and competitive. The full force of this failure was not experienced, in part because of the passage of the Merchant Marine Act of 1936, but more importantly because of World War II. This does not change the fact that for most of the interwar period, with its important developments in marine technology, the maritime policy of the United States was as inappropriate as it had been during the 19th century.

The availability of cheap war-built ships and the protection and preference afforded U. S. -built ships combined to render foreign building impractical. Domestic building was available, but a ship built in the United States cost considerably more than it would in a foreign country because of the higher labor costs and general backwardness of American yards. This made the operation of the World War I vessels more attractive than it would have been if foreign tonnage was effectively available.

NOTES

1. Senate, Hearings on U.S. Maritime Policy, 1967, p. 477.

2. Arnljot Stromme Svendsen, Sea Transport and Shipping Economics (Bremen: Institute for Shipping Research, 1958), p. 175.

3. John G. B. Hutchins, The American Maritime Industries and Public Policy 1789-1914 (New York: Russell & Russell, 1941), p. 542.

4. Ibid., p. 400.

5. Quoted in ibid., p. 455.

6. Interagency Maritime Task Force (IMTF), The Merchant Marine in National Defense and Trade; A Policy and a Program (Washington: IMTF, 1965), p. 28. Cited hereafter as IMTF Report.

7. Hutchins, op. cit., p. 475.

8. Ibid., p. 533.

9. Ibid., pp. 474-75.

10. 41 Stat. 988 (1920) Sec. 2, 46 U.S.C.A. 861 (1958).

11. 41 Stat. 991 (1920) Sec. 7, 46 U.S.C.A. 866 (1958).

12. 41 Stat. 998 (1920) Sec. 24, 46 U.S.C.A. 880 (1958).

13. 41 Stat. 999 (1920) Sec. 28, 46 U.S.C.A. 884 (1958).

14. 45 Stat. 689 (1928), 46 U.S.C.A. 891 (1958).

15. 45 Stat. 690 (1928) Sec. 203, 46 U.S.C.A. 891c (1958).

16. Samuel A. Lawrence, United States Merchant Shipping Policies and Politics (Washington: Brookings Institution, 1966), p. 43.

17. Wytze Gorter, United States Shipping Policy (New York: Harper Brothers, 1956), pp. 131-32.

18. 41 Stat. 997 (1920) Sec. 21, 46 U.S.C.A. 887 (1958). Became effective Feb. 1, 1922.

19. 33 Stat. 518 (1904), 10 U.S.C.A. 2631 (1959).

3

INTRODUCTION

The national maritime policy of the United States during the years since 1936 has been, to a large extent, a continuation of principles developed in earlier periods. The fundamental principle of promoting a domestic shipbuilding capacity has remained intact. The domestic trades have remained an American-flag preserve. The principle of protection applied to U.S. military shipments in 1904 has been retained and extended in part (50 percent) to other government-generated cargoes. However, there also have been major alterations in policy and administration superimposed on the old structure.

The two most important modifications of existing maritime policy were features of the Merchant Marine Act of 1936. The first was an effective citizen crew requirement that tied the seagoing labor force to the American economy for the first time. This caused the wages of American seamen to catch up with, and then parallel, wages ashore. The effective citizen crew requirement was the beginning and major cause of the significant labor-cost disadvantage faced by the U.S. flag in the postwar period.

The second important change was the introduction of the concept of cost parity. A subsidy system was devised that supposedly equalized construction and operating costs between American and foreign-flag ships.

Most of the operating-differential subsidy (ODS) initiated by the 1936 legislation has been employed to offset the labor-cost disadvantage imposed on the flag by U.S. maritime policy. The construction-differential subsidy (CDS) has been similarly employed to offset the effective policy requirement that ships be built only in high-cost domestic yards.

The ship-cost disadvantage faced by the U.S. shipping industry has been described. This chapter will first explain the development of

the more recent problem, the labor-cost disadvantage, and will then
outline the major elements of U.S. maritime policy for the period
1936-70.

THE LABOR-COST DISADVANTAGE

The first two failures of the U.S. shipping industry are directly
attributable to a ship-cost disadvantage and an inability to employ the
latest technology. Both result from U.S. maritime policy. Since the
1930s the maritime problem of the United States has become complicated by a labor-cost disadvantage. In addition to facing a 100 percent
disadvantage in the purchase price of a ship, an American operator in
the postwar period has had to pay several times as much for his crew
than has his foreign-flag counterpart.

The maritime unions have universally been given credit (or blame)
for raising the wages and improving the working and living conditions
of American seamen. Undoubtedly, the unions have had an effect on
the timing of wage increases and have improved working and living
conditions on the ships in many ways. They also have prevented seagoing wages from declining during period of weak demand for labor and
from rising to heights they would otherwise have reached during periods
of high employment. The latter case is most true of such groups as
marine engineers and electricians. It is questionable, however,
whether the unions have had a major long-run impact on the level of
seagoing wages.

Seafaring wage rates would have increased enormously from
their prewar levels regardless of the efforts of the unions. This was
inevitable and followed from the combined effects of the reduced
immigration into the United States legislated during the 1920s and
the feature of the Merchant Marine Act of 1936 that required all officers
and crew members on subsidized ships to be native-born or fully
naturalized citizens of the United States. [1] An earlier law already
required that all watch-standing officers on all U.S. ships be citizens. [2]

These requirements are not absolute. Passenger ships are
allowed to carry 10 percent foreign nationals in the crew of the steward's department. [3] Furthermore, on nonsubsidized vessels only 75
percent of the crew (excluding officers) must be citizens. [4] These
exceptions are relatively unimportant, and by the 1950s they were
meaningless except for a few specialized personnel on passenger ships.

During the late 1940s and early 1950s, the impact of the immigration restrictions and the citizen-crew requirement was made virtually
absolute by the wide acceptance of the union-operated hiring halls.
Although the shipowners could legally employ 25 percent foreign seamen on nonsubsidized vessels, the companies effectively surrendered
this right when they entered into hiring-hall agreements with the unions.

Foreign seamen usually are not interested in, or able to become members of, American unions. For one thing, they would first have to obtain seamen's papers, which is usually difficult and time-consuming. Also, the crew unions often are effectively "closed" to new entrants and are always selective on various criteria in regard to new members. Though the officers' unions accept anyone with a valid license, the Coast Guard requires that a man serve a certain length of time on U. S. -flag ships before he can "sit" for a license. The examinations are fairly rigorous and in English. Foreign seamen thus are effectively kept out of the U. S. maritime labor market. The very few exceptions would have no impact on wage rates. Since the passage of the Merchant Marine Act of 1936, it is safe to say that U. S. ships have been manned by citizen crews.

The end result of this was to tie the seagoing labor force to the American economy for the first time. Once the shipping industry had to compete with shoreside industry for its labor, it had to pay competitive wages. It was inevitable that the wages of seamen would catch up with those of workers ashore and thereafter keep pace with them. Since the wages of all American workers have increased considerably since the 1930s, it is not surprising to find that seagoing wages have gone up as well.

Although it is difficult to compare seagoing and shoreside employment, Table 3.1 demonstrates approximately the movement of seagoing wages relative to average earnings in manufacturing, relating the monthly base rate of an able seaman to the monthly pay of the average worker in manufacturing. The latter was obtained by multiplying the hourly rate in manufacturing by a factor of 173. However, prior to 1946 seamen worked 56 hours per week at sea and 48 in port. In 1946, after strong urgings from the government, the shipowners granted a 48-hour week for watch standers at sea and a 40-hour week for day workers at sea and for everyone in port. [5] In 1951 seamen obtained the 40-hour week for all ratings at sea as well as in port. [6] Thus the gains in base wages underestimate the improvement in the earnings of seamen by 20 to 40 percent.

From the employer point of view, the seaman's improved earnings were directly translated into additional operating cost. Between 1936 and 1951 the base rate of an able seaman went up by 310 percent, while his workweek decreased by 40 percent at sea and 20 percent in port. Between 1936 and 1968 the monthly base had gone up by 640 percent without regard to the shorter workweek.

Of course, figures of this sort can be used to prove anything, and the game should not be overplayed. For instance, between 1951 and 1968 the monthly base wage for able seamen went up by only 79 percent, compared with 91 percent for the average manufacturing worker.

The point important to the present discussion is the cause of the increase in seamen's wages. The additional labor costs are directly

TABLE 3. 1

Relative Earnings of U. S. Able-Bodied Seamen and
Production Workers in Manufacturing, 1925-68

Year	U. S. Able-Bodied Seamen's Monthly Base Wage (in dollars)	Average Monthly Earnings of Production Workers in Manufacturing (in dollars)	Differential	
			Dollars	Percent
1925	59	95	36	61. 0
1930	61	95	34	55. 7
1935	55	95	40	72. 7
1940	73	114	41	56. 1
1945	145	164	19	13. 1
1946	163	180	17	10. 4
1947	192	204	12	6. 1
1948	223	223	0	0
1949	226	232	6	2. 7
1950	226	240	14	6. 2
1951	248	261	13	5. 2
1952	263	275	12	4. 6
1953	302	291	-11	- 3. 6
1954	314	298	-16	- 5. 1
1955	314	310	- 4	- 1. 3
1956	314	327	13	4. 1
1957	333	344	11	3. 3
1958	353	355	2	0. 6
1959	353	367	14	4. 0
1960	369	381	12	3. 3
1961	384	389	5	1. 3
1962	393	400	7	1. 8
1963	393	410	17	4. 3
1964	393	422	29	7. 4
1965	393	434	41	10. 4
1966	393	448	55	14. 0
1967	423	470	47	11. 1
1968	444	498	54	12. 2

Sources: Seamen, 1925-55, U. S. Department of Commerce, Maritime Administration, The Handbook of Merchant Shipping Statistics Through 1958 (Washington: U. S. Government Printing Office, 1959), Table 4, p. 192; 1956-68, from relevant years of Maritime Administration, Seafaring Wage Rates, for 1964, 1967, and 1968 (Washington, U. S. Government Printing Office, 1965, 1968, 1969), pagination varies. Manufacturing, 1930-40, Statistical Abstracts of the United States, 1949, Table 238, p. 215; 1945-68, U. S. Office of Business Economics; Business Statistics 1969, p. 81. These data were given as hourly earnings and multiplied by 173 to get monthly earnings.

attributable to a national maritime policy requiring citizen crews that coincided with an immigration policy that effectively ended the free flow of foreign-born seamen into the United States. The result was that American ships had to be manned by American citizens during a period in which the cost of labor increased for all U.S. industries. Most industries, however, were protected to some extent by tariffs, distance (transportation costs), and an ability to employ more efficient and capital-intensive technology. The shipping industry, or at least that part of it engaged in competitive international shipping during the postwar period, had no tariff or distance protection and was generally unable to adopt the new technology. The result was the third failure of the U.S. merchant marine.

ELEMENTS OF RECENT U.S. MARITIME POLICY

The Merchant Marine Act of 1936

The Merchant Marine Act of 1936, the first comprehensive approach to the problems of the U.S. shipping industry, emerged from the political climate of the depression. Many of its supporters represented forces and positions only remotely concerned with the problems of building a viable merchant marine. [7] This resulted in the inclusion of such features as the citizen crew requirement and a "buy American" provision[8] that added to the industry's existing cost disadvantage.

The Act of 1936 did not attempt to free the shipping industry from the effective requirement that it build in domestic yards. Indeed, it greatly reinforced it. Its operating-differential subsidy, for instance, was available only to ships built in the United States. Neither did it make any attempt to reduce or eliminate the labor-cost disadvantage. What the Act did do, however, was shift the cost of building in domestic yards, manning with citizen personnel, and a few other costs (crew subsistence, repairs, insurance costs) associated with the "buy American" principle to the federal government for a few operators.

Ship Construction

Title V of the Act established a system of construction-differential subsidies (CDS) whereby the government, through the Federal Maritime Commission (now the Maritime Administration) paid the differential between the cost of building a vessel in an American yard and a representative foreign shipbuilding center. Initially, there was a maximum limit of 33.3 percent on the CDS (excluding national defense features, which are wholly paid for by the government). However, if there was "convincing evidence" that the actual differential was greater and four of the five Commission members agreed, the CDS could be as much as 50 percent. [9] There has been an abundance of "convincing evidence" throughout the postwar period, and the effective CDS ceiling was 50 percent until it was raised to 55 percent for construction and 60 percent for reconditioning in the 1960s. [10]

There are two less well-known features of the Merchant Marine Act of 1936 that complement the CDS. One is the "capital reserve funds" and "special reserve funds" established by Title VI of the Act. The other is the Federal Ship Mortgage and Loan Insurance Program of Title XI. They will be discussed in turn.

Capital and Special Reserve Funds

Section 607 (b) of the Merchant Marine Act of 1936 provides that an operator receiving operating-differential subsidy (ODS) will deposit an amount equal to the annual depreciation of his subsidized vessels, plus the proceeds of all insurance and indemnities due to a total ship loss and the proceeds of sales of ships, in a capital reserve fund. The Commission (Maritime Administration) may additionally require a subsidized operator to deposit profits in excess of 10 percent that are not recaptured under the provisions of Section 606 (5) in a capital reserve fund. The only purposes for which these monies may be withdrawn are to pay the principal on notes secured by mortgage on subsidized vessels and to construct, reconstruct, or purchase replacement tonnage.

Section 607 (c) provides that a subsidized operator shall deposit profits in excess of 10 percent, which the Commission does not require deposited in the capital reserve fund, in a special reserve fund. Withdrawal from special reserve funds may be made for a number of business-connected reasons, usually subject to the approval of the government.

The principal of the capital and special reserve funds may be invested by the operator in interest-bearing securities approved by the Commission. Also, 50 percent of the amount of the funds may be placed in trust and invested in common stocks. [11]

The most important feature of the capital and special reserve funds is that taxes on the money so deposited are deferred. The actual language of the law states that they are "exempt from all federal taxes."[12] However, in the late 1940s the subsidized operators and the Treasury Department reached an agreement in regard to funds deposited during the war that amounts to tax deferment. [13] If an operator puts up $2 million of his own money from a reserve fund toward a $10 million ship, the depreciation base of that ship will be $8 million, not $10 million. [14] Thus the government eventually taxes the funds, although it will take many years to do so. In the meantime the operator has an instrument for the rapid accumulation of ship replacement capital and the ability to invest those funds in interest- and dividend-bearing assets.

The corporate income tax rate in the United States is 48 percent. It thus would take a nonsubsidized operator twice as long to accumulate a given amount of investment capital for shipbuilding purposes as it would a subsidized operator. In addition, he would not be receiving interest or dividends on those funds not yet accumulated. Further, he would find it more difficult to escape taxation on the profits of unusually prosperous years than would a subsidized operator, who may deposit his excess profits in a reserve fund.

The reserve funds are a very important feature of the Merchant Marine Act of 1936. For the subsidized operator they alone go a long way to offset the ship-cost disadvantage. Rather, they would do so if it were not for the fact that many other countries give similar benefits to their merchant marines.

Unfortunately, the United States granted the reserve funds only to the subsidized liner sector.* As may be seen in Table 3.2, the funds reached a peak in the late 1950s and decreased through 1970.

Mortgage Insurance

In addition to the CDS and the capital and special reserve funds, the Merchant Marine Act of 1936 provides a system of federal ship mortgage insurance under Title XI, whereby the "faith of the United States is solemnly pledged to the payment of interest on and the unpaid balance of the principal amount of each mortgage and loan insured under this title."[15] In practical terms this means that an operator building a ship can borrow $3 for every $1 of "seed money" that the ship owner provides.[16] Title XI guarantees are available for all ship operators, subsidized and unsubsidized but of course are of more benefit to the subsidized operator. He can combine the lower interest rate resulting from the guarantee with the CDS and reserve funds features of the Act to finance new construction. The nonsubsidized operator cannot. However, a number of tanker operators found the provisions of Title XI beneficial. Table 3.3 presents the experience under Title XI.

The combination of construction subsidies, tax deferment on reserve funds, and mortgage guarantees has effectively offset the ship-cost disadvantage for the subsidized liner segment of the industry. The 13 companies that made up that sector in 1970 had, in fact, taken advantage of these provisions and operated a relatively modern

---

*Section 511 of the Merchant Marine Act of 1936 permitted unsubsidized operators to establish construction reserve funds. Tax deferment was not allowed on earnings deposited in such funds, and they were little used.

TABLE 3.2

Capital and Special Reserve Funds of U.S.
Subsidized Operators, 1955-70
(million dollars)

Year	Capital Reserve Funds	Special Reserve Funds	Total Capital and Special Reserve Funds
1955	130	104	235
1956	136	110	246
1957	142	133	276
1958	162	163	325
1959	180	166	345
1960	167	156	323
1961	153	146	299
1962	117	134	251
1963	114	132	247
1964	116	142	258
1965	100	143	243
1966	109	131	240
1967	140	105	244
1968	144	72	217
1969	75	61	136
1970	46	48	95

Notes: 1955-68 are as of December 31; 1969 and 1970 are as of June 30.
Totals do not sum because of rounding.

Sources: 1955-68, U.S. Department of Commerce, Maritime Administration, "Special and Capital Reserve Funds: Summary," unpublished table and chart (313.51), dated Dec. 31, 1968; 1969 and 1970, MARAD 1970, Year of Transition, annual report of the Maritime Administration for Fiscal Year 1970 (Washington: U.S. Government Printing Office, 1971), App. XI, p. 77.

TABLE 3.3

Federal Ship Mortgage and Loan Insurance Program
(Title XI), 1958-70

Year	Total Approved Applications and Contracts in Force (million dollars)	Number of Vessels Covered
1958	219	26
1959	257	34
1960	449	53
1961	464	64
1962	459	67
1963	431	70
1964	454	82
1965	422	79
1966	485	98
1967	562	113
1968	652	129
1969	752	144
1970	919	171

Source: U.S. Department of Commerce, Maritime Administration, "Federal Ship Mortgage and Loan Insurance Program," unpublished table and chart (325.10), dated June 30, 1970.

and sizable fleet. A number of tankers also have been constructed with the aid of Title XI, primarily for operation in the domestic trades.

Ship Operation

The 1936 legislation also applied the concept of cost parity to ship operation. Title VI provides for a system of operating-differential subsidies designed to offset the difference in operating costs between U.S.- and foreign-flag ships on a given trade route. A subsidized operator enters into a contractual relationship with the Maritime Administration for up to 20 years. The agreement provides that the operator will perform an approximate number of voyages per year over a designated trade route and take certain other actions that are spelled out in the Act (such as making deposits in the capital and special reserve funds). In return he receives an operating subsidy on the additional costs of insurance, maintenance, repairs, and the wages and subsistence of officers and crew that are associated with flying the American flag. [17] The most important ODS account is wages. In 1969, it amounted to 85.6 percent of total ODS costs. [18]

The operating-differential subsidies of 1936 Act, unlike the construction subsidies, were limited by statute to liner operation. In practice, however, both forms of subsidy have been granted only to part of the liner sector. The Maritime Administration has had statutory authority to grant CDS to bulk carriers since 1952. It has gone unused, however, because of a lack of funding and the high cost of replacing the tramp fleet.[19]

Cargo Preference

The second pillar of U.S. maritime policy is cargo preference and related programs. This is a massive system of indirect aid to both the subsidized and the nonsubsidized operators, and is as important and perhaps as costly as the ODS program. It completely supports the operation of the tramp and unsubsidized liner fleets, and the subsidized lines are dependent upon it for much of their cargo.

A distinction must be made between route preference and rate preference. All shipping countries route their "establishment traffic" over their home flags, officially or unofficially. This is widely accepted and there is nothing wrong with it, provided the cargo moves at internationally competitive rates. Much of the movement of U.S. military and preference cargo carried by American liners at conference rates falls into this category. However, large amounts of preference cargo move at rates substantially above world market rates. The indirect subsidy resulting from such movement has been estimated at $80 million annually.[20]

The practice of restricting certain cargoes to U.S.-flag ships began with the 1904 law requiring that all military cargoes be moved in American bottoms. In 1934, Public Resolution 17 stipulated that surplus agricultural products exported with the aid of Reconstruction Finance Corporation loans had to be carried exclusively in U.S.-flag ships.[21] In practice this means that 50 percent of the cargoes may be lifted by U.S. ships and 50 percent by the ships of the recipient country.[22] In 1948 Congress passed the first cargo preference provision for aid cargoes. This practice continued on an ad hoc or annual basis until 1954, when Public Law 664 made it permanent. Cargo preference, the so-called 50-50 program, became Section 901 (b) of the Merchant Marine Act of 1936. Public Law 480 applies to Department of Agriculture (USDA) cargoes and contains its own 50-50 provision.

The Agency for International Development (AID) and the USDA are by far the largest shippers of nonmilitary government-impelled cargo. In calendar 1969, they shipped 14.3 million tons between them. U.S.-flag ships carried 52.7 percent of this, or 7.5 million tons.[23] This compares with a total of 20.7 million tons of commercial cargo lifted by U.S. ships in calendar year 1969, including government cargo

46

(but excluding military shipments). As may be seen in Table 3.4, this is not a new condition. AID and USDA shipments have made up over one-third of what is reported as "commercial" cargo for many years. This does not include other government agency-impelled cargo, such as that financed by the Export-Import Bank. Nor does it reflect the importance of Department of Defense (DOD) cargoes to U.S. operators.

The DOD pays approximately $70 million per year to U.S. ship operators above what it would pay if it used foreign-flag ships.[24] In fiscal 1969 the Military Sea Transport Service (MSTS) shipped 18.3 million measurement tons of dry cargo (16.9 million of which was non-bulk) and 14.1 million long tons of petroleum.[25] (A measurement ton is equal to 40 cubic feet, and four measurement tons equal approximately one long ton.)[26] Thus MSTS shipped about 4.6 million long tons of dry cargo in fiscal 1969, for a total of 18.1 million long tons. Note that this approaches the 20.7 million tons of commercial cargo carried, including preference cargo.

Prior to World War II there was virtually no U.S.-flag tramp fleet.[27] American tramping is a postwar development and is dependent upon preference and military cargoes. If the programs ended, the tramp companies would disappear.

Liners have also grown increasingly dependent upon reserved cargoes. The nonsubsidized liner companies are almost as dependent upon preference and military cargoes as are the tramps. The subsidized liner companies also have grown to favor the easy access to preferred cargoes over the rigors of international competition.

Until recently each government agency procured its own ocean transportation without coordination.[28] This resulted in each agency striving to minimize its shipping costs and, in consequence, the amount of cargo it placed in American bottoms. A continuing complaint arose from the industry and its friends in Congress of bad faith on the part of the agencies (mainly AID and USDA). The problem was remedied from the point of view of the industry in 1970, when Congress directed the Maritime Administration to "exercise general surveillance over the administration and observance of the Cargo Preference Act."[29] The Maritime Administration subsequently established a Cargo Preference Control Center to insure that the cargo preference laws are obeyed both as to tonnage and as to revenue. A regulation has been issued requiring that the 50 percent share of full shiploads of preference cargo be fixed prior to that of foreign vessels. A procedure also has been established to handle carrier complaints against shipping agencies.[30] This presumably will result in an expansion of cargo preference, since the Maritime Administration is charged with promoting the merchant marine and usually identifies its interests with those of the industry.

TABLE 3.4

Nonmilitary Preference Cargo Carried by
U.S.-Flag Ships, 1955-69
(million long tons)

Year	Total Commercial Cargo	AID Cargo	USDA Cargo	Total AID and USDA Cargo	Preference Cargo as a Percentage of Commercial Cargo
1955	53.1	4.9	1.4	6.3	11.9
1956	53.9	4.0	2.8	6.8	12.6
1957	50.8	3.4	4.3	7.7	15.1
1958	30.9	3.0	5.1	8.1	26.2
1959	27.1	2.4	5.0	7.4	27.3
1960	31.0	2.7	7.5	10.2	32.9
1961	26.3	4.1	6.8	10.9	41.4
1962	29.6	4.6	8.3	12.9	43.6
1963	28.5	6.2	7.8	14.0	49.1
1964	30.5	4.1	7.9	12.0	39.3
1965	27.7	3.8	6.6	10.4	37.5
1966	26.2	2.8	5.8	8.6	32.8
1967	20.5	2.5	3.9	6.4	31.2
1968	25.5	3.2	4.3	7.5	29.2
1969	20.7	3.3	4.2	7.5	36.2

Note: AID and USDA cargoes only.

Sources: U.S. Maritime Administration, "U.S. Oceanborne Foreign Trade: Commercial Cargo Carried (Tonnage)," unpublished table and chart (233.01), prepared Nov. 9, 1970; "Cargo Preference: Agency for International Development Cargo," unpublished table and chart (322.23), prepared Sept. 10, 1970; "Cargo Preference: Department of Agriculture Cargo (P.L. 480)," unpublished table and chart (322.24), prepared Sept. 10, 1970.

Cabotage

The third pillar of United States maritime policy is cabotage, or protected domestic trades. This includes coastal, intercoastal, and what is known as the noncontiguous trades (Alaska, Hawaii, Puerto Rico). Foreign-flag ships were excluded from the U.S. coasting trades in the early 1800s. [31] The Merchant Marine Act of 1920 expanded the restriction to the noncontiguous trades. [32]

This is an absolute restriction. Not only must the ships be documented in the United States, but they must have been built in the United States. [33] However, because of the complete absence of foreign competition in these trades, the problems and benefits of national maritime policy are different from those in the offshore trades.

Ships in the coastal and intercoastal trades are in competition with overland transportation, especially railroads. They are regulated in a way similar to other domestic transportation. In 1933 the Intercoastal Shipping Act charged the Shipping Board with rate regulation. [34] This was strengthened in 1938 and common carriers in the coastal trades were brought within the jurisdiction of the Shipping Board's successor agency, the Maritime Commission. [35] The Transportation Act of 1940 transferred jurisdiction to the Interstate Commerce Commission, and the provisions pertaining to water carriers became Part III of the Interstate Commerce Act. [36]

In 1939 there was a sizable fleet in the dry-cargo coastal and intercoastal service. World War II resulted in a complete shutdown of these trades, and the industry never recovered. [37] Industry spokesmen are critical of the decisions of the Interstate Commerce Commission, but the main reason for the failure of the trade to revive after the war was the growth of population centers away from the ports and the development of an extensive trucking industry operating on metaled roads. [38]

Coastwise tanker operation has fared better. Indeed, U.S.-flag tankers seldom operate anywhere else. Virtually all U.S. tankers are engaged in domestic operation.

The noncontiguous trades have done better than dry-cargo coastal and intercoastal operation, although it is difficult to measure their performance. The same ships that operate in other trades call at the noncontiguous ports as well as those ships that serve them regularly. The reason for this success is obvious. There is no competition.

SUMMARY

The maritime policy of the United States consists of three major elements: subsidy, preference, and cabotage. This is an oversimplification. There are important features of postwar maritime policy involving the sale and exchange of war-built tonnage, National Defense Reserve Fleets, nuclear ship construction and development, and other things that have been omitted from the above description. They will be introduced when appropriate in the chapters that follow.

There are also important areas of overlap that blur the issues. A few tankers go offshore. Subsidized ships occasionally carry domestic traffic. Nonsubsidized and subsidized liners compete at the margin for commercial cargoes, and liners and tramps compete for bulk shipments. Military cargo and shipments covered by Public Resolution 17 are sometimes carried by foreign-flag ships. For the most part, these "exceptions" will be ignored in the following chapters. The industry will be treated as though it contained defined sectors with single-purpose interest groups within them. This will do little damage to the truth. Prior to 1970 the interests of the various parties were overwhelmingly within one sector and they acted accordingly. Thus, the operation of U.S. maritime policy has divided the industry into well-defined segments with conflicting interests.

Maritime policy does not exist in a vacuum. It is most strongly tested during eras of rapid change in marine technology. The maritime policy of the United States proved inadequate during the first two technological revolutions, when it was largely one of default or of continuing past practices. Since 1936, however, the United States has had a more positive and directed maritime program.

Before evaluation of the operation of U.S. maritime policy in recent years, the technological, economic, and institutional changes with which the policy has had to contend will be examined.

NOTES

1. 43 Stat. 153 (1924), 8 U.S.C.A. 201 (1970), rep. 1952; 49 Stat. 1992 (1936) Sec. 302 (a), 46 U.S.C.A. 1132 (1958).

2. 1 Stat. 287 (1792), 46 U.S.C.A. 221 (1958).

3. 49 Stat. 1992 (1936) Sec. 302 (b), 46 U.S.C.A. 1132 (1958).

4. 49 Stat. 1930 (1936) Sec. 1, 46 U.S.C.A. 672 (b) (1958).

5. Charles W. Uhlinger, "The Wages of American Seamen, 1939-1952" (unpublished Ph.D. diss., Fordham University, 1956), p. 21.

6. Ibid., p. 190.

7. Samuel A. Lawrence, United States Merchant Shipping Policies and Politics (Washington: Brookings Institution, 1966) p. 49.

8. 49 Stat. 1998 (1936) Sec. 505 (a), 46 U.S.C.A. 1155 (1958).

9. 49 Stat. 1996 (1936) Sec. 502 (b), 46 U.S.C.A. 1152 (1958).

10. U.S. Department of Commerce, Annual Report of the Secretary of Commerce (Washington: U.S. Government Printing Office, 1960), p. 73.

11. 49 Stat. 2005 (1936) Secs. 607 (d) (2, 3), 46 U.S.C.A. 1177 (1958).

12. 49 Stat. 2005 (1936) Sec. 607 (h), 46 U.S.C.A. 1177 (1958).

13. U.S. Congress, House, Committee on Merchant Marine and Fisheries, Subcommittee on Merchant Marine, Hearings on Long-Range Maritime Program, 90th Cong., 2nd sess. (Washington: U.S. Government Printing Office, 1968), p. 512. Cited hereafter as House, Hearings on Long-Range Maritime Program, 1968.

14. Ibid., p. 499.

15. 49 Stat. 2017 (1936) Sec. 1103 (d), 46 U.S.C.A. 1273 (1958).

16. House, Hearings on Long-Range Maritime Program, 1968, p. 483.

17. 49 Stat. 2002 (1936) Sec. 603 (b), 46 U.S.C.A. 1173 (1958).

18. The percentage of ODS going to insurance was 7.4, to maintenance and repair 5.8, and to subsistence 1.2. U.S. Department of Commerce, Maritime Administration, "Operating-Differential Subsidy (From Inception of 1936 Merchant Marine Act)," unpublished table and chart (311.61), prepared Nov. 17, 1970.

19. William B. Dickinson, Jr., "National Maritime Policy," Educational Research Reports 2 (Sept. 29, 1965): 712.

20. Congressional Quarterly Weekly Report, Mar. 19, 1965, p. 440.

21. 73rd Congress, Mar. 26, 1934.

22. Wytze Gorter, United States Shipping Policy (New York: Harper Brothers, 1956), p. 107.

23. U.S. Department of Commerce, Maritime Administration, "Cargo Preference: Agency for International Development Cargo," unpublished table and chart (322.23), prepared Sept. 10, 1970; "Cargo Preference: Department of Agriculture Cargo (P.L. 480)," unpublished table and chart (322.24), prepared Sept. 10, 1970.

24. Senate, Hearings on U.S. Maritime Policy, 1967, p. 37.

25. Military Sea Transportation Service, Sealift Command, "Financial and Statistical Report, Part 2, Fiscal Year 1969," unpublished (Washington: 1969) pp. 1, 2. MSTS reports this information as ". . . Cargo Subject to Public Law 664 (50-50 Law)."

26. Letter to the author from Larry C. Manning, Department of the Navy, Military Sealift Command (MSTS), dated Apr. 6, 1972.

27. Gorter, op. cit., p. 116.

28. Senate, Hearings on U.S. Maritime Policy, 1967, p. 111.

29. MARAD 1970, p. 29.

30. U.S. Department of Commerce, Maritime Administration, MARAD 1972, A New Wave in American Shipping, annual report of the Maritime Administration for fiscal year 1972 (Washington: U.S. Government Printing Office, 1972), pp. 34-36. Hereafter cited as MARAD 1972.

31. Gorter, op. cit., p. 131.

32. 41 Stat. 999 (1920) Sec. 27, 46 U.S.C.A. 883 (1958).

33. Ibid.

34. 47 Stat. 1425 (1933), 46 U.S.C.A. 843 (1958).

35. Philip D. Locklin, Economics of Transportation (6th ed.; Homewood, Illinois: Richard D. Irwin, Inc., 1966), pp. 743-44.

36. Ibid., p. 747.

37. Wytze Gorter and George H. Hildebrandt, The Pacific Coast Maritime Shipping Industry, 1930-1948, Volume II: An Analysis of Performance (Berkeley and Los Angeles: University of California Press, 1954), p. 118.

38. Ibid., p. 83.

4

INTRODUCTION

The development of marine technology in the 20th century has been greatly influenced by the two World Wars. From a maritime perspective, World War II was of greater importance than World War I. The seas were practically swept clean of prewar tonnage. The United States lost 519 ships in the first 180 days of hostilities. [1] Table 4. 1 shows the number of ships and deadweight tonnage of the major belligerents for 1939 and 1949. Even after four years of peace and the acquisition of large numbers of U. S. war-built ships, the fleets of the Allies were a fraction of their former size. All of the major maritime powers involved in the war lost large numbers of vessels. Germany and Japan were especially hard-hit and were not permitted to acquire U. S.-built vessels under the provisions of the Ship Sales Act of 1946. [2]

The decline of certain national fleets and the slight growth of the world fleet between 1939 and 1949 indicates nothing of the qualitative change that had taken place. The United States built 5, 037 merchant vessels of 2, 000 gross tons and over between 1940 and 1945. [3] A total of 1, 956 of these ships were sold under the provisions of the Ship Sales Act of 1946 before it expired on January 15, 1951. Of these, 843 were acquired by American-flag operators and 1, 113 were sold abroad. [4]

With the exception of the Liberty ship, all of the war-built vessels employed recent, and very similar, technology. The Victory and C-type freighters and the T-2 tanker established a standard against which subsequent developments are measured. It is now common to gauge supertanker size in "T-2 equivalents."

The current revolution in marine technology is occurring on many fronts. No part of the industry is immune to it unless isolated by

TABLE 4.1

Merchant Fleets of World War II Belligerent
Maritime Powers, 1939 and 1949

Country	Sept. 1, 1939		Dec. 31, 1949		Difference Ships
	No.	dwt (1,000)	No.	dwt (1,000)	
Total, all flags	12,798	80,600	12,868	103,461	+70
United States	1,379	11,681	3,513	37,445	+2134
British Empire	3,319	24,053	3,115	25,010	-204
United Kingdom	2,850	21,857	2,571	21,697	-279
Denmark	379	1,575	298	1,552	-81
France	555	2,998	494	3,476	-61
Germany	854	5,177	47	149	-807
Greece	436	2,791	223	1,930	-213
Italy	667	3,910	378	3,180	-289
Japan	1,180	7,145	292	1,679	-888
Netherlands	537	3,424	492	3,622	-45
Norway	1,072	6,931	912	7,177	-160
USSR	354	1,597	432	1,801	+78

Source: U.S. Department of Commerce, Maritime Administration, Handbook of Merchant Shipping Statistics Through 1958 (Washington: U.S. Government Printing Office, 1959), pp. 28-31.

governmental protection (such as the U.S. tramp fleet). The liner trades are rapidly becoming containerized. Large bulk carriers have taken over the traditional international tramping trades, and oil tankers have so grown that they hardly resemble their sisters of a few years ago. Meanwhile, the business of transporting people from one place to another by ship has all but ended, while the quite different cruise business is expanding rapidly.

Automation, a term loosely used in shipping to cover anything that reduces crew size, adds to the pace of change and its impact. To complete the list, several current and impending market and institutional developments complicate and intensify the technological revolution. The general demand for sea transport has increased enormously in the postwar era, and will continue to grow in the future. However, there are important structural changes within the larger market development that greatly alter the patterns of world shipping. The present international system is more structured and complex than it has ever been. Unions are politically and economically strong in many countries, especially in the United States. Taxes are high and there is considerable regulation, control, and encouragement of shipping under most flags.

The high cost and rigidity of operating under the American and, to a lesser extent, West European flags has encouraged the flow of capital to the "flags of convenience" fleets. Meanwhile, Japan has reemerged as a major shipping and shipbuilding power, and a large and expanding East European bloc shipping presence has suddenly appeared around the world. Many developing and semideveloped countries have entered world shipping, to the discomfort of the established flags, especially such cross-traders as Norway and Greece.

The effect of most of these political and institutional changes has been to reinforce the impact of the technical developments on the United States and other high wage countries. The combination of technological and institutional changes makes it critical that a nation desirous of maintaining a shipping industry adopt an appropriate maritime policy. It is equally critical that it prevent that policy from being made ineffective by poor administration or the activities of special interest groups. Unfortunately, the United States has failed on both counts.

TECHNOLOGICAL CHANGES

Although the components of the postwar technological revolution in shipping overlap and interrelate, examination requires that they be treated separately. This section will discuss the technological revolution, and the remaining two sections will discuss market and institutional changes, respectively.

Cargo Handling

The most striking aspect of the current revolution in marine technology is the way ships are loaded and unloaded, and the most impressive feature of that is containerization. Though conceptually simple, containerization is one of the greatest improvements in the movement of goods ever devised.

The container concept has been with us for well over a decade, but its full impact is only now being felt. The United States, especially in the person of Malcolm McLean, founder of Sea-Land Service, Inc., forced the concept on the shipping world during the mid-1960s. The predecessor of Sea-Land, Pan Atlantic Steamship Co., was incorporated in 1933. It was acquired by McLean in the early 1950s and began containership operations between the port of New York and Houston, Texas in 1956.[5] It then expanded to other domestic trades. Thus containerization developed under the protection of the cabotage restrictions.

Sea-Land began, and in 1970 operated, with a fleet of converted World War II-built ships. The first ones carried their own cranes and were self-loading and -unloading. As a trade route was developed for container traffic, large cranes were built on the docks and the crane-carrying vessels were shifted to new runs.

The other early introduction of container service was by Matson Navigation on the West Coast-Hawaii run. Matson converted three war-built vessels to full containerships in 1960.[6] Compared with the Sea-Land operation this was a modest development. It is interesting, though, that the only other early introduction of containerization also occurred in a protected domestic trade.

In 1966 Sea-Land tested the container concept on the North Atlantic with great success.[7] By 1970 its operations had spread throughout much of the world. It has been charged that the United States forced containerization on the rest of the world.[8] It would be more accurate, however, to say that Sea-Land forced the concept on the world, including the United States operators, before it was ready. Of course, containerization would have developed eventually. The surprising feature is that it was developed by an American-flag company.

The United States maintained a lead in container shipping throughout the 1960s. At the beginning of 1970 it continued to operate more containership tonnage and more containers than all other countries combined. After that, however, the balance began to shift in favor of foreign flags. The gap will continue to widen thereafter. *

---

*This view is not unanimous. A study commissioned by the Maritime Administration predicted that the U. S. share of container shipment will drop to 40 percent by 1975 and remain at that level until 1980. Traffic World, July 10, 1972, p. 62.

Containerships are rapidly displacing traditional break-bulk liners, and liner operators have suddenly found themselves in a very different economic and business situation. Capital requirements per ship have mushroomed. The cargo-carrying capacity of a fleet of a given size has been multiplied by a factor of from three to five, and the shipping companies are being forced to integrate their operations with other modes of transportation. It is essential that these expensive and rigidly scheduled ships be kept running without interruption, a requirement that presents the industry's industrial relations system with an intensified challenge.

The European response to the container revolution has been giant international consortia, such as Atlantic Container Lines, made up of Cunard Line, French Line, Holland America Line, Swedish America Line, Swedish Transatlantic Line, and Wallenius Line. By 1970 the consortium operated 10 containerships between the United States and Europe. The American response has been less organized, but there have been a few mergers. Considering the economies of scale available, the magnitude and structure of capital requirements, and the operating demands of a containership fleet, there undoubtedly will be pressure for additional mergers.

The economies of scale available are impressive. A containership pier can achieve loading and unloading rates of 1,000 tons per berth hour, compared with 60 tons per hour for break-bulk operation. [9] Full utilization of port facilities under the higher loading and unloading rate requires a larger number of ships. As the number of vessels in a fleet increases, fewer "suits" of containers are needed per ship. [10] That is, the number of boxes needed at each end of the run for port operation and pickup and delivery does not expand in proportion to the number carried by the ships.

The carrying capacity of a fleet of a given size has also increased because of higher steaming speeds, greater size, and especially the faster turnaround of the new ships. In general, a three-to-one displacement of conventional vessels by containerships is a conservative estimate, since the speed and carrying capacity of newly built ships are growing rapidly. The ships that will replace the break-bulk vessels still in service will be more efficient than the containerships now on berth. In addition, the number and efficiency of container ports and other related services is also increasing.

The "third generation" containerships under consideration in Europe will steam at over 30 knots and carry about 2,000 boxes each (presumably 20-foot equivalents). [11] In the United States the basic designs developed by the Maritime Administration's project "Competitive Merchant Ship" (CMX) are more modest. The larger models will carry about 1,500 20-foot equivalents and steam at 23 or 24 knots. [12]

Accepting a three-to-one displacement ratio and ignoring the partial containership as a passing phenomenon, it is interesting to note that at the beginning of 1970 there were 76 full containerships in

operation under the U.S. flag, out of a world total of about 130.[13]
There were an additional 41 full containerships under construction or
on order to be delivered by 1973 to U.S.-flag operators.[14] This does
not include several barge-carrying vessels (to be discussed separately).

It appears that even if we allow for some replacement of older,
less efficient containerships by newer ones, and for considerable
growth in that part of U.S. oceanborne foreign trade carried by American-
flag ships, the United States will have enough containership capacity
to replace its entire break-bulk liner fleet with containerships by the
mid-1970s. Other countries, and especially the European consortia,
will experience even greater expansion.

Forecasts of containership growth seem overly conservative.
Litton Systems predicted that by 1973, 23 percent of total U.S. liner
trade would be transported by containerships. A longer-range study
by the New York Journal of Commerce estimated 41.5 percent by 1983.[15]
When one considers the excess capacity now developing and the impact
it is having on rates on the North Atlantic, it is difficult to accept these
estimates. When the inevitable worldwide rate war begins in earnest
between underutilized containerships and those companies and flags
that fail to adopt the new technology, the conventional liners will be
driven from most trade routes.[16] These routes will thereafter be served
by a small number of large containership operators.[17] At the rate container technology is being adopted, the transition will soon be completed.

Some observers think that containerships will be employed only
on the routes between the developed countries and that the trades with,
and between, the developing nations will be left to the traditional
liners. There are two factors working against this. First, as the
developing excess capacity of containership tonnage results in the
newer generation of vessels displacing still-usable container capacity
from the more lucrative trades, owners of the latter will seek employment on the less competitive routes to and between the developing
countries. There are few countries engaged in world trade that do not
have a highway and/or rail system capable of supporting a container
operation. The few exceptions are rapidly building a transport network
as an essential element of economic development.

Second, those situations that do not lend themselves to the usual
container operation seem especially well suited to its cousin, the barge-
carrying ship. The two models so far developed are the lighter aboard
ship (LASH) and the Sea-Bee. This modification of the container concept has much to offer a region with a good river or coastal transport
system or only shallow-draft ports. It may also be a solution to
chronic port congestion or longshore labor problems. One or all of
these conditions prevail in most developing countries.

There were two LASH-type ships in operation in 1970 between
the U.S. Gulf Coast and Europe: Central Gulf's Japanese-built,
Norwegian-manned and -registered Arcadia Forest and Atlantic Forest.

The ships are 43,541 dwt and carry 73 lighters that hold up to 27,000 tons of cargo each.[18] Fourteen more LASH and Sea-Bee ships were on order for delivery by 1973 for U.S.-flag operation alone.[19] By June 30, 1973, there were 10 such ships in operation under the American flag.[20]

Except for a few ships equipped with heavy-lift gear, there will be no economic justification for traditional break-bulk liner service in international shipping by the late 1970s. That which survives will owe its existence to the protectionist policies of certain countries.

In addition to the dramatic developments of containerization, including barge-type containers, there have been other important developments in cargo handling that have received much less notice. Little liner cargo is ever moved today in real break bulk, the way the term was once used. The simple expedient of strapping individual cases to pallets and moving them with fork-lift trucks has greatly facilitated the loading and unloading of both ships holds and containers. We are used to this concept now, but 20 years ago it was still new.

Another cargo-handling development that is often overlooked but, with palletization, is part of the technological revolution, is the way bulk cargoes are now loaded and unloaded. The specific method varies with the commodity and the port, but most use some sort of continuous movement by conveyer or vacuum action. In a related development, many liquid cargoes once shipped in drums are now moved in bulk and are pumped in and out of ships tanks.

Although less spectacular, the effect of palletization and continuous-flow loading and unloading is similar to containerization. They all greatly reduce the amount of time a ship spends in port. As the ratio of sea time to port time is increased, it becomes profitable to invest more in ship size and speed.

Ship Size

The second dimension of the technological revolution is size. Prior to World War II, freighters went up to about 9,000 dwt and tankers 15,000. The wartime shipbuilding program did not push these dimensions much further. The Liberty ship was 10,800 dwt and the T-2 tanker 15,850.[21] The effect of the war was to make these respective sizes standard throughout the world. Because of the similarity of the war-built ships and the loss of most of the older ones, the immediate postwar world fleet was the most homogeneous in history. Practically all tankers were T-2s and all freighters either Liberties, Victories, C-2s, or C-3s. Although the ships built later in the war were considerably faster than the Liberty, their capacity was not much greater.

Liners

As with other aspects of the technological revolution, the increase in the size of ships has occurred throughout the industry. The conventional freighter, however, has grown little in comparison with other types of vessels. In addition to the effects of the supply of war-built ships, liner operation prior to containerization did not lend itself to increasing ship size.

Liners spend too much time in port, working a few holds at a time, to tie up more capital than necessary. Furthermore, since the 1930s it has been necessary for break-bulk ships to call at a range of ports in order to acquire a reasonably full load before sailing abroad and to offer delivery to a range of ports at the other end. If a liner's draft is increased significantly, access to many ports is eliminated. Consequently, the growth of conventional break-bulk liners has been modest since the war.

The containership is different. An efficient container operation requires a very fast turn-around to fully utilize the technical capacity of the ship. This requires that it call at one or two ports at each end. [22] Since there is less need to call at "out ports," the containership is released from their draft requirements.

The influence of World War II has been felt on the growth of containerships, too, however. All of the early ones were converted war-built vessels. This automatically excluded the possibility of much growth. Next came the conversion of the somewhat larger, recently built freighters, such as the 13,300 dwt American Racer of the United States Lines. This allowed a modest increase in size but still reflected the limitations of the conventional freighter. The full containerships now being built and ordered are free of such restraints. The model designs solicited by the Maritime Administration from the Bath Iron Works and the Newport News shipyards are each approximately 20,000 dwt. [23] In 1971 Japan was building one of 35,250 dwt. [24]

This, of course, is not the final development. The CMX designs may, in fact, be overly modest. Since a containership ideally calls at one port at each end, the optimal ship for that run should be tailored to the minimum draft of its particular pair of ports, assuming sufficient cargo is available and economies of scale remain.

There will probably develop a range of containership sizes going from very large vessels totally specialized to a pair of busy deep-water ports to comparatively smaller ones similarly specialized by their dimensions. There will also be a number of very small vessels operated as feeders in areas such as the Baltic, Mediterranean, or Caribbean. It is expected, however, that considerable economies of scale remain and that the largest ships usable on a run will dominate that trade—assuming enough cargo is available to maintain an adequate schedule. This implies considerable growth for the containership in the years ahead.

Bulk Carriers

A more impressive expansion of size has occurred among bulk carriers. In fact, the bulk carrier concept is primarily the application of size to the transport of traditionally tramp cargoes. Bulk carriage on a large scale became commonplace only in the late 1950s and early 1960s.[25] Since then it has grown to such an extent that it is rapidly becoming synonymous with long-haul tramping for most commodities.

Size is the most important factor in the economics of bulk carriage.[26] The larger the ship, within the limits set by port and canal draft limitations, the more cheaply it can deliver cargo. The lower the unit cost of supplying transport service, the lower the rate necessary to cover the costs of operation and to stay in business. Since international tramp shipping is a highly competitive business subject to periodic contraction, this is a very significant point. Thus, within the limits mentioned, there is a strong inducement to build the largest ships for which cargoes can be found.

There are limits, however, on the size to which a bulk carrier operated as a tramp may expand. They are not technical but, rather, are due to the inability of most ports to accommodate deep-draft ships. Few ports in the world have a depth greater than 35 feet.[27] As the required draft of a ship is increased, the number of ports in which it can acquire or deliver a full load is reduced. Since tramping requires maximum flexibility of operation, there exists an economic force offsetting the benefits available from large size bulk carriers.

It should be noted that this limitation does not apply to industrial bulk carriers or to ships under long-term contract. In such cases the drafts of a single pair of ports are the limiting factor. Since channels can be dredged and plants located where there is access to deep water, the limit is not overly restrictive. It should also be noted that even in tramp operation, draft limitations are not absolute. A partially loaded large bulk carrier can carry more cargo more cheaply than a conventional tramping freighter, even when limited to the draft of the smaller ship.[28]

There has been considerable growth in bulk carriers, and more is promised. The first ones, like the first containerships, were converted from war-built tonnage. The T-2 tanker, sometimes "jumboized" by welding in an additional midsection, was most commonly used. In 1966 the average size of a bulk ship on order was 41,000 dwt.[29] Obviously, the average size has grown and is growing rapidly. It must be remembered that an average includes some ships of very large dimension. Some combination ore-bulk-oil ships, fitted and designed to carry any kind of liquid or dry bulk cargo, are now in the range of 150,000 tons and may go up to 200,000 tons in the near future.[30]

As indicated above, there are definite limits to the growth of the bulk carrier. One estimate, based on cargo studies and Panama Canal limitations (36-38 feet), considers the largest size feasible for general tramp operations to be about 60,000 dwt.[31] Not all bulk carriers will attain this size. Some, especially those operated as industrial carriers, will greatly exceed it. However, it probably represents the typical bulk carrier of the future.

If we accept the 60, 000 dwt size as a rough yardstick, we can get an idea of the magnitude of this part of the technological revolution. Unlike the development of the containership, the United States has lagged in the bulk carrier field. In fact, it is hardly in it at all.

Tankers

In many respects the tankship is similar to the dry bulk carrier; but because it operates in a different market and has had an independent development, it will be discussed separately. As with the bulk carrier, the principal feature of recent tanker development has been the expansion in size. However, the growth in the size of tankers had an earlier beginning than that of the bulk carrier, and its upper limit is not as easily foreseen.

During World War II, the 16, 000-dwt T-2 tanker was considered a large ship. The tankships built immediately after the war ranged from 22, 000 to 35, 000 dwt. [32] Today there are many tankers in operation over 200, 000 dwt and several over 300, 000. It is estimated that the average size of the tankers now under contract is about 100, 000 dwt (compared with 40, 000 dwt for dry bulk carriers). [33]

After such a development one is reluctant to speculate about the upper limit tankers will eventually reach. At each level of development, there are technical limits beyond which further expansion is impractical. As technology improves, this "maximum" limit is pushed higher and higher. [34] Presumably there is an upper limit somewhere, but it is difficult to define what the limiting criteria are on a route not hampered by draft limitations. Unlike the dry bulk carrier, the giant tanker can expect to operate between a given number of ports—and may remain on the same run for its entire life. Furthermore, it can load and discharge via pipelines extending miles out to sea. [35] On some trades there is virtually no draft limitation.

The impetus to employ larger and larger tankships is the same as in the case of dry-bulk carriers. The larger the ship, the more cheaply it can deliver a given cargo and the lower the rate it can accept in order to remain in operation in a depressed market. This point can best be made by an example. In 1970 a 50, 000-ton tanker could deliver oil from Kuwait to Rotterdam via the Suez Canal for $3. 36 a ton at prevailing oil prices (if the Canal were open). A 200, 000-tonner going by way of the Cape of Good Hope could deliver for $2. 40 a ton. [36]

The example illustrates two points besides the $. 96 a ton difference in delivered price. First, it has not been so many years since a 50, 000-ton vessel was considered a very large "supertanker." Furthermore, a 200, 000-tonner is not an uncommonly large ship today and will, in fact, soon be dwarfed by some of the ships now on order.

The other point involves an additional impetus to the development of the giant tanker: the desire of operators to be free of the uncertainties of the Suez Canal and similar waterways. [37] Recent history has strengthened this desire and, as indicated above, the goal has been attained.

The importance of the supertanker portion of the technological revolution must not be blown out of perspective. Its impact will be lessened by the inability of the largest tankers to enter any but the deepest ports. They may, in fact, be excluded from whole areas of the world, such as the North Sea, the Baltic, the Mediterranean, and the Gulf of Mexico, because of draft limitations and the pollution problems caused by shipwrecks.

Speed

Speed is the most complex factor in ship capacity. At first glance, it would appear that a faster ship has a higher transport capability than a slower one. At slow speeds this is true, but above 15 knots or so it becomes more complicated and a decision on the appropriate designed speed must include many other factors. The optimum speed declines with an increase in the cost of fuel, while an increase in cargo rates raises the optimal speed. Relatively high sea-going wage costs justify higher speeds, but high construction costs work in the opposite direction. [38]

As speed is increased, fuel consumption goes up disproprotionately, which means that more bunker (fuel) space is required. This reduces the amount of space available for cargo. On the other hand, a fast ship may have a market advantage if fast service is valued by shippers. Of course, each of these factors is influenced by the level of marine technology.

At any level of technology there is an absolute limit to the rate at which a ship of a given dimension may be propelled through the water. There is also a more important and elusive range beyond which it is impractical to go. Because of this economic barrier, speed is better thought of as a dependent variable—dependent upon the other values in the capacity equation.

As ships spend less time in port, it becomes profitable to invest more heavily in speed. Additional speed allows a company to maintain a given schedule with less tonnage and, consequently, less labor. Within limits, speed may be a good investment in itself. As container shipping becomes increasingly competitive, the advantage of early delivery may become critical.

The containership models of the Maritime Administration's CMX have speeds in the 23-24 knot range. [39] This is modest compared with containerships capable of over 30 knots being built in Europe.

Containerships of over 30 knots will be common within a few years on the North Atlantic and trans-Pacific runs.

High speed is of less importance for bulk carriers and tankers. The shippers of liquid and dry bulk commodities do not value speed in transport, providing the charter is fulfilled in a timely fashion. Tanker and bulk carrier operators have found it more profitable to utilize additional horsepower for the propulsion of larger and larger ships. The economies of ship size are so overwhelming in bulk transport that they offset everything else. Both bulk carriers and tankers are now in the 15- to 18-knot range, not much faster than the T-2 tanker of World War II. This will not change in the near future. One recent study found the optimal speed for bulk carriers to be 16-18 knots, and the CMX models call for 16-17 knots. [40]

Developments in ship speed are predictable—at least for the near future. We may expect containerships of 30 knots, while the speeds of large bulk carriers and tankers will not go beyond 20 knots. [41]

At present there is relatively little economic difference between steam and diesel. [42] The gas turbine also is competitive. Nuclear propulsion has been an expensive experiment on the N. S. Savannah of the United States and the Otto Hahn of West Germany, but its value at very high levels of horsepower cannot be denied. The threshold at which nuclear power becomes competitive is 50,000 shaft horsepower (shp). [43] In the 100,000-shp range, nuclear propulsion is definitely competitive. [44]

The main advantage of the nuclear plant at high levels of horsepower is its complete elimination of bunker requirements. In the fall of 1968, the N. S. Savannah underwent its first partial refueling. The ship had sailed 331,680 miles on 122.4 pounds of uranium since going into service six years earlier. [45]

When the economies of nuclear propulsion at high horsepower levels are viewed in the context of the projected growth in the sizes and speeds of ships in the near future, there is no question that it will be employed extensively within a few years. The Japanese have committed themselves to a nuclear ship experiment. There have been important expressions of interest in nuclear propulsion in the United States, and the Maritime Administration has received an application for construction subsidy to build 12 nuclear-powered tankers of 415,000 dwt and 120,000 shp each. [46] Notwithstanding such interest, nuclear propulsion remains uncompetitive for most ship operation at present.

Automation

The last front of the technological revolution is an internal one. Automation in shipping means crew reduction, which can be accomplished in many ways. It has been well known for years that ships of the future will carry fewer men than they do today or did yesterday. The technology to do this has been available for years, and much of it is already in operation ashore. Some of it has already been introduced on board ships.

It is technically feasible to operate a medium-size freighter, with available equipment, with 17 men. [47] Some engineers have indicated that it is possible to operate a fully automated ship with as few as 12 men. [48] Estimates of this sort are unrealistic for the immediate future. Technical feasibility is only one factor in the determination of crew size. In the United States, and in other countries where shipping is unionized, crew size will be determined, at least in part, by collective bargaining and, to a lesser extent, through legislation and regulation.

Crew complements on some of the newer U.S.-flag liners have been reduced from 56 men to 32 men in recent years. [49] The manning requirements of a new tanker or bulk carrier will not be very different from that of a liner. Their operating requirements, in terms of crew size, are very similar. Perhaps the size of ships' crews will be reduced slightly in the future, but it is doubtful that they will go significantly below the 30-35 man level of recently built ships within the next 10 to 20 years for the United States. There are three reasons for this.

First, labor relations realities are against it. As crews become smaller through the elimination of unnecessary jobs, each union's determination to protect the jobs remaining to it is strengthened. Interunion rivalry and organizational requirements insure that future cuts will be met with increased resistance. This is especially true for the officers' unions, which have proportionately more to lose from the elimination of each job. Meanwhile, ships are becoming more costly to build and more expensive to be strike-bound. As the unions' will to resist additional cuts in manning is strengthened, the employers' ability to withstand prolonged strikes for limited objectives will be weakened.

Much of the interest in manning levels is misplaced. Increased size, speed, and other technological developments like containerization have increased labor productivity by several hundred percent over the past few years and promise to increase it much more in the near future. Meanwhile, crew reductions of one man with a productivity increase of 2 or 3 percent (unrealistically assuming a net marginal product of labor of zero) have been met with bitter resistance by labor. [50]

A second reason why crew sizes are unlikely to go much below the level of 30-35 in the near future is that it is easier to design a ship to run with, say, 17 men than it is to run it with 17 men. Seamen miss ships, get sick, hurt, drunk, etc. The Coast Guard requires 24 men (all watchstanders) on a conventional freighter. [51] Most union manning scales are higher. The safety demands of a semiautomated ship may require fewer than 24 watchstanders, but there is a minimum. When steward's department personnel and some other nonessentials, such as an electrician and a boatswain are added, the "reasonable" minimum may prove higher than the engineers estimate.

Finally, these estimates are based on assumptions of having practically all maintenance done ashore. This may not be economical. A ship's engineer can pack a pump or perform one of the thousand other minor maintenance jobs on a ship in a few hours, with little cost other than his wages. If the same job is done in a shipyard, it involves job orders, requisitions for supplies, and coordinating the efforts of machinists, electricians, riggers, and others. This may be workable for large jobs; but if the typical shipboard job is to be shifted ashore, a different kind of shipyard will be needed.

Crew size on American-flag ships will remain at the 30 to 35-man level for the near future. There will be attempts to lower manning scales by shipping management and other attempts by labor to raise them. Eventually a balance will be reached that will hold for as long as the present institutional arrangements last. An estimate of an average crew size of 35 men per ship for the next 20 years is probably realistic for the United States, with the actual average being above 35 for the 1970s and below it for the 1980s.

THE DEMAND FOR SEA TRANSPORT

The technological developments discussed above are complemented by important market developments. The economic context of the industry has undergone considerable change since World War II and will experience more change in the future. Much of this development either relates to other components of the maritime revolution or is the continuation of long-run market developments. A few factors, however, are independent enough to consider as contributing to the maritime revolution.

Passenger Service

With a few exceptions, the movement of passengers across oceans by ship has all but ceased, and the future of that which remains is uncertain. [52] A ship, regardless of its size, speed, or luxury, is unable to compete with the airplane. In addition to its speed and cost advantages, the airplane is a relatively small unit, which insures a generally high load factor and more operational flexibility than a ship. While a ship such as the S.S. United States must deliver its 1,000 or so passengers to one or two major ports, regardless of their ultimate destination, the air lines can transport the same number to 10 cities nonstop and still maintain a profitable load factor. This is especially important in Europe, where many of the major cities are inland. Because of the relatively high labor intensity of passenger service, the United States was the first to feel the squeeze; but it is only a matter of time before there will be no long-haul passenger liner service left under any flag.

A related development is the phenomenal growth of the cruise trade. The two trades are linked in the minds of most people. However, they are quite different in terms of market, type of operation, and even in the ships that should be employed. The last is quite important. In recent years many passenger liners have entered the cruise trades during slack periods. This was better than going into layup and disbanding their large and highly skilled crews, but they are not efficient at such operation. The ships have too much horsepower and speed for the run and too much luxury, with its attending labor costs, for the clientele served.

Growth in Demand

Demand for shipping service is derived from an infinite number of specific product demands that are, in turn, determined by such factors as population size, the level of consumption, and the degree of international specialization of production. The much-discussed population explosion is very real. One of its less Malthusian implications is an expansion in the demand for sea transport. The relationship between population and demand for shipping may not be proportional, but it undoubtedly is strongly positive. World population has grown from 1 billion in 1850 to 2 billion in 1930 to 3 billion in 1960. In 1980 it will be about 4 billion. [53] Even the most conservative estimate of the impact of the population explosion on world shipping must be enormous. However, population is but one factor in the demand for sea transport.

The level of consumption as expressed in gross national product (GNP) is of equal importance. The fact that this growth has been concentrated in developed countries increases its impact on the demand for shipping service by creating an imbalanced trade between the rich and poor nations. This results in more voyages in ballast.

If we limit our focus to the United States and employ an approach developed in the IMTF Report, but update it by using an approximate GNP of $950 billion for 1970 and a 4 percent annual growth rate based on recent work, [54] we gain an idea of the expansion in the level of consumption in the United States and perhaps of the other industrialized countries.

The GNP of the United States has grown from $503 billion in 1960 to $685 billion in 1965 to approximately $950 billion in 1970.[55] Based on our rough estimate, GNP will reach $1,156 billion by 1975 and $1,406 billion by 1980. The IMTF Report based its now-obsolete projections of the value of oceanborne trade on 4.5 to 4.8 percent of GNP.[56] Using the 4.5 percent figure with updated estimates of GNP, it is estimated that the value of the oceanborne foreign trade of the United States will reach $52 billion in 1975 and $63 billion in 1980, compared with approximately $43 billion in 1970.

Drawing another relationship from the IMTF Report, the volume of oceanborne foreign trade in long tons is related to its value by a factor of 11. On this basis the volume of U.S. oceanborne foreign trade will be an estimated 572 million long tons in 1975 and 693 million long tons in 1980, compared with only 473 million in 1970 and 340 million as recently as 1966.

The reader is cautioned that no claim to accuracy is made. These figures only indicate direction of movement and general magnitude. The expansion of the oceanborne foreign trade of the United States over the next decade will be very large. If anything, the above analysis understates the case because the elasticity of demand for imports is thought to be rather high. Furthermore, the shipment of low-value bulk commodities is growing at the expense of higher-valued general cargo for the United States.

The oceanborne foreign trade of the United States has expanded and will continue to expand greatly. This statement is true for the rest of the world as well. One source estimates that between 1960 and 1967 world trade increased at a rate of 8.9 percent per year, and seaborne trade by 8.7 percent.[57] Another estimates that world trade rose by 10 percent between 1967 and 1968.[58]

Changes in Demand

The growth predictions of world trade conceal several important developments in the trade patterns that affect shipping. Developments in passenger carriage have been discussed. A second phenomenon of much greater importance is the growth of bulk carriage. This topic has been partially treated under the development of the dry bulk carrier. It remains to indicate the magnitude of this development. World bulk carrier shipments have grown at a rate of 24 percent per year since 1960.[59] Of course, some of this growth was the transfer of conventional tramp cargoes to the newer type of ship, but much of it was genuine growth in bulk commodity trade. There is every reason to expect this to continue.

In addition to the overall growth of bulk transport, other events have served to increase the demand for shipping service. Mines in the industrialized countries are becoming depleted, resulting in the need to transport huge quantities of ore from foreign sources. The best example of this is exhaustion of the Mesabi Range in the United States.

Another important change in the pattern of world trade is the virtual end— even reversal— of the traffic in coal from Europe to the rest of the world, especially to the developing countries. [60] The coal trade has traditionally balanced the trade between Europe and the less developed countries in terms of volume. Its end will result in more voyages in ballast, and thus more demand for ships.

This list is not complete. The closing of the Suez Canal and the Cold War could be added. The enormous growth in world oceanborne trade is an important factor in the maritime revolution. Its effect is to accelerate the adoption of the new technology while mitigating some of the displacement effect.

POLITICAL AND INSTITUTIONAL DEVELOPMENTS IN WORLD SHIPPING

An examination of the third maritime revolution would not be complete without mentioning the more important developments in the political and institutional framework within which it is taking place. Their effect is to greatly complicate the already complex technological and market phenomena.

Flags of Convenience

The practice of nationals of one country documenting ships under the flag of another is an old one. In its simpler form it is of limited concern to most nations. The significance of the modern development of registering ships under the so-called flags of convenience (or flags of necessity) is due to its magnitude, its concentration under a few nonmaritime flags, and especially its economic rationale.

The growth of the flags-of-convenience problem is best illustrated by its most striking example, Liberia. In 1949 there were 15 ocean-going ships, totaling 374,000 dwt, under Liberian registry. [61] By June 30, 1970, there were 1,754 Liberian-flag ships totaling 56,668,000 dwt. [62] The combination of political stability, close business and legal ties with the United States, a dollar-based currency, and virtually no taxation or regulation has proved irresistible to American (and other) shipping capital.

Since there is little chance of the wage and tax structure in the United States lowering or of a complete reversal of U.S. maritime policy, the flags of convenience are here to stay. Indeed, they will continue to grow, with new flags, such as those of Bermuda and some of the Arab countries, joining the ranks of the traditional Panamanian, Liberian, and Honduran (Panlibhon) convenience flags.* The U.S. government has accepted this fact as implied by its program of effective United States control (EUSC). If the owner of a Panlibhon ship enters into a contractual arrangement with the Maritime Administration that agrees to make the vessel available to the United States in the event of national emergency or war, the ship is entitled to interim war risk insurance. [63] In 1970 there were 394 ships of 18.4 million dwt deemed under effective control by the U.S. Navy. Of these, 272 were tankships and 87 bulk carriers. [64] Although this controversial program may not be foolproof, it is reasonable to assume that most of the ships under EUSC, as well as many additional flags-of-convenience ships, will be available to the United States in case of national emergency. [65]

An important feature of the flags of convenience is that they present a very attractive alternative to the registration of ships under the American or other established flags. This increases the displacement effects of the technological revolution on high-cost national fleets by widening the differential between alternatives. The difference in operating costs between an American and a European ship may be relatively large because of the high wage level of the United States. This distance is lessened to some extent, however, by the high levels of taxation and comparable degree of regulation of most European flags. This militating effect is not present in the case of Panlibhon. In consequence, the existence of the flags of convenience makes the adoption of an appropriate national maritime policy of even greater importance to high-cost flags.

Emergence and Ambitions of New Flags

Another development pertaining to the flag of documentation is the emergence and ambitions of new shipping centers. This development consists of the natural expansion of a few flags, based on economic growth and diversification, and those that are, or will be, encouraged in the hothouse of flag preference.

Most striking among the first group has been the rise of Japan, whose meteoric reemergence as a major shipping and shipbuilding power has no parallel. This has been a natural corollary of the general economic growth of this island industrial power. In fact, it would be unrealistic not to expect the Japanese marine to keep pace with the country's economic development.

_____

*Honduras is no longer an important flag of convenience.

To date, the Japanese have been largely engaged in the carriage of their own rapidly growing foreign trade. The influence of the growth of their fleet on other flags has been limited. If the Japanese enter cross-trading in the future, they will present extremely sharp competition to other established flags. Their wages are relatively low, their ships good, and their management excellent.

The other explosive expansion of national tonnage has been that of the Russians and, to a lesser extent, the East Germans and Poles. Their expansion dates from the Suez crisis of 1956 and especially the Cuban missile crisis of 1962. The teeth in the U.S. quarantine was the blacklisting of neutral ships that carried commodities from Eastern Europe to Cuban ports.[66] The blockade proved effective and presented the Soviets with a visible weakness in their ability to pursue an aggressive foreign policy at a distance.

Of course, the Russians are not as "red" as they are usually painted. If the events of 1956 had not impressed them with the value of a merchant fleet, their expanding economy soon would have. The motives of trade expansion and foreign exchange earnings are less dramatic, but their influence probably is more lasting and is as consistent with Cold War strategy as are more purely militaristic ones.

The Russian fleet has grown from 716 ships of 2,510,000 gross tons in 1956, to 1,766 ships of 10,418,000 gross tons as of June 30, 1970.[67] Much of this increase is an expansion into international shipping and cross-trading for the first time. The USSR is suddenly one of the major shipping powers in the world. Unlike the Japanese, the Russians do not intend to limit their interests to their own trades. The East European ships are subject to no real cost limitations in a competitive struggle, so their entry into cross-trading is disturbing to the Western maritime powers. When it is learned that both the USSR and East Germany are building containerships, it is alarming.[68]

Ambitions worthy of equal alarm exist in many of the developing and semideveloped countries. Although unwelcome, observers consider the emergence of the East European fleets as inevitable. A different attitude prevails toward developing nations that aspire to enter the shipping business. It is considered proper for the established shipping powers to lecture the developing countries on the difficulties they will encounter and admonish them to leave shipping to those who know how.

The most disturbing feature of this development to the established maritime countries is not the added competition of the new flags but, rather, the manner in which some of them have supported, and will support and protect, their relatively inefficient fleets.

There is no question that many developing and semideveloped countries intend to establish national fleets despite advice to the contrary and formidable economic hurdles. Among the more popular rationales for their decisions are the shortage of tonnage experienced during World War II and its disastrous effects on their foreign trade; a way of preserving and perhaps earning precious hard currency, thereby improving their balances of payments; an expression of national pride and independence from former colonial powers; and part of a program to develop and diversify their economies. [69]

An evaluation of the motives of the developing countries or of the economic arguments of the established maritime powers is not called for here. The important points are that the emerging nations are not likely to be dissuaded from their ambitions and that most of them will find their national fleets a disappointment. Since few developing countries can afford to support their fleets with direct subsidies, the new flags will resort to some form of national or regional discrimination. Both are already operating in Latin America. In 1964 Brazil established a quota system on its coffee trade with the U.S. East Coast that restricted 80 percent of the trade to the Brazilian carriers <u>Lloyd Brasiliero</u> and <u>Netumar</u> and certain American operators. This is the first time on recent record that one country has unilaterally decided to restrict its trade with another country to the ships of the two countries involved. [70] Uruguay and Argentina have since taken similar steps.

There undoubtedly will be more instances of such action in the future, especially in Latin America, where 60 percent of the total tonnage is owned and operated by governments. [71] As these fleets continue to find themselves in trouble, flag discrimination is such an obvious solution that it is bound to be employed. It must be remembered that the developing countries have not shared in the fruits of free trade and unrestricted shipping to the extent that the developed countries have— or, at least, they do not think they have. At the United Nations Conference on Trade and Development at New Delhi in 1968, the practice of flag discrimination was defended by the emerging nations on the grounds that they are denied suitable shares of the existing trade by the conferences and cannot afford subsidies. [72]

This is not a black-and-white issue. Flag discrimination will reduce aggregate world income and will especially hurt established third-country traders, such as Norway. On the other hand, the assumption of equal marginal utility of income between countries is questionable, and the benefits of unrestricted shipping have not been evenly distributed. [73] If flag discrimination proves to benefit the poorer nations at the expense of the rich ones, it will have a considerable appeal (to the poorer nations). *

South America has presented the world with another innovation in flag preference besides unilateral action. The Latin American Free

---

*Some 30 countries currently employ some form of flag discrimination. It is most popular in Latin America but has also appeared in West Africa. Traffic World, Apr. 17, 1972, p. 29; Aug. 28, 1972, p. 11.

Trade Area (LAFTA) has attempted to establish a form of regional flag discrimination among its member nations.[74] If successful, this practice is sure to spread to other regional organizations.

SUMMARY

The technological developments taking place in ocean shipping should operate to the relative advantage of a high-wage flag. All are in the direction of increasing capital intensity. When the improvements in cargo handling, ship size, speed, and reduced crew sizes are combined in a modern containership, large bulk carrier, or supertanker, the importance of wage costs per se is greatly reduced. Thus, the wage-cost disadvantage of the United States should be of less importance in the years ahead.

The capital requirements associated with the new technology are enormous. This too should be to the advantage of the United States relative to other flags, because of its well-organized capital markets. The difference of a fraction of a point on the financing costs of a $50 million, 20-year mortgage goes a long way in offsetting the remaining wage-cost disadvantage to a modern American-flag vessel.

The large capital expenses of the new ships are largely fixed cost. Fixed cost diminishes as a unit cost as volume increases, and increases as volume decreases. It is therefore more important than ever that the new ships sail "full and down." Also, it is essential that there be no interruptions in service due to work stoppages.

If the United States is to maintain a competitive shipping presence, it is essential that it adopt the new technology. The new ships are so productive in relation to those being displaced that a flag cannot possibly compete without the new technology. In the past it has been possible for some flags to compete internationally with outdated tonnage on the basis of lower labor costs, but this is not now possible. Wage costs are no longer that important, and they will become even less important in the future.

NOTES

1. Senate, Hearings on U.S. Maritime Policy, 1967, p. 56. The United States lost almost 750 ships during World War II. Traffic World, Mar. 6, 1965, p. 31.

2. 60 Stat. 41 (1946), 50 U.S.C.A. App. 1735 (1951).

3. John J. Clark and Margaret T. Norton, "The Merchant Marine: Subsidies and Competition," U.S. Naval Institute Proceedings 93 (Jan. 1967): 75.

4. U. S. Department of Commerce, Annual Report of the Secretary of Commerce (Washington: U. S. Government Printing Office, 1951), p. 70.

5. House, Hearings on Long-Range Maritime Program, 1968, p. 677.

6. U. S. Department of Commerce, Maritime Administration, Containerships, as of June 30, 1970 (Washington: Maritime Administration, ca. 1970), p. 3. Hereafter cited as Containerships, 1970.

7. James R. Barker and Robert Brandwein, The United States Merchant Marine in National Perspective (Lexington, Mass.: D. C. Heath, 1970), p. 24. A number of companies were exploring containerization around 1965-66, most notably American Export Isbrandtsen Lines.

8. Container News, Feb. 1970, p. 8.

9. Barker and Brandwein, op. cit., p. 25.

10. Ibid., p. 27.

11. "Container Revolution," German International 14 (Feb. 1970): 38.

12. Container News, July 1970, p. 48.

13. "Container Revolution," p. 34.

14. Container News, Feb. 1970, p. 21.

15. Norwegian Shipping News, Feb. 7, 1969, p. 30.

16. Ibid. A rate war raged out of control from some time in 1969 to the end of 1972. Traffic World, Jan. 10, 1972, p. 69.

17. Norwegian Shipping News, Feb. 7, 1969, p. 30.

18. Traffic World, Aug. 3, 1970, p. 18.

19. Container News, Feb. 1970, p. 21.

20. U. S. Department of Commerce, Maritime Administration, Vessel Inventory Report, United States Flag Dry Cargo and Tanker Fleets 1000 Gross Tons and Over as of June 30, 1973, Report no. MAR-560-19 (Washington: Maritime Administration, 1973). Hereafter cited as Vessel Inventory Report, 1973.

21. Samuel A. Lawrence, United States Merchant Shipping Policies and Politics (Washington: Brookings Institution, 1966), p. 95.

22. Norwegian Shipping News, Feb. 7, 1969, p. 29.

23. Fairplay, June 11, 1970, p. 45.

24. Traffic World, May 24, 1971, p. 28.

25. Kaare Petersen, "Trends in Shipping— 1945-1970, the Most Momentous Quarter Century in the History of Shipping," Norwegian Shipping News 26, no. 10C (June 1970): 38.

26. Booz-Allen Applied Research, Inc., Bulk Carrier Program Technical Requirements, P. B. 185, 763 (Washington: U. S. Department of Commerce, 1969), p. 66.

27. P. B. Buck, "Technological Change and the Merchant Seaman," International Labor Review 92, no. 4 (Oct. 1965): 304.

28. Booz-Allen, op. cit., p. 17.

29. Ibid., p. 7.

30. Rolf Stodter, "The Future of Shipping," Norwegian Shipping News 25, no. 10C (June 6, 1969): 46.

31. Booz-Allen, op. cit., p. 73.

32. Petersen, op. cit., p. 37.

33. Ingebrigt Borsheim, "Financing Problems in Shipping," Norwegian Shipping News 23, no. 21 (Nov. 10, 1967): 1054.

34. Petersen, loc. cit.

35. The United States has no such deep-water terminals. However, there has been considerable recent interest in their development by government and industry. Traffic World, May 5, 1972, p. 83; June 26, 1972, p. 62.

36. Houston Chronicle, July 24, 1970 as reported by Todd Daily Maritime, July 28, 1970.

37. Borsheim, op. cit., p. 1051.

38. Harry Benford, "Engineering Economy in Tanker Design," Society of Naval Architects and Marine Engineers Transactions 65 (1957): 824-25.

39. Fairplay, July 11, 1970, p. 45.

40. Booz-Allen, op. cit., p. 67; Fairplay, June 11, 1970, p. 45.

41. Stodter, op. cit., p. 49.

42. Booz-Allen, op. cit., p. 68.

43. Ibid., p. 45.

44. Stodter, loc. cit.

45. U.S. Department of Commerce, Annual Report of the Secretary of Commerce (Washington: U.S. Government Printing Office, 1970), p. 91.

46. Traffic World, Sept. 7, 1970, p. 63; July 2, 1973, p. 63; Nov. 26, 1973, p. 58.

47. Aaron W. Warner, "Technology and the Labor Force in the Offshore Maritime Industry," Industrial Relations Research Association Proceedings, 1965, p. 141.

48. Buck, op. cit., p. 299.

49. Aaron W. Warner and Alfred S. Eichner, "Analysis of Labor-Management Relations in the Off-Shore Operations of the East Coast Maritime Industry," a study prepared for the Maritime Administration of the United States Department of Commerce (June 1969), p. 263. Recent developments in crew-size reduction include a 32-man crew for Delta Lines LASH ships; a 38-man crew for the LASH vessels operated by Prudential-Grace and Pacific Far East Lines; and a 26-man crew for a 37,000-dwt tanker owned by Falcon Tankers. Traffic World, Apr. 26, 1971, p. 67; Jan. 4, 1971, p. 37; Jan. 1, 1972, p. 78.

50. Buck, op. cit., p. 307.

51. Quoted: Hirsch Samuel Ruchlin, Manpower Resources of the U.S. Maritime Industry: A Definitional and Descriptive Analysis of the Maritime Labor Force, P.B. 178, 727 (Washington: U.S. Department of Commerce, 1968), p. 54.

52. Petersen, op. cit., p. 41.

53. Encyclopaedia Britannica, 14th ed. (1969), "Population," p. 239.

54. IMTF Report, pp. 46-47; Stanley W. Black and R. Robert Russel, "An Alternative Estimate of Potential GNP," Review of Economics and Statistics 51, no. 1 (Feb. 1969): 70-76.

55. Richard M. Nixon, Economic Report of the President, 1970 (Washington: U.S. Government Printing Office, 1970), p. 177.

56. IMTF Report, Exhibit I.

57. Stodter, op. cit., p. 45.

58. Norwegian Shipping News, Feb. 7, 1969, p. 17.

59. Booz-Allen Applied Research, Inc., Forecast of U.S. Ocean-borne Foreign Trade in Dry Bulk Commodities, P.B. 183, 250 (Washington: U.S. Department of Commerce, 1969), p. 36.

60. Petersen, op. cit., p. 30.

61. Handbook of Merchant Shipping Statistics Through 1958, p. 31.

62. MARAD 1970, App. II, p. 63.

63. U.S. Department of Commerce, Maritime Administration, Effective United States Control of Merchant Ships, a Statistical Analysis, 1970 (Washington: U.S. Government Printing Office, 1970), pp. 7-8.

64. Ibid., p. 9.

65. Booz-Allen Applied Research, Inc., The National Need for a Dry Bulk Fleet (Washington: U.S. Department of Commerce, 1969), p. 36.

66. Petersen, op. cit., p. 33.

67. Handbook of Merchant Shipping Statistics Through 1958, p. 45 (83 of these ships, totaling 518,000 gross tons, were acquired from U.S. lend lease); MARAD 1970, App. II, p. 64.

68. Container News, Feb. 1970, p. 8. Soviet ships began calling regularly on the U.S. West Coast in January 1971 and on the East Coast in June 1973. Traffic World, Sept. 10, 1973, p. 11.

69. Norwegian Shipping News, Jan. 26, 1968, pp. 48-49.

70. Ibid., Feb. 1965, p. 30.

71. Dag Tresselt, "Shipping and Shipping Policy in Latin America," Norwegian Shipping News 23, no. 22 (Nov. 25, 1967): 1099.

72. Petersen, op. cit., p. 46.

73. S. G. Sturmey, "National Shipping Policies," Journal of Industrial Economics 14, no. 1 (Nov. 1965): 27.

74. Petersen, op. cit., p. 42.

INTRODUCTION

The main elements of U. S. maritime policy are subsidy, cargo preference, and cabotage restrictions. Although there is some overlap, each has become the main support of an important segment of the industry.

This chapter will examine the operation of U. S. maritime policy and evaluate its effectiveness. Much of it has been less than successful, but the results are not black-and-white.

The relative success of each element of maritime policy will be measured by the performance of the segment of the industry to which it primarily applies. Some of the data available do not lend themselves to such an analysis. However, there will be enough light shed upon the subject to answer the major questions.

The criteria used to evaluate each sector will be the size of the fleet, the quality of the ships in terms of age and technology, and, where relevant, the ability to compete.

All of the technological developments described in Chapter 4 should operate to the advantage of a high-wage country, and most of the market and institutional developments should enhance the benefits of adopting the new technology or make it more costly to fail to do so. Yet the American-flag shipping industry steadily declined throughout the period, and in 1970 much of it was about to disappear.

A problem that must be noted is the transition taking place among nonsubsidized liner operators. Until a few years ago Isthmian, States Marine, Waterman, and Central Gulf were essentially liner companies, although they also engaged in tramping and chartered ships to MSTS. However, with the closing of the Suez Canal in 1967 and the Vietnam buildup they increasingly entered the military charter and tramp markets.

In 1970 much of the nonsubsidized liner sector was in the midst of a transition from liner to quasi-tramp operation. However, the discussion that follows will refer to nonsubsidized liners as they existed about 1965. This should do little damage. The nonsubsidized liners are closely related to the tramp sector in matters of maritime policy, economic interests, and labor-management affiliations.

THE MERCHANT MARINE ACT OF 1936
AND THE LINER SECTOR

It may be argued that the Merchant Marine Act of 1936 has been either a great success or a dismal failure. There is evidence to support either position. The most vigorous supporters of the subsidy program are the subsidized operators and their unions, the shipbuilding industry and its unions, the Maritime Administration, and those members of Congress who find it in their interest to be members of the committees that handle maritime affairs. Criticism of the program is most strong from nonsubsidized operators and their unions and from economists. Both friends and enemies of the subsidy program have a history of overstating their cases and casting the issues in black and white. As often happens, the truth lies somewhere between.

The 1936 legislation has been partially successful in terms of its original objectives. Unfortunately, those objectives have long been out of date, and some of the side effects of the operation of the subsidy program have been regrettable.

Title I of the 1936 Act declares it the policy of the United States to promote efficient American-built, -owned and -manned merchant marine sufficient to carry a substantial portion of the nation's ocean-borne foreign trade over routes deemed essential to the United States and capable of serving as a military auxiliary in time of national emergency.[1] The language of this declaration of policy and the provisions of Title VI of the Act dealing with the ODS program have effectively limited the legislation to liner operation.[2] A 1952 legislative attempt to expand eligibility for CDS to all operators in the foreign trades proved ineffective.[3] The Maritime Administration continued to grant CDS only to companies with ODS contracts. Thus, an appraisal of the 1936 legislation must be limited to its effect on the liner sector.

The Liner Fleet

As of June 30, 1970, there were 13 subsidized companies operating 247 American-built and citizen-manned liners on trade routes designated as essential to the United States.[4] About 156 of the ships

TABLE 5. 1

Containership Capacity of U. S. Subsidized
Operators, 1970

Company	Subsidized Number Ships	Number of Container Ships	Partial Container Ships
American Export-Isbrandtsen			
Lines	33	9	
American Mail Line	10	0	10
American President Lines	24	0	10
Delta Steamship Lines	12	0	
Farrell Lines	14	2	
Gulf & South American			
Steamship Company	5	0	
Lykes Bros. Steamship			
Company	55	0	
Moore McCormack Lines	27	0	15
Oceanic Steamship Company	4	0	
Pacific Far East Lines	10	2	9
Prudential-Grace Lines			
(merger 12/18/69)	26	0	10
States Steamship Company	13	0	13
United States Lines	14	6	12
Total	247	19	79

Sources: U. S. Department of Commerce, Maritime Administration
MARAD 1970, Year of Transition, annual report of the Maritime Administration for fiscal year 1970 (Washington: U. S. Government Printing
Office, 1971), App. X, pp. 75-76; and Containerships, as of June 30,
1970 (Washington: Maritime Administration, ca. 1970).

had been built since 1956. [5] Nineteen were full containerships and
another 79 had partial container capacity. [6] Table 5. 1 lists the subsidized companies, their ships, and the degree to which they had
adopted containerization.

Table 5. 2 lists the important nonsubsidized liner companies with
a primary interest in foreign trade carriage. It excludes Matson Navigation and Seatrain Lines. Matson is overwhelmingly involved in
domestic carriage, although it also traded in Japan. Seatrain is an
amorphous and dynamic organization. In 1970 Seatrain and its affiliates
(Cefor, Hudson Waterways, Manhattan Tankers, and Transeastern)
operated a total of 29 ships. Six were tankers and 19 were containerships or partial containerships. Seatrain was very heavily engaged in

TABLE 5.2

U.S. Nonsubsidized Companies with Important
Operations in the Foreign Trades, 1970

	Total Ships	Full Container Ships	Partial Container Ships	Estimated Ships in Foreign Trade
Central Gulf	11			11
Isthmian Lines	24			24
Sea-Land Service	42	42		34
Containerships Chartering				
Donmac Corporation				
Madison Transportation				
Monterey Transportation				
Litton Industries Leasing				
Sea-Land Service				
States Marine	16			16
Waterman	17		2	17
Total	110	42	2	101

Notes: Matson Navigation and Seatrain excluded.
         Isthmian and States Marine were "affiliated" organizations
in 1970.

Sources: U.S. Department of Commerce, Maritime Administration,
Vessel Inventory Report, United States Flag Dry Cargo and Tanker Fleets
1000 Gross Tons and Over as of June 30, 1970, report no. MAR-560-19
(Washington: Maritime Administration, 1971); Containerships, as of
June 30, 1970 (Washington: Maritime Administration, ca. 1970).

military charter operation. However, it was also engaged in domestic
liner operation between New York and Puerto Rico and the West Coast
and Hawaii, and had recently entered the North Atlantic container
trade. In addition Seatrain had leased a portion of the old Brooklyn
Navy Yard and was building its own ships.* This company defies
classification and will be omitted from the discussion that immediately
follows.

---

    *On June 30, 1973, Seatrain launched the 225,000-dwt tanker
S.S. Brooklyn, the largest ship ever built in the United States. A
sister ship was two-thirds complete. Traffic World, July 9, 1973, p. 25.

Sea-Land operates extensively in both domestic and several offshore trades. Its foreign trade component has been placed at 34 ships, based on an estimate that 20 percent of Sea-Land's business was in the domestic trades. [7]

Table 5.3 shows that the nonsubsidized liner fleet engaging in foreign trade consisted of about 110 ships. Although considerably fewer than the subsidized liner fleet of 247 ships, the nonsubsidized liners are an important element of the U.S. merchant marine.

The condition of much of the liner fleet was poor, with a curious imbalance in the adoption of containerization. In 1970 all of the new ships belonged to subsidized companies, but most of the full container-ships were operated by one nonsubsidized line, Sea-Land.

New ship construction got off to a slow start after World War II. The massive war-built fleet made available to the operators under the provisions of the Ship Sales Act of 1946 made new construction unnecessary or unprofitable, even with construction subsidies available. The first construction of ships of any magnitude that took place in the United States after the war was the Mariner program. The Maritime Administration built 35 Mariner-type ships under the provisions of Title VII of the Act in order to keep the domestic yards busy and to strengthen the reserve fleet. The ships were designed for easy conversion to military use. It was expected that the operators would be happy to get them, but the government was disappointed and had to greatly reduce their price in order to get the Mariners into civilian operation. [8]

Important building did not begin in the United States until the late 1950s. Between 1956 and 1970 the subsidized operators contracted for 182 new ships. [9] However, 285 ships had been planned for under the Maritime Administration's replacement program. [10] This number was adjusted to 242 on the basis of the higher productivity of the new ships, which allowed the Maritime Administration to report that 74 percent of the program had been completed by 1970. [11]

The claim is a bit heroic. As of February 2, 1970, only 156 of the ships had been delivered. Moreover, with the exception of three ships for American Export-Isbrandtsen Lines (AEIL)* and six for United States Lines (USL), all of the ships were built as break-bulk freighters and passenger ships. [12] Thus whether the subsidy program is to be deemed a success or a failure depends, at least in part, on whose numbers are used and how they are interpreted.

The nonsubsidized foreign-trade liner fleet stands in marked contrast with the subsidized sector. All of its ships were of World

---

*Effective July 18, 1972, this company changed its name to American Export Lines. Traffic World, July 13, 1972, p. 56.

TABLE 5.3

Full Containerships Operated by Subsidized and Nonsubsidized
U.S.-Flag Companies, June 30, 1970

	Full Container Ships	Built New or Converted Ship Built Since 1960	Converted Pre-1960 Ship
Subsidized Lines			
American Export-			
Isbrandtsen	9	3	6
Farrell Lines	2	2	
Pacific Far East Lines	2		2
United States Lines	6	6	
Total Subsidized:	19	11	8
Nonsubsidized Lines			
Containerships	2	2	
Sea-Land Service	42		42
Containerships Chartering			
Donmac Corporation			
Madison Transportation			
Monterey Transportation			
Litton Industries Leasing			
Sea-Land Service			
Seatrain Lines	9		9
Greyhound Leasing			
Hudson Waterways			
Seatrain Lines			
C.I.T. Corporation			
Matson Navigation	7	2	5
Total Nonsubsidized	60	4	56
Total Subsidized and			
Nonsubsidized:	79	15	64

Sources: U.S. Department of Commerce, Maritime Administration, Vessel Inventory Report, United States Flag Dry Cargo and Tanker Fleets 1000 Gross Tons and Over as of June 30, 1970, report no. Mar-560-19 (Washington: Maritime Administration, 1971); Containerships, as of June 30, 1970 (Washington: Maritime Administration, ca. 1970).

War II vintage, and there had been no new construction. However, there were a relatively large number of full containerships.

Tables 5.3 and 5.4 illustrate the preponderance of Sea-Land in the field of containerization as of 1970. It operated 42 full container-ships, 34 of which were in the foreign trades, compared with 19 oper-ated by all 13 subsidized companies.

It will be noted in Tables 5.1 and 5.2 that the subsidized operators sail 79 partial containerships, compared with 2 nonsubsidized. Partial container capacity is unimportant or, at best, is of only passing interest. The loading characteristics of a break-bulk ship and a con-tainership are quite different, and do not work well together. A break-bulk vessel loads and unloads at right angles to the ship from several holds (usually five). A containership, in contrast, works two large cranes that allow the trucks (or railroad cars) to approach the ship longitudinally. If a break-bulk operation is under way, it prevents efficient container handling and vice versa. Of course, it is possible to work break-bulk during the day and containers at night, but this requires longer stays in port and leads to the second problem of partial containerization.

TABLE 5.4

Characteristics of Full Containerships Operated
by Selected Countries, June 30, 1970

Flag	Number	Built New	Reconverted Hull Built Since 1960	Reconverted Hull Built Before 1960	Average Age of Hull (yrs.)
Belgium	4		4		7
France	2	2			2
West Germany	20	20			1
Japan	12	12			1
United Kingdom	25	25			3.4
United States	79	14*	6	58	20.4
Subsidized	19	10	6		
Nonsubsidized	60	4	0	56	
Sea-Land (and affiliates)	42	0	0	42	25.8

*Includes Seatrain New York, built in 1932.

Source: U.S. Department of Commerce, Maritime Administration, Containerships, as of June 30, 1970 (Washington: Maritime Adminis-tration, ca. 1970).

The main feature of containerization is rapid service allowed by the fast turnaround of the ship. If a container service is limited to the port-time requirements of a break-bulk ship, it cannot compete effectively with full containerships. The partial containership is a stop-gap measure designed to retain customers while the company has a chance to adopt the full containerships needed to stay in business.

The leading role of the United States in developing containerization and introducing it to the foreign trades occurred without the aid of the Merchant Marine Act of 1936. Indeed, it occurred in spite of U. S. maritime policy rather than because of it. Sea-Land and Matson were required by law to operate only American-built ships in the domestic trades. When Sea-Land went offshore, it was effectively required to continue to operate with domestic-built tonnage or lose access to the sizable trade in government-generated cargo. This again limited the operator to reconstructed war-built tonnage.

The old ships served well and permitted Sea-Land to hold the lead in containerization as long as there was little full containership competition. As indicated above, the partial containership was of minor importance. In the late 1960s, however, the Europeans and Japanese, as well as the subsidized American companies, entered the field. All had access to new, fast, and highly productive container tonnage, whereas Sea-Land remained effectively tied to rapidly aging war-built ships.

The impressive U. S. containership lead of 79 ships is misleading. With the exception of Sea-Land, the nonsubsidized container operators are almost exclusively engaged in the domestic trades. A significant part of the Sea-Land fleet is also engaged in domestic carriage. Thus, in the foreign trade U. S. containership capacity was the 19 subsidized ships and about 34 Sea-Land ships. Though still an impressive fleet in terms of numbers, it must be noted that the average age of the U. S. fleet was 20. 4 years. The Sea-Land fleet had an average age of 25. 8 years.

The precariousness of Sea-Land's position is clear. Though it was the leader in containerization and operated a very efficient service, it did not have access to new tonnage. In fact, it did not even have access to relatively recent tonnage to rebuild as did the subsidized operators, who were able to convert ships built during the 1960s to containerships with the aid of reconstruction subsidies.

Sea-Land's answer was to attempt to lease 16 new containerships from U. S. Lines, one of the subsidized operators having trouble filling its ships. The lease was to run for 20 years, and Sea-Land would have an option to buy the ships at the end of the period. The parent organization of Sea-Land, R. J. Reynolds Industries, was to purchase U. S. Lines from its owner, Walter Kidde Co. , as part of the deal. Sea-Land also contracted to have eight containerships built in Germany and Holland for American-flag operation. [13] This is one of two important exceptions to the effective prohibition on foreign building and reflects the desperate situation faced by Sea-Land.* The other exception was two containerships ordered by Matson from German yards. Sea-Land acquired these vessels also.[14]

Although the subsidized U.S. operators represent a major threat to Sea-Land because of their access to preference and military cargoes in the foreign trades, they are themselves in trouble relative to the Europeans and Japanese. To succeed in the impending competitive struggle in liner shipping, it will be necessary to have large numbers of containerships in the water within the next few years. The subsidized operators, however, are still tied to the domestic shipbuilding industry. Even though part of the problem is offset by the CDS, the number of ships built per year remains a function of the funding of the program. That in turn depends on the mood of Congress. During the late 1960s the U.S. subsidized operators did not have access to the funding necessary to acquire the needed containership tonnage under the subsidy program, yet they could not build abroad. Since 1970, as will be seen, appropriations have increased dramatically. However, the backlog in American shipyards has proved just as effective as a lack of funds in preventing rapid adoption of new technology.

Liner Cargo

The cargo data by industry sector available do not differentiate between subsidized and nonsubsidized operators. According to Table 5.5, the 247 subsidized liners and the approximately 110 nonsubsidized liners in the foreign trades lifted 11.5 million, out of a total of 53.9 million long tons of U.S. foreign trade liner cargo in calendar year 1970 This represented 21.4 percent of the total. In value terms U.S.-flag liners lifted $9.4 million out of a total of $32.7 million or 28.7 percent.

---

*This deal remains in litigation at the time of this writing. In September 1972 the Federal Maritime Commission approved the merger, provided certain conditions were met. One condition was that the merged company operate only American-built ships. Twenty-four hours later a clarification excepted the SL-7s, to the great relief of Sea-Land. Another condition was that the two companies be operated competitively. The conditions were accepted by the two parent organizations in March 1973, and the merger was formally approved by the FMC soon after. However, in November 1973 American Export Lines legally challenged the workability of the FMC requirement that the companies be operated competitively. No doubt this matter will remain in litigation for some time. Wall Street Journal, Oct. 22, 1971. Traffic World, Oct. 2, 1972, p. 14; Oct. 9, 1972, p. 62; Mar. 26, 1973, p. 68; Apr. 2, 1973, p. 136; Nov. 12, 1973, p. 75.

TABLE 5.5

Tonnage and Value of Commercial Cargo Carried in U.S.
Oceanborne Foreign Trade, Calendar Year 1970

	Tonnage (1,000 long tons)			Value ($1,000)		
	Total Tons	U.S. Flag Tons	U.S. Percent	Total Value	U.S. Flag Value	U.S. Percent
Total	472,535	26,527	5.6	48,638	10,040	20.6
Liner	53,867	11,535	21.4	32,729	9,378	28.7
Nonliner	236,634	6,513	2.8	11,838	431	3.6
Tanker	182,034	8,479	4.7	4,071	231	5.7
Exports	193,753	12,391	6.4	24,794	5,272	21.3
Liner	33,113	7,009	21.1	16,935	4,853	28.7
Nonliner	143,002	3,600	2.5	6,632	314	4.7
Tanker	17,638	1,782	10.1	1,226	105	8.6
Imports	278,782	14,136	5.1	23,844	4,768	20.0
Liner	20,754	4,526	21.8	15,794	4,525	28.7
Nonliner	93,632	2,913	3.1	5,206	117	2.2
Tanker	164,396	6,697	4.1	2,845	126	4.4

Source: U.S. Department of Commerce, Maritime Administration, "Value and Tonnage of Commercial Cargo Carried in United States Oceanborne Foreign Trade," unpublished table dated July 21, 1971. Data preliminary.

At first glance the fact that U.S. liners carried 21.4 percent of U.S. liner cargoes by volume may appear encouraging. When it is compared with the 2.8 percent for nonliners (tramps) and 4.7 percent for tankers, it looks even better. In addition, the liner traffic appears well-balanced between imports and exports, whereas that of tramps and tankers does not.

A closer examination of the cargo carried by American-flag liners brings less comfort. When the 1936 legislation was enacted, the oceanborne foreign trade of the United States was overwhelmingly liner traffic. [15] Throughout the postwar years the balance swung in the other direction, until in 1970 only 54 out of 473 million tons, or 11.4 percent of the total, was in liner cargoes. Another 182 million tons, or 38.4 percent of the total, was in tanker cargoes; and 237 million tons, or 50.1 percent in nonliner or tramp cargoes.

American-flag liners carried 21.4 percent of 11.4 percent of U.S. oceanborne foreign trade, or about 2.4 percent of the total by volume. A significant part of this was carried by nonsubsidized liners. In comparison, tramps carried 2.8 percent of 50.1 percent of the total, or 1.4 percent. Tankers carried 4.7 percent of 38.4 percent, or 1.8 percent of the total.

Whether or not the U.S.-flag liners and their patron, the 1936 Act, have been successful in terms of cargo carried depends, to some extent, upon who is doing the arithmetic. The flag is holding its own within the liner sector, but liner cargo has declined in importance as a part of total U.S. oceanborne foreign trade. The liner is doing better than the tramp and tanker sectors in terms of cargo carried; but when the comparison is between 2.8 percent and 1.4 or 1.8 percent of the total, there is little comfort for a champion of the industry.

Cost of the Subsidy Program

Whether or not the subsidy program is judged successful should have some relationship to its cost. That is, the relative merit in lifting 21.4 percent of liner cargo or 2.4 percent of total cargo should depend on how much it costs the taxpayer.

The subsidy program began modestly. It was discontinued during World War II and resumed operation in 1947. [16] There was little ship construction during the late 1940s and 1950s except for the Mariner program. The labor-cost disadvantage was also of rather modest size at the beginning of the period. However, it became increasingly costly after the war.

Table 5.6 lists the cumulative expenditures for ODS, CDS, and their total for the period 1936-54 and annually thereafter through 1970. The total cost of the program rose steadily between 1955 and the early 1960s because of the increase of both ODS and CDS expenditures.

TABLE 5.6

U.S. Maritime Subsidy Expenditures, 1936-70
($ million)

Fiscal Year	ODS	CDS	Total
1936 through			
1954	$ 225.7	$ 246.2	$ 471.9
1955	115.4	5.4	120.7
1956	135.3	16.0	151.3
1957	108.3	20.3	128.6
1958	120.0	27.3	147.4
1959	127.7	28.7	156.4
1960	152.8	74.0	226.7
1961	150.1	103.3	253.5
1962	181.9	141.0	323.0
1963	220.7	94.7	315.4
1964	203.0	78.9	282.0
1965	213.3	87.7	301.0
1966	186.6	73.4	260.0
1967	175.6	82.5	258.2
1968	201.1	97.7	297.8
1969	194.7	95.5	290.2
1970	205.7	96.7	302.4
Total	2,917.9	1,369.3	4,286.5

Note: Columns do not sum because of rounding.

Source: MARAD 1970, Year of Transition, annual report of the Maritime Administration for fiscal year 1970 (Washington: U.S. Government Printing Office, 1971), Chart III, p. 22.

Beginning in 1963, CDS expenditure fell and then leveled off at less than $100 million in the late 1960s. ODS continued to climb, with considerable fluctuations from year to year.

These numbers tell little. Is $302 million for 1970 too much or too little? Compared with many government programs, it is insignificant. On the other hand, the whole shipping industry is of modest size compared with many others, and the direct subsidy expenditures were available only to part of it.

According to Table 5.5 and 5.6, in 1970 it cost the federal government $302 million to subsidize the movement of 11,535,000 tons of liner cargo. This amounts to $26.18 per ton. However, a significant portion of this cargo was lifted by the 110 nonsubsidized liners. Approximately 35 percent of the American-flag liners in the foreign trades in 1970 did not participate in the direct subsidy program.* Assuming the subsidized and nonsubsidized liners carried proportionately the same amount of cargo per ship, the volume of commercial cargo carried by the subsidized operators becomes roughly 7.5 million tons, which brings the subsidy per ton to over $40. This is a rather startling value, but it is not the whole story. The 11,535,000 tons of "commercial" cargo includes a large amount of government-generated shipments covered by the cargo preference laws (but excludes military shipments).

In calendar year 1970, U.S.-flag vessels carried 6.8 million tons of PL 480 and PL 664 cargoes. In addition, they carried enough cargo financed by the Export-Import Bank to generate revenue of over $79 million.[17] It is not known how much of this preference cargo was lifted by liners and how much by tramps. It is safe to assume, however, that a significant portion of the estimated 7.5 million tons carried by subsidized liners in 1970 was preference cargo reserved for American-flag ships. The actual cost per ton of strictly commercial cargo moved by subsidized operators is very high.

This is an important point. The subsidy program of the Merchant Marine Act of 1936 was designed to help U.S. ships compete with foreign-flag ships, not with other American vessels. In addition to raising the per-ton cost of the direct subsidy program, it may be argued that the carriage of preference cargo by subsidized ships reduces the effectiveness of the cargo preference program. This matter will be developed in the next section.

If the CDS is considered a subsidy to the shipyards rather than to the shipping industry, it is appropriate to use only ODS expenditure in computing the subsidy cost of moving cargo. In that case the cost of inducing the movement of one ton of cargo on a subsidized ship becomes roughly $27 per ton for 1970.

The CDS cost another $96.7 million in 1970. Because of the long production period in shipbuilding and the fact that ships are not delivered in the year they are funded, it is better to relate the number of ships contracted for to their cost.

Table 5.7 shows the number of ships contracted for per year during 1956-70 and the CDS paid on them. The CDS expenditure shown differs from that in Table 5.6 as it does not include reconstruction subsidies (which were relatively unimportant until fiscal 1970), the cost of national defense features, and certain other outfitting and engineering costs.

The per-ship cost of the CDS program varied from $4.6 million in 1959 to $12.7 million ten year later, with the trend being upward.

---

*This estimate allows for the foreign-trade liner operations of Seatrain and Matson Navigation.

TABLE 5.7

Cost of CDS, 1956-70

Year	New Ships Contracted for	CDS ($ million)	Cost per Ship* ($ million)
1956	4	38.6	9.7
1957	0	0	0
1958	15	77.9	5.2
1959	14	65.0	4.6
1960	13	81.5	6.3
1961	31	147.1	4.7
1962	13	63.4	4.9
1963	18	106.3	5.9
1964	15	84.0	5.6
1965	14	89.6	6.4
1966	17	133.0	7.8
1967	1	8.5	8.5
1968	12	124.8	10.4
1969	10	127.2	12.7
1970	5	96.7	9.9
Total	182	Total 1,196.6	Average 6.6

*Does not include cost of national defense features, reconstruction subsidies, and certain other outfitting and engineering costs.

Source: U.S. Department of Commerce, Maritime Administration, "Ship Replacement Program," unpublished table and chart dated June 30, 1970.

The average subsidy cost to the government for the 182 ships contracted for was $6.6 million each. When it is remembered that most of these ships were outmoded by the container revolution, which was based on converted war-built tonnage, the price seems high. Many of these ships have been or are being converted to containerships with additional government subsidy.

It is debatable whether the direct subsidy program has been successful. It has given the flag a fairly new, if not modern, liner fleet. U.S. liners ply established trade routes and compete with foreign operators for cargoes. But the cost of the program is very high, much higher than most observers realize.

Whether the cost of the subsidy program is too high is a value judgment. The most relevant unit of costing is the cost per ton lifted of strictly commercial cargo. ODS expenditure has gone up considerably over the years, but the real cost of moving a ton of commercial cargo has gone up much more. For as the subsidized liners have become increasingly dependent upon preference cargo, the cost of subsidizing their remaining competitive efforts has risen. A not overly absurd extreme would be a subsidized fleet engaged entirely in the carriage of preference and military cargo.

The CDS is also expensive. If CDS is considered a subsidy to the shipyards, however, the hidden escalator associated with the carriage of preference cargo does not apply. The CDS program has become more costly on a per-ship basis partly because ships have become more sophisticated and expensive.

What success the direct subsidy program has had in the liner sector must be heavily qualified. It has been extremely costly in terms of carrying strictly commercial cargo. It has not encouraged the subsidized operators to lead the way technologically. In fact, the red tape and rigidity associated with the CDS program may have hindered the sector's efforts to initiate change.

Another qualification that must be placed on the success of the direct subsidy program is the detrimental impact if has had on the nonsubsidized sector. One effect involves the "double subsidy" created when subsidized operators compete with nonsubsidized ones for the carriage of preference cargo. An important effect of the 1936 legislation is that it masked the deterioration of the U.S. shipping industry for so long and helped to hide the flaws in U.S. maritime policy. Throughout the postwar period the liner sector was pointed to as proof of the success of the subsidy program. By offsetting the ship-cost disadvantage of part of the fleet by construction subsidies, the Congress was able to ignore the deterioration of the rest of the fleet.

CARGO PREFERENCE AND THE U.S.-FLAG TRAMPS

The nonsubsidized operators in the foreign trades are almost entirely dependent upon preference and military cargo. None, with the possible exception of Sea-Land, could survive without it. The other nonsubsidized liners and the many tramp operators would have disappeared in the absence of cargo preference. Also, the few U.S. tankers that go offshore with government cargoes would have changed flags or retreated to the domestic trades without access to preference cargoes.

As of June 30, 1970, there were approximately 126 dry cargo ships identifiable as tramps under the U.S. flag. [18] They were operated by 67 nominally different companies, many of which were affiliated with each other through common parent organizations.

The fluctuation of the U.S. merchant marine falls most heavily on the tramp sector. The number of subsidized liners is relatively stable by definition. The nonsubsidized liners may increase to some extent by chartering ships when demand is high, but the demands of maintaining a schedule keep their fleets at fairly constant size. The demand for tankers in the domestic trades has been fairly stable over the years. But the number of active dry cargo tramps fluctuates in response to demand.

Anything said about the tramp sector must refer to a specific date. However, the 126 vessels identifiable as tramps on June 30, 1970, are representative of the postwar period (prior to the advent of the present contraction).

With one exception,* the U.S. tramp fleet was entirely of World War II construction in 1970. There had been no replacement, nor could there have been; the effects of national maritime policy precluded it. Consequently, there was almost no adoption of the new technology.

The cargo program upon which the American tramp sector depends provides a large amount of cargo at preferential rates. This is, in effect, an operating subsidy that has kept the U.S.-flag tramp fleet running. However, it has provided no means of replacing the ships.

Initially a ship need only have been registered under the U.S. flag to carry preference cargoes. This technically allowed operators to build abroad; but with one exception, none did. In 1961 the cargo preference provisions of Section 9(b) of the Merchant Marine Act of 1936 were modified to require that after September 21, 1961, a ship built, rebuilt, or registered abroad must be documented under the U.S. flag for three years before it may carry preference cargo. [19] This effectively closed the possibility of building or even rebuilding abroad. The chances of a tramp ship remaining in operation for three years under the U.S. flag without access to preference cargo or the domestic trades are slim. To lay such a ship up for three years is out of the question.

While there was (almost) no foreign building during the postwar period, there was some reconstruction. In the late 1950s it became popular to convert T-2 tankers into bulk carriers by welding additional midsections into the hulls. Between 1958 and 1962, 12 bulk carriers

---

*The S. S. Tamara Guilden, a bulk carrier of 22,900 dwt, was built abroad in 1961.

92

(and one jumboized tanker) were converted in foreign yards.[20] Such reconstruction turned a 16, 000-dwt war-built tanker into a relatively efficient bulk carrier of 21, 000 to 25, 000 dwt. Though four additional conversions of T-2's into bulk carriers were done by American yards using foreign-built midsections, this type of work ended about 1963.

As of June 30, 1970, 27 of the 126 ships identifiable as tramps were bulk carriers. With the exception of the S. S. Tamara Guilden, all were at least 25 years old. They averaged 20, 700 dwt, and none was of the multi-cargo (OBO) type.[21] Yet these 27 ships represented the most advanced part of the U.S. tramp fleet. The remainder were war-built freighters operating as tramps.

Tramp Cargo

Nonliner or tramp cargo has grown enormously in both absolute and relative terms. In calendar year 1969 it totaled 206. 5 million long tons (including government-sponsored cargo but excluding military shipments). Of this, U.S. ships carried 4. 4 million long tons, or 2. 1 percent.[22] Probably all of the American share was preference cargo.

In calendar year 1969 the Department of Agriculture and Agency for International Development alone shipped over 7. 5 million short tons (about 6. 7 long tons).[23] Apparently the 2. 3 million-ton difference was carried by subsidized and nonsubsidized liners.

This is not an enviable record. The U. S. tramp fleet is entirely noncompetitive in international trade, and its sole source of cargo is the cargo preference program.

Cost of the Program

Rates on government-sponsored cargoes lifted by U.S.-flag tramps are perhaps twice those of foreign-flag ships.[24] A recent estimate places rate preference costs at about $60 million annually.[25] This means that the government is subsidizing the movement of each long ton of nonliner cargo by about $13. 63. Though this figure is very rough, it gives an idea of the relative cost of the cargo preference program.

As with the direct subsidy program, the indirect subsidy contained in the cargo preference program is very expensive. However, there is even less to show for the expenditure. At least the direct subsidy program has resulted in a fairly modern fleet and some international competitiveness. The cargo preference program, in contrast, has kept an aging fleet of inefficient ships in operation. Though it allowed some reconstruction of war-built ships for a while, this practice was stopped. The program contains no means of replacing the fleet. As a result the U.S. tramp fleet is woefully inadequate. Had it not been for the Ship Exchange Program initiated in 1960, and the limited amount of conversion prior to 1963, it would be in even worse condition than it is.

THE CABOTAGE LAWS AND THE DOMESTIC FLEET

The domestic trades are by definition noncompetitive internationally. Ships in the coastal and intercoastal trades are in direct competition with overland transport, mainly railroads. No attempt will be made to evaluate the competitiveness of domestic water transport relative to railroads. The obvious conclusion is that water transport has not fared well. Nor will any attempt be made to judge the competitiveness of U.S. ships engaged in domestic carriage relative to what would prevail if foreign-flag operators were allowed into these trades. This section will examine only the outcome of the cabotage element of U.S. maritime policy in terms of the size of the fleet it supports and its ability to participate in the technological revolution.

The Domestic Fleet

The U.S. domestic fleet consists of two distinct segments, dry cargo and tanker. They will be discussed separately.

Dry Cargo

Most of the dry-cargo coastal and intercoastal fleet was requisitioned by the government at the beginning of World War II. The cargo it had carried was taken over by the railroads, and the domestic fleet never recovered. With one exception, there was practically no important coastal or intercoastal dry-cargo shipping in 1970. The exception was part of Sea-Land's domestic operation.

The coastal and intercoastal trades are hard to separate from the noncontiguous trades. The same companies may operate in both. Furthermore, there is no prohibition on nonsubsidized foreign trade ships operating in the domestic trades. The same ship may operate in both foreign and domestic trades at different times.

There were three sizable domestic liner operations in 1970. Sea-Land Service operated in the coastal, intercoastal, and noncontiguous trades, running an estimated nine ships in this trade. Seatrain operated from the West Coast to Hawaii and from New York to Puerto Rico

TABLE 5.8

Characteristics of U.S. Domestic Dry-Cargo
Fleet, as of December 31, 1968

Year Built		Type of Ship	Number
1932	2	Containership	27
1940	1	Partial containership	1
1942	2	Freighter	17
1943	11	Bulk Carrier	11
1944	20	LST	1
1945	12	Refrigeration ship	1
1946	4	Total	58
1948	2		
1960	2		
1967	1		
1968	1		

Source: Derived from Labor-Management Maritime Committee, The U.S. Merchant Marine Today, Sunrise or Sunset? (Washington: LMMC, 1970), Tables 63 and 64, pp. 194, 195.

with about five ships. Matson Navigation operated 17 ships, primarily in the West Coast-Hawaii trade. [26] There are several other companies in the domestic trades, operating a few ships each.

As of December 31, 1968, there were 58 ships employed in the domestic trades. [27] Table 5.8 shows the characteristics of the fleet. With the exception of three containerships of fairly recent construction, all of them were built during the 1940s. Most of the 11 bulk carriers and some of the "freighters" operated as tramps, shifting in and out of domestic carriage. Hence, it is concluded that the domestic trade supported about 50 dry-cargo vessels.

A large segment of the dry-cargo domestic fleet consisted of full containerships. All of Sea-Land's operation was in containerships. Seven of Matson's 17 vessels were full containerships, and most of the remainder had partial container capacity. Two of Matson's full containerships were of new construction (1967 and 1970). [28]

The domestic dry-cargo fleet has incorporated the new technology to a considerable degree. In fact, as was discussed earlier, container-ization developed in the domestic trades. Nevertheless, the fleet is a relatively unimportant part of the U.S. shipping industry. There are relatively few dry-cargo ships supported by the cabotage restrictions, and they are quite old. With a few exceptions, this element of U.S. maritime policy has failed to replace the dry-cargo fleet dependent upon it.

Tankers

In 1970 U.S.-flag tankers were employed almost exclusively in the domestic trades. The exceptions were those commercial ships chartered to MSTS or carrying government cargo in some other form. None competed internationally in any important way, although occasionally a U.S. tanker is in a position, after delivering a government shipment, to bring back a commercial cargo.*

A second exception is the recent entry of U.S.-flag tankships into the carriage of grain. Though technically in the foreign trades, this usually involves government cargo and is more related to bulk carriage and cargo preference than to the present discussion. The impact of this development is to expand the U.S. bulk carrier fleet.

As of June 30, 1970, there were 252 privately owned tankers of 1,000 gross tons and over operating under the U.S. flag. Sixty-nine were listed as "supertankers" by the Maritime Administration. Most of the supertankers were between 30,000 and 50,000 dwt, of modest dimension by current world standards. Seven U.S.-flag tankers were over 50,000 dwt. The largest was the S. S. Manhattan, 115,000 dwt. The smallest was 1,450 dwt. In addition to the 69 vessels listed as supertankers were eight others of 30,000 dwt or more. Thus, 77 out of the 256 tankships were larger than a jumboized T-2. [29] A year and a half earlier, December 31, 1968, there were 277 tankships in operation with an average age of 18 years. [30]

The oil transportation business is divided into two parts, proprietary and independent. Proprietary tankers seldom go offshore. They are integral parts of the operations of the large oil companies. They are not leased to MSTS and do not participate in the carriage of grain or other preference cargo. In 1970 there were 146 proprietary tankers, 38 of which had been designated supertankers by the Maritime Administration. [31] This fleet is solely a product of the cabotage restrictions.

The independents are greatly involved in the transport of oil under charter to the oil companies and are, to some extent, a product of cabotage. They also charter to MSTS, carry preference cargo, and, on rare occasions, engage in the international carriage of oil. As of June 30, 1970, there were 106 independent tankers, 31 of which were designated supertankers. They were operated by 69 nominally independent companies although, as with tramp operation, many of them are affiliated with common parent organizations. [32]

There has been some new construction of U.S.-flag tankers for the domestic trades. This was made possible by two government

---

*An exception was the 115,000-dwt S.S. Manhattan of Northwest Passage fame, which began shuttling oil from the Persian Gulf to Europe in 1970. Traffic World, Aug. 10, 1970, p. 18.

programs that represent a rare success in U.S. maritime policy. The tanker Trade-In and Build Program was added to the Merchant Marine Act of 1936 as Section 510(b). [33] It began in 1952 and expired on July 1, 1958, and resulted in 192,000 dwt of new tanker construction. [34] This represents about five new tankers.

The tanker Trade-Out and Build Program was more important. It was established in 1955 by the Maritime Administration under the provisions of Section 9 of the Shipping Act of 1916 and later given statutory authority. [35] Between 1955 and 1958, 136 World War II vessels of 2,177,000 dwt were sold abroad. The proceeds from the sales were applied to the construction of 59 new tankers totaling 2,383,800 dwt. [36] The average tonnage of the ships built was 40,000, and the program went a long way toward upgrading the U.S.-flag fleet.

The Cost of Cabotage Protection

There were about 50 dry-cargo ships and 146 proprietary tankers engaged almost entirely in the domestic trades in 1970. Another 106 independent tankships were more or less dependent on the cabotage restrictions, although at times they carried military and preference cargoes. Thus a fleet of approximately 300 ships was supported by the cabotage restrictions.

There are no data available on the cost of maintaining the domestic fleet. Most of it is paid by consumers in the form of higher prices for goods that have been transported by water. In a few cases this may be considerable, but there are limits on how much ships in the domestic trades may charge. Presumably the costs are higher than if the trades were open to foreign-flag ships.

In the coastal and intercoastal trades, ships compete with overland transportation. Thus there is relatively little dry-cargo movement in these trades today. Oil tankers compete mainly with pipelines, and on long hauls they do so successfully.

At first glance the noncontiguous states and possessions may appear captives of the domestic ship operators. There are limits here also. If the cost of transporting, say, cars from the West Coast to Hawaii goes too high, they will be imported from Japan on Japanese ships. If the transportation costs of, say, paper go too high, Hawaii can import wood or pulp and manufacture paper within the state. As tariffs have been lowered in recent years, this limit on ship operators in the noncontiguous trades has become more effective.

The problem with supporting a domestic fleet in the cabotage trades is that its cost falls most heavily on a small part of the population. The obvious cases are Alaska, Hawaii, and, to a lesser extent because of its proximity to the mainland, Puerto Rico.

The cabotage pillar of U.S. maritime policy has been a qualified success. The cost of the program is probably not so high as one would think. Although most of the coastal and intercoastal dry-cargo traffic was lost to the railroads as a result of World War II, some of it has been recovered through containerization.

There has been some new construction of tankers. Much of it is of rather modest size by world standards, but this is to be expected. A large number of the tankships operate between the Gulf and East Coasts. Draft restrictions on this route rule out real supertankers.

The fact that containerization was developed in the domestic trades is of some encouragement. Apparently domestic trade operation allows technological innovation as well as new ship construction. Of course, the requirement that ships in the domestic trades be built in U.S. yards adds to the cost to the industry and undoubtedly has retarded its technological development. There are no comparable restrictions on its overland competitors; and if the ship operators could build abroad, they would be able to compete better. However, because of the relatively captive nature of the market, they are able to pass some of the additional costs forward through the price system.

SUMMARY

The subsidy program, cargo preference program, and cabotage restrictions have left their mark on the industry. The 1936 legislation promoted the interests of a favored group of subsidized liner operators. Cargo preference, while of great importance to all U.S. operators in the foreign trades, is the sole support of the tramp sector. The cabotage laws also have their clients. Each group has developed interests vested in the existing situation. Each would be affected differently by a major change in U.S. maritime policy.

By the 1960s everyone was aware of the plight of the U.S. merchant marine. Much of the industry was on the brink of obsolescence, and was saved only by the Vessel Exchange Program and the buildup associated with the Vietnam war.

The Johnson administration had pledged to come forward with a program to revitalize the U.S. fleet. In 1965 a proposal was made public that called for foreign building and the elimination of cargo preference. This was a bombshell of the first magnitude to the shipping industry.

The shipping industry on the East Coast had been organized by two large crew unions and a number of small but important officers' unions. A bitter and complex interunion rivalry had raged in the industry since it was organized in the 1930s. One of its causes was that the two crew unions had their respective main sources of jobs in different sectors of the industry. The impact of the proposed policy changes thus promised to affect them differently.

Like the companies, the unions had seen the inevitable debate over maritime policy coming. Alliances had been made and organizations formed to influence the change prior to 1965. When the time came, sides were quickly formed. The battle took place, to a large extent, in the Congressional hearing rooms and in the press. Before examining that development, however, it will be helpful to trace the development of the parties to the dispute.

NOTES

1. 49 Stat. 1985 (1936) Sec. 101, 46 U.S.C.A. 1101 (1958).
2. 49 Stat. 2001 (1936) Sec. 601, 46 U.S.C.A. 1171 (1958).
3. 49 Stat. 1995 (1936) Sec. 501, 46 U.S.C.A. 1151 (1958), historical note.
4. MARAD 1970, App. X, pp. 75-76.
5. U.S. Department of Commerce, Maritime Administration, "Ship Replacement Commitments: Subsidized Operators," unpublished table and chart (315.14) dated Feb. 2, 1970.
6. Containerships, 1970, Pts. 1 and II.
7. House, Hearings on Long-Range Maritime Program, 1968, p. 627.
8. Wytze Gorter, United States Shipping Policy (New York: Harper Brothers, 1956), pp. 55, 62.
9. MARAD 1970, Chart IV, p. 23.
10. U.S. Department of Commerce, Maritime Administration, "Ship Replacement Commitments: Subsidized Operators," unpublished table and chart (315.14) dated Feb. 2, 1970. The number was reported as 285/286. To avoid confusion, the possible last ship will be ignored.
11. Ibid.
12. Containerships, 1970, Pt. I.
13. U.S. Congress, House, Committee on Merchant Marine and Fisheries, Subcommittee on Merchant Marine, Hearings on President's Maritime Program, Pt. II, 91st Cong., 2nd sess. (Washington: U.S. Government Printing Office, 1970), p. 425. Cited hereafter as House, Hearings on President's Maritime Program, Pt. II, 1970.
14. Traffic World, Apr. 26, 1971, p. 67.
15. W. B. Dickinson, Jr., "National Maritime Policy," Editorial Research Reports 2 (Sept. 29, 1965): 706; A. W. Warner and A. S. Eichner, "Analysis of Labor-Management Relations in the Off-Shore Operations of the East Coast Maritime Industry," 1966, p. 149.
16. Gorter, op. cit., p. 82.
17. U.S. Department of Commerce, Maritime Administration, MARAD 1971, Year of Breakthrough, annual report of the Maritime Administration for fiscal year 1971 (Washington: U.S. Government Printing Office, 1971), Table 7, p. 30. Hereafter cited MARAD 1971.

18. Derived from Vessel Inventory Report, 1970.

19. 75 Stat. 565 (1961), 46 U.S.C.A. 1241 (1962).

20. Labor-Management Maritime Committee, The U.S. Merchant Marine Today, Sunrise or Sunset? (Washington: Labor Management Maritime Committee, 1970), Table 46, pp. 152-53. Cited hereafter as LMMC, The U.S. Merchant Marine Today.

21. Derived from Vessel Inventory Report, 1970.

22. U.S. Department of Commerce, Maritime Administration, "Value and Tonnage of Commercial Cargo Carried in United States Oceanborne Foreign Trade," unpublished table dated July 21, 1971.

23. MARAD 1970, Table IX, p. 26.

24. LMMC, The U.S. Merchant Marine Today, p. 79. S. A. Lawrence, United States Merchant Shipping Policies and Politics (Washington: Brookings Institution, 1966), pp. 90, 178, cites 2.2:1 for 1963. In 1968 a specific preference rate was 75.6 percent above world rates. Traffic World, Oct. 19, 1968, p. 92.

25. J. R. Barker and Robert Brandwein, The United States Merchant Marine in National Perspective (Lexington, Mass.: D. C. Heath, 1970), p. 99.

26. Derived from Vessel Inventory Report, 1970.

27. LMMC, The U.S. Merchant Marine Today, p. 193.

28. Containerships, 1970, Pt. I.

29. Derived from Vessel Inventory Report, 1970.

30. A Statistical Analysis of the World's Merchant Fleets, 1968, p. 89.

31. Derived from Vessel Inventory Report, 1970.

32. Ibid.

33. 49 Stat. 2000 (1936) Sec. 510(b), 46 U.S.C.A. 1160 (1958).

34. LMMC, The U.S. Merchant Marine Today, p. 144.

35. 39 Stat. 730 (1916) Sec. 9, 46 U.S.C.A. 808 (1958); 68 Stat. 680 (1954), 46 Stat. 1160 (1958). Discussed in LMMC, The U.S. Merchant Marine Today, pp. 143-46.

36. LMMC, The U.S. Merchant Marine Today, p. 143.

6

**MARITIME UNION
RIVALRY**

INTRODUCTION

The dominant industrial-relations consideration in the shipping industry throughout the period under study (1936-70) is interunion rivalry. Maritime union rivalry has features that are unique to the industry. Initially it was only a conflict between the National Maritime Union (NMU) and the Atlantic and Gulf District of the Seafarers' International Union of North America (SIU). During the 1950s the NMU-SIU rivalry expanded to embrace several officers' unions, and by the 1960s it involved the employer organizations as well. In its recent form the conflict is more of a dispute between sectors than a rivalry between unions.

The casual observer might conclude that the behavior of the seamen's unions has been irrational and self-defeating. In terms of the industry as a whole this may be true; but from the point of view of the NMU and SIU, nothing could be further from the truth. The behavior of the unions has been rational, understandable, and predictable, considering the industrial situation within which they operate. It is the situation that must be explained rather than the actions of the unions.

The context within which maritime industrial relations occurs has been most influenced by two things. The first is the operation of national maritime policy. One of its effects has been a chronically declining shipping industry after each war-induced expansion. The other is the operation of the union hiring halls. Together they have encouraged the development of labor unions to which the control of seagoing jobs are critical.

THE IMPORTANCE OF JOBS

One feature of the hiring halls is that the control of jobs is critical to each union's members as individuals. The primary criterion upon which the members judge the performance of their union and its leaders is job control or, more accurately, the ratio of members to available jobs. The higher this ratio the more difficult it is to "ship out," which results in greater membership dissatisfaction. The ratio of members to jobs can be controlled, within limits, by manipulating the size of the membership. However, as the membership decreases, the dues base of the union is reduced. This is no solution to the loss of jobs, from the point of view of the organization.

The union is an institution in control of a number of jobs. If it has jobs under contract, it usually has no trouble getting members. When it loses jobs, it loses members. In fact, it loses more members than jobs, because it takes at least 1.5 members to fill each job. [1]

The critical nature of the pool of union-controlled jobs to the member and to the labor organization means that none can be given up without a fight. Furthermore, if an opportunity to acquire additional jobs presents itself, it must be taken regardless of cost.

The situation has been aggravated by the decline the industry has experienced since World War II, punctuated by the short-run expansions associated with the Korean and Vietnam conflicts. With each expansion, thousands of additional men are added to the sea-going work force. Many others "upgrade" and sail higher-rated jobs than they did before. When the boom ends and the industry contracts, many of the new entrants remain committed to the industry and those who have bettered themselves are reluctant to return to their previous jobs.

A contraction of the industry increases the member-job ratio. Eventually the membership is reduced. Entry is restricted, men leave the industry, and others get used to sailing as, say, able seamen rather than boatswain. But this takes several years, and in the mean-time many of the members of the various unions are extremely job-conscious. This job-consciousness goes a long way towards explaining the union rivalry that has plagued the industry as well as the importance of national maritime policy to the unions.

The combined effect of a declining industry and unions that are concerned primarily with the protection of the jobs they have under contract and the acquisition of new jobs whenever possible created a situation in which interunion rivalry was inevitable. That bitter and complex interunion rivalry is the subject of this chapter.

ORIGINS OF MARITIME UNION RIVALRY

Early History

Although some of the origins and many of the characteristics of today's maritime unions can be traced deep into the 19th century, most of the industry has been organized since 1936. In 1921 the existing union, the International Seamen's Union (ISU), suffered a defeat in a strike and lockout that left the industry practically unorganized until after 1934. The little effective union action in the interim was on the West Coast, where the Sailors' Union of the Pacific (SUP), one of the many autonomous affiliates of the ISU, was permeated with the philosophy and members of the Industrial Workers of the World (IWW).

The renaissance of maritime labor organization began in 1934. The ISU shared the general union growth induced by the National Industrial Recovery Act. [2] A new and militant leadership emerged from the rank and file on the West Coast. When the longshoremen struck in 1934 against the employer-dominated "blue book" hiring hall, the seamen spontaneously joined them. The conservative ISU leaders were against the walkout, but were forced to proclaim a strike or lose their positions to the insurgent radicals within the union or to the (Communist) Marine Workers' International Union (MWIU).

Under the influence of one of those radicals, Harry Lundeberg, the seagoing unions joined with the longshoremen, under the leadership of Harry Bridges, to form what became the Maritime Federation of the Pacific (MFP) in 1935. The Federation continued in existence until 1937.

The strike soon spread to the East Coast affiliates of the ISU, the main issue being the elimination of the wage differential between the East and West Coasts. The ISU leadership succeeded in breaking the strike by supplying strikebreakers from among the unemployed. However, the weakness of their hold had been demonstrated. On the West Coast the strike continued, and reached a dramatic climax from July 16-19, when the shoreside labor force of San Francisco proclaimed a general strike.

On July 31 the three-month-old strike was called off and the West Coast ISU affiliates were recognized by the companies. Terms were to be settled by arbitration. Although some gains were made by the seamen, the crucial question of hiring was left in the position favored by the ISU leadership. The companies had the option of hiring from the union hall or off the dock.

Meanwhile the Communists were making gains on the East Coast. The failure of the ISU to respond to membership demands allowed the MWIU to attract members by advocating a militant program and the liberal use of "job action." The ISU finally called a strike for

October 8, 1934, and the MWIU did the same. When the ISU called off the strike at the last minute in return for recognition by 28 companies, the Communist strike proved a fiasco. The ISU supplied replacements for the few jobs they left. Shortly thereafter the Communists changed their tactics and began "boring from within" by dissolving the MWIU and joining the ISU as individuals. They soon gained a hold within the union at the expense of the entrenched leadership, and later carried this influence into the National Maritime Union. [3]

Shortly after the MWIU went underground in February 1935, an "ISU Rank and File Committee" was formed. It started publishing the ISU Pilot, and stated that its purpose was to build "one powerful ISU and organize every seaman in the industry."[4] The Committee attacked the ISU leadership for signing a contract that retained a five-dollar intercoast differential and for failing to organize the bulk of the industry. The old leadership retorted by calling the committee "Communist-inspired," and resorted to packing meetings and changing the constitution in an attempt to strengthen its hold on the union. When the contract expired in January 1936 and the old leadership announced it had accepted the operators' terms, which retained the intercoast differential, there was a strong rank-and-file reaction that forced it to submit the contract to a referendum. It was defeated three to one.

On March 2, 1936, a group of sailors led by Joseph Curran refused to cast off lines as the S.S. California was about to sail from San Pedro, California, until the company agreed to pay West Coast wages. After a promise of the "good offices" of Secretary of Labor Frances Perkins, the ship sailed; but on arrival in New York the men involved were fired and logged (fined) two days' pay. There was also some talk of "mutiny charges." The ISU refused to back the men—which, under the circumstances, constituted its practical acceptance of the charges.

On the West Coast the Communists had their greatest success among the longshoremen. Among the sailors the prevailing ideological influence was from the IWW. Its Marine Transport Workers (MTW) found cooperation with the SUP easy because of a mutual fondness for "job action" and a dislike for the Communist clique in control of the International Longshoremen's and Warehousemen's Union (ILWU). [5] Undoubtedly most of the MTW membership was made up of the members of the SUP. Since the MTW had no ships under contract its main influence was through the SUP. Much of the controversy between Bridges and Lundeberg reflected the ideological and tactical differences of the Communists and the "Wobblies."

Harry Lundeberg was thirty-four years old when he rose to leadership during the 1934 strike. He had been born in Norway and went to sea at the age of 14. After sailing under several flags, in the early 1920s he began shipping out of Seattle, where he joined the SUP and was influenced by the "Wobblie" doctrines of industrial unionism, antipoliticalism, and direct action. He opposed any restriction on the use of "job action" by seamen. This was the cause of much conflict with

Harry Bridges. Once the longshoremen had attained control of hiring, Bridges thought this tactic should be controlled by the Maritime Federation in order to prevent small groups from weakening the union's position in the pursuit of limited economic gains.[6]

Bridges was a left-wing militant Australian who came to leadership among the longshoremen during the 1934 revolt against the company-dominated hiring system. If not a member of the Communist Party, he was at least a fellow traveler. He followed much of the party line in succeeding years while becoming one of the more colorful personalities in American labor. Bridges' ideological coloration did not prevent him from becoming an effective trade unionist, and he has retained his position in the ILWU despite the popular disenchantment with Communism. His preference for the "hot cargo" tool over "job action" was consistent with the principle of centralized control, but it was also in the best interests of his union. The longshoremen were then trying to protect the gains made on the docks by organizing inland and by aiding unionization on the East Coast. The ILWU also wanted to dampen the animosity and allay the fears of the companies by appearing "responsible" and of the labor movement by retaining friendly relations with the American Federation of Labor (AFL).

Lundeberg, on the other hand, had no great admiration for "responsibility," and the SUP was not affiliated with the AFL after the desperate conservative leadership expelled it from the ISU in January 1936.* Bridges' urgings that the SUP should reaffiliate with the ISU were resented by the SUP, as was his effective veto of Lundeberg's desire to merge the SUP with the National Union of Marine Cooks and Stewards (NUMCS) and the Marine Firemen, Oilers, Watertenders, and Wipers (MFOW).

Despite their differences in ideology and strategy and the clash of two strong and ambitious personalities, the longshoremen and seamen continued to cooperate within the Maritime Federation of the Pacific when under attack by the shipowners, and on several occasions were able to act on each other's behalf.

Formation of the NMU

Although the weak position of the old-line ISU leadership was obvious after 1934, the owners continued to deal with it rather than

---

*The ISU was a federation consisting of over 20 autonomous affiliated unions. In structure it resembled the AFL, to which it was itself affiliated. The SUP's connection with the AFL was through the ISU. When the SUP was expelled from the ISU, it was automatically out of the AFL.

allow the militant rank-and-file leaders to gain control. Of course this enhanced the position of the new leaders and insured their eventual success. After much in-fighting, the AFL authorized an election for the Eastern and Gulf Sailors' Association of the ISU and recognized the results of a previous election in the MFOW.[7] These measures were too late. The split between the AFL and the Committee for Industrial Organizations (CIO) resulted in delays while the insurgency within the ISU continued to grow. Finally, under the leadership of Joseph Curran, the National Maritime Union (NMU) was established in May 1937. The new union grew rapidly while the ISU virtually disintegrated. By the time of its first convention in July, the NMU claimed 35,000 members. In June, with the new union in effective control of most East Coast shipping and making daily gains, the old-line leaders filed a petition with the National Labor Relations Board (NLRB) alleging that "a question had arisen concerning the representation of the unlicensed personnel employed by more than fifty companies."[8] The provisional officers of the NMU accepted the challenge, and that was the de facto end of the ISU.

The first NMU convention in 1936 reflected the character and philosophy of the new union and its leadership. The constitution approved by the convention was very democratic, and stated the goals of the NMU to be "the unification of all workers in the industry regardless of creed, color, nationality, or political affiliation." Advancement was to be sought by "legislative and/or economic action."[9] The union affiliated with the CIO and organized as an industrial union.

From the beginning the NMU was beset with internal-factional disputes and external attacks. It was immediately, and with justification, branded as Communist and linked with Harry Bridges by the conservative ISU leadership, the owners, and the press.[10]

Before the first election in 1938, an internal rank-and-file movement developed that made similar charges of Communist domination against Curran and the political clique around him. They began printing the Rank and File NMU Pilot and marshaled enough strength to elect Jerome King secretary-treasurer and gain control of the National Council and the NMU Pilot. Curran was elected president, however, and soon undermined the position of the insurgents by pinning the failure of an attempt to organize the East Coast tankers on them. King and a number of his followers were brought up on charges and suspended from the union for 99 years. Despite these problems, by 1939, when the AFL challenged the NMU hegemony, the union had 51,000 members and contracts with most of the large carriers on the East Coast. This head start was a major factor in the rivalry and eventual fight over national maritime policy in the 1960s.

Formation of the SIU

Because of its preoccupation with the CIO, the AFL could do little to challenge the initial growth of the NMU. At first it tried to ignore the ISU leadership. It encouraged an attempt by Joseph Ryan, president of the International Longshoremen's Association (ILA), to set up a Maritime Labor Council of longshoremen, seamen, and harbor workers; but this made little headway. The AFL then established a board, which included Ryan and William Green, to incorporate the remains of the old ISU. In October 1937 it revoked the charter of the ISU and established an AFL Seamen's Union directly under the Federation, composed mainly of the Gulf Coast remnants of the ISU that were opposed to the political (and probably racial) makeup of the NMU.

Meanwhile, on the West Coast the rapid growth of the NMU was seen as a threat by the SUP. Although Lundeberg's trade union philosophy favored the industrial form of organization, he had no desire to have the SUP absorbed by the much larger NMU. The NMU affiliation with the CIO practically forced the SUP into the AFL camp. The SUP affiliated with the AFL, and in August 1938 the Federation issued an international charter in the name of the Seafarers' International Union of North America (SIU, NA) under the direction of the SUP and Lundeberg. The SUP became the autonomous Pacific District of the SIU, NA, with the Atlantic and Gulf District having similar autonomy. Lundeberg became president of the SIU, NA, while retaining his position as secretary of the SUP. The SUP has no president.

On the East Coast the SIU was set up as an industrial union. All three departments were represented by the SIU, as in the NMU. On the West Coast the SUP continued to represent only the sailors.* In the maritime industry the AFL-CIO conflict had nothing to do with the industrial versus carft form of organization. It was caused mainly by the personalities of the leaders, differences in ideologies, and preferences for tactics.

In accord with the "Wobblie-SUP" philosophy, the early SIU relied on "job action" and cared little for public opinion. It was rabidly anti-Communist from the beginning, and its attacks on the NMU have often been in the form of "Red-baiting." The SIU immediately started an aggressive and rough organizing campaign on the East and Gulf Coasts. This, of course, brought it into conflict with the well-established NMU. Despite its late start, the SIU could claim a membership of 15,000 by October 1939.

---

*In maritime parlance "sailor" refers to a crew member in the deck department. "Seaman" is a more general term that applies to anyone who works on a merchant ship.

The Early Rivalry

The fact that the SIU was created by the AFL to challenge the NMU precluded the possibility of a peaceful relationship between the two unions. Although they were rivals from the beginning, their behavior and the form of the rivalry were determined by several factors within the unions and within the maritime industry. The ideologies, preferences for tactics, affiliations, and alliances had already been determined by circumstances.

By the time the SIU was in the field, the NMU had most of the subsidized dry-cargo companies on the East Coast under contract. The early East Coast gains of the SIU were mainly among the small independent operators. On the Gulf Coast, where the SIU inherited the remnants of the ISU, it was most successful. Either in order to attract, or as a result of attracting, a large southern membership, the SIU developed a strong racist policy that it retained until recently. * The NMU, in contrast, adopted a nondiscriminatory racial policy and as a result is largely nonwhite and "Latin." This has been the cause of considerable animosity and has created hostility between large segments of the two memberships.

In keeping with the tradition of unions at war, one of the first things the rivals did was to obtain allies. By 1939 the basic alliance system, stripped of the small unions and temporary frills, consisted of the SIU and ILA against the NMU on the East Coast. On the West Coast the SUP was in general conflict with the ILWU. The NMU and ILWU were connected through the CIO, and in the early years they had an ideological bond. The SUP cooperated with the SIU, and aggressively fought the NMU when the latter became active on the West Coast.

One of the early constructive aspects of the rivalry followed an NMU drive to organize the West Coast tankers in 1941. To meet the challenge, the SUP reorganized into an industrial union; and within three years it had unionized all three departments on virtually all West Coast tankers. [11]

On the dry-cargo ships the clash between Bridges and Lundeberg prevented horizontal amalgamation of the departments. Of the other two ex-ISU West Coast affiliates, the MCS, with 8,200 members, came within the ILWU orbit by 1938, when it ousted its Lundeberg supporters. Nevertheless, it was able to resist a bid by Bridges to join the NMU as an autonomous union in 1941. The MFOW, with 4,000 members, succeeded in retaining its independence under the able leadership of Vincent J. Malone, who rejected bids by both Bridges and Lundeberg.

---

*This statement is based on personal observation.

Between 1937 and 1939 both the NMU and the SIU renewed their contracts without change because of the general interunion warfare, the widespread unemployment caused by the 1937 recession, and the large number of ships sold to the Allies.[12] The contracts negotiated in 1939 made some gains and, with an eye on Europe, all contained provisions for reopening on economic matters after a specified period of notice.

The prewar manifestations of the rivalry usually were direct drives to organize the unorganized parts of the industry. Neither union tried to raid ships organized by the other. Although there was much name-calling and a few clashes, they largely expanded into new territory. Some of the invective was undoubtedly engineered for internal political reasons in each union, and much of it concerned the impending war. Both the NMU and the ILWU followed a straight "party line." Before the Nazi-Soviet nonaggression pact they were strong anti-fascists; after it they were vocal "neutrals." Along with other left-wing unions they strongly opposed U. S. aid to the Allies in any form. The SIU and SUP were strongly anti-Communist and made capital of the NMU-ILWU position whenever possible. Of course, once Germany invaded Russia and the NMU and ILWU came out in support of the war, everyone was on the same side—almost.

CONSOLIDATION

World War II was a period of consolidation for the NMU and SIU. The immediate impact of the opening of hostilities in Europe was a decrease in the number of deep-sea jobs available, as U. S. companies sold ships to foreign-flag operators and affiliates. Seagoing employment fell from 54,280 on March 31, 1938, to a low of 45,580 on September 30, 1942, before responding to the war-induced expansion.[13]

As the demand for seamen increased and the hazards of seagoing employment multiplied, the unions were able to demand several emergency wage increases.* Once the United States entered the war. wages remained stable for the duration except for a few minor adjustments.[14] By January 1, 1942, the base wage of an able-bodied seaman reached $100 per month, where it remained throughout the war.[15]

The question of area and attack bonuses was more important than wages. It was brought to a head when the SIU struck nine ships over the bonus issue. The Maritime Commission seized and manned three

---

*May 1, 1940, 10 percent or $10; Jan. 1 to Feb. 10, 1941, 15 percent or $15; May 15 to Nov. 1941, 5 percent for licensed personnel only. C. W. Uhlinger, "The Wages of American Seamen, 1939-1952" (doctoral diss., Fordham University, 1956), p. 176.

vessels of the Alcoa fleet, and within a week 25 ships were tied up. The 12-day strike was settled by the acceptance of a National Defense Mediation Board recommendation for a $100 bonus for the port of Suez and smaller amounts for less dangerous runs.

Within a week of Pearl Harbor a conference was held between the unions and shipowners under the auspices of the Maritime Commission and the Department of Labor. On December 19 the parties arrived at a Statement of Principles including a no-strike pledge and an agreement that all collective bargaining relationships and procedures would remain unchanged for the duration of the war.

The Statement of Principles was an agreement between private parties without the force of law, but circumstances insured that it would be respected. Both parties knew that the government would not tolerate a restriction of shipping due to labor disputes.

Union fears that the War Shipping Administration (WSA) might man the tonnage being built by the government with Navy crews were allayed when the WSA adopted a policy of letting the companies operate the ships as "government agents" and agreed to respect existing arrangements for obtaining crews, including the union hiring halls. By May 1942 the foundation had been laid for a labor relations policy that allowed the industry to operate without a single strike and only a few minor delays for the remainder of the war. [16]

Although the unions contributed to the labor peace of World War II, much of the credit must be given to the Maritime Labor Relations Organization (MLRO) of the WSA. In order to retain stability in the face of union rivalry, the MLRO adopted the realistic policies of maintaining the existing national uniformity of wages and conditions and maintaining the same relative strength between the rival unions that existed before the war. Wage equality had been achieved before the war began; but it required several War Labor Board decisions to bring East Coast conditions up to West Coast levels, thus removing a potential source of trouble. In assigning ships to the various operators, the WSA considered the effect on relative union strength. When a dispute between the NMU and SUP broke out in December 1942 over ships built in West Coast yards that were operating out of East Coast ports with West Coast crews, the WSA ruled that the ships involved be manned by the NMU. After that, ships remained on the coast where they were built, thus avoiding clashes of this type.

Much of the labor peace of World War II was attributable to the enormous expansion of the industry. Shipboard employment went from about 50,000 to 168,000 in five years. The seagoing work force expanded much more, since it takes more than one man to fill each job.

Some 168,000 new recruits came from the government-operated training schools. Trouble from the unions in this area was avoided by the WSA policy of manning the new ships allotted to the companies through the union hiring halls. When the unions ran short of men, they called on the Recruitment and Manning Organization (RMO) of the WSA for replacements. The new men then joined the unions.

There was an interesting difference in the attitudes of the rival unions toward the expanded role of government in the industry. The difference was consistent with their respective trade-union philosophies. Although suspicious of RMO intentions, the NMU cooperated fully with the WSA and strove for more union participation in government decision-making.

The position of the SIU and SUP was just the opposite. While fully supporting the war effort, the SIU opposed any extension of the government into maritime labor relations and was highly critical of NMU behavior. Its members refused to sign RMO draft deferment cards, equating them with the hated "fink book." It also attacked an RMO requirement that seamen take an annual physical examination, on the ground that it threatened the elimination of older members. Subsequent legislation prevented such a possibility. The SIU also successfully fought a WSA plan to establish an incentive system to reduce turnover on the ships, which it considered an attempt to undermine the unions.

As stated above, the war was a period of consolidation for both unions. They emerged much stronger, in terms of membership and resources, into a peace that promised severe dislocation. The immediate problem was an announcement by the Maritime War Emergency Board that all bonuses would end on October 1, 1945. As a rule of thumb the combined area bonus, attack bonus, and port bonus for unlicensed personnel added up to approximately the base pay. [17] The elimination of the bonus would thus cut earnings in half and leave seamen to face postwar prices with prewar wages. To avoid an immediate strike and unwanted delays in bringing the soldiers home and in the European Recovery Program, the National War Labor Board ordered a general $45 per month increase effective October 1.

DEPOLITICIZATION

The NMU-SIU rivalry emerged from the forced peace of World War II slightly modified but as strong as ever. One of the main factors of the early conflict had been a strong ideological difference between the two unions, which was reinforced by the AFL-CIO alignment. With the growth of the Atlantic and Gulf Coast district of the SIU relative to the more radical SUP within the parent organization (SIU, NA), what remained of the old IWW influence was overshadowed by the more pressing demands of "pork-chop unionism." The unemployment promised for the expanded membership by the conversion to a peacetime economy made the SIU policy of avoiding involvement with government less feasible. Although the SIU was more anti-Communist than ever, the elimination of a strong left-wing within the NMU after 1948 reduced what had been a real issue to occasional rhetoric.

The Communist faction in the NMU had lost ground throughout the war and afterward. This coincided with a general change in attitude of the American people, but seamen are so isolated from public opinion and insulated from prolonged exposure to the media that the causes of the shift are better sought within the industry. Many East Coast seamen made runs into Murmansk, Archangel, and other Russian ports. The realities of the USSR fighting for its life were a shock to many of its erstwhile friends.

Another factor that reduced the importance of radicalism was the changing character of the merchant seaman himself. The prewar seaman was often a rough character, seldom married, and with attitudes toward employers and society that reflected the conditions in the fo'c'sle when the industry was unorganized. If he was not a "reformer" by nature, he often became one in response to his own conditions or to those he witnessed. The casualness of the seaman's employment and his extreme mobility insured that he came in contact with many radicals and foreign-born seamen sailing American ships who had been influenced by Marx and other "isms" in their native lands.

The young men who took to the sea during World War II were different. The new seaman was usually recruited and trained by the WSA. His main reason for going to sea was the money or a desire to stay out of the army. These were the replacements of the large number of casualties during the first half of the war. This process of replacement of the older, more radical men by younger ones just off the farm or out of high school involved thousands of men and changed the composition of the union memberships. The extent of the replacement is indicated by the fact that 5,600 seamen lost their lives during the war. [18]

Another drain on the radical segment of the crew unions came from "top side." The shortage of licensed officers gave many of the more able experienced men a chance to get out of the crew. Since the more intelligent, or at least the more intellectually oriented, men probably had been attracted to radicalism in general and Communism in particular, this had the effect of further reducing the ranks of the radicals. In addition, since new entrants could "sit" for a license after only 18 months' sea time, as opposed to the usual 36, the radicals were denied many of their "natural" recruits.

Another factor contributing to the "depoliticization" of the NMU membership was its changing racial and ethnic composition. Its non-discriminatory admittance policy attracted many black members while the SIU continued its segregationist policies. Until recently the American black has been relatively uninterested in radical doctrines and has remained politically aloof. This attitude was undoubtedly carried into the uncertain environment of the NMU of the 1940s.

114

The most important factor in altering the political complexion of the seagoing work force, and keeping it so temperate, is the better wages paid since the war. For the first time the average seaman could afford to get married and keep a home ashore. This caused a closer tie with the larger community. No longer was the "jack ashore" restricted to the pleasures of the waterfront, and with his integration came a change in attitude.

The new social attitudes of American seamen had an impact on all maritime unions, but nowhere was it as dramatic or as decisive as in the NMU, where the group led by Joseph Curran succeeded in ousting a strong Communist faction. This necessitated a break with the NMU's traditional ally, the ILWU and Harry Bridges.

The NMU was allied with the ILWU and other left-wing maritime CIO affiliates through the Committee for Maritime Unity. The Committee was formed in 1946 with the announced purpose of "developing coordination of policy and unity of action in important matters of common concern such as strikes, legislative proposals, and government regulations." It was to have considerable policy-making authority and required the surrender of a significant measure of union sovereignty. [19] The Committee had a short but hectic life. The efforts of Bridges and the left-wing faction within the NMU to use it to direct the policies and strategies of the affiliated unions along lines favored by the Communists kindled resentment and resistance among the non-Communists. Curran's resignation from the cochairmanship of the Committee in December 1946, on the ground that the Committee was dominated by its other cochairman, Bridges, brought the simmering NMU to a boil. When the NMU National Council refused to endorse the resignation, the fight was out in the open and the lines clearly drawn.

Curran charged the left-wing-controlled organizing department of the NMU with using union funds and organizers in a drive on Isthmian Line—to campaign rather than to organize. As a result the line was lost to the SIU. Curran's hand was strengthened by gains achieved through a successful strike in 1947 that had been opposed by the left wing. When the Bridges-dominated unions settled for an extension of the existing contracts, it made the NMU gains look even better.

The battle for control of the union climaxed at the NMU convention in September 1947. Curran's group won a 24-day floor fight, and the victory was verified in the elections of July 1948. The left-wing faction was swept completely from office, and Curran eventually had it expelled from the union. An insurgent movement then developed among the "non-party Communists" but was quashed at the 1949 convention, when Curran succeeded in carrying a proposal to bar the admission of Communists to the union. Another proposal to expel all Communists from the NMU was not carried, but the victory of business unionism was complete. [20] The left wing made one final stand. On

November 14, 1949, 400 insurgents seized the NMU hall and held it by force until routed on Thanksgiving Day. [21]

The SUP attacked the Communists on the West Coast. The Seattle branch of the SUP was the home of a "radical" movement that resented SUP's support of an SIU raid on the Communist-dominated Canadian Maritime Union (CMU) through its new affiliate, the SIU of Canada. The insurgents were quickly branded "Trotskyites" and expelled from the SUP. [22]

Another attack on the left was in the form of a complicated and extended battle between the SUP and ILWU. The fight lasted from 1948 to 1955 and resulted in a new unit of the SIU, the Marine Cooks and Stewards, AFL, replacing the Communist- and Bridges-dominated National Union of Marine Cooks and Stewards (NUMCS) as the principal West Coast representative of steward's department personnel. The NUMCS had been an ally of the ILWU since 1938, and with it was expelled from the CIO in 1949 for Communist domination. Its destruction completed the purge of Communists from positions of leadership in the seagoing unions and ended the influence of Harry Bridges among the seamen. Since 1950 ideology has played no part in the NMU-SIU rivalry. However, what impetus to fight was lost was more than made up by the ambitions of Paul Hall.

Hall rose to the position of secretary-treasurer of the East Coast SIU in 1948 and replaced Lundeberg as president of the SIU, NA on the latter's death in 1955. Hall's dynamic and effective leadership made the SIU challenge to the NMU stronger than ever and expanded the rivalry into a complex maze that covers the whole maritime industry.

Lundeberg had been president of the Seafarers International Union of North America (SIU, NA) as well as secretary-treasurer of its West Coast affiliate, the SUP. Therefore, prior to 1955 it is appropriate to think of the SIU, NA as one organization. Hall's assumption of its presidency effectively split the national union in two. It was to be expected that the larger Atlantic and Gulf District (SIU, A&G) would dominate the SIU, NA. However, this resulted in the West Coast affiliates' withdrawing to a degree from East Coast and national affairs.

Although the SUP and other Pacific Coast SIU affiliates remained within the national organization and continued to cooperate with their East Coast brothers in relation to the NMU, it is more accurate to think of the SIU, A&G and the SUP as separate unions. In the pages that follow reference to the SIU means the Atlantic and Gulf Districts of the SIU, NA. The distinction usually is not overly important, since Paul Hall heads both organizations and the West Coast affiliates have been relatively inactive on nationally important matters.

At the end of the war both the NMU and the SIU began drives to organize the rest of the industry. The SIU had an advantage, since the NMU was in the throes of "civil war." Besides picking up many small companies, the SIU won the Isthmian Lines (mentioned above in connection with the NMU purge) and the very resistant Cities Service tanker fleet.

After the postwar organizing drive, the industry was completely unionized in terms of the rivalry. There were several East Coast tanker companies with company unions, but the chance of organizing them was (and is) very slim. Their conditions were as good as on union ships, and many of the men involved were either strongly anti-union or had been thrown out of the national unions for one reason or another. [23] The only other large unorganized area was the Navy-owned and civilian-manned Military Sea Transport Service (MSTS). At that time government regulation prevented these men from organizing.

With the "closing of the frontier" the rivals turned on each other. After a decade of conflict each union had become a highly efficient machine with a "personality" geared for a continuation of the rivalry. Neither union was interested in enticing the other's members away. The objective of the conflict was the job, not the man who held it. It is also an industrial peculiarity that the hiring hall of each union has the effect of enforcing a completely closed shop. Thus neither union had direct access to the jobs of the other. However, the officers' unions overlap the crew jurisdictions. When the SIU shifted its emphasis "top side," it involved the whole industry in the rivalry.

Most jurisdictional disputes since the mid-1950s have followed a consistent pattern. Every dispute, no matter how complex and multi-partied, has been between, and never within, the camps of the two rivals and their respective allies. Some of the disputes arise on the spur of the moment and have not always appeared in the best interests of one or both of the central figures. However, the fact that disputes within coalitions either do not occur or do not result in strikes, and clashes between unions of different loyalties always result in bitter conflict, can be explained only in terms of an expanded NMU-SIU rivalry.

NOTES

1. H. S. Ruchlin, Manpower Resources of the U.S. Maritime Industry: A Definitional and Descriptive Analysis of the Maritime Labor Force, P.B. 178, 727 (Washington: U.S. Department of Commerce, 1968), pp. 120-21.

2. 48 Stat. 195 (1933) Sec. 7(b), 15 U.S.C.A. 705-707 Elim. (1963); Joseph P. Goldberg, The Maritime Story: A Study in Labor-Management Relations (Cambridge, Massachusetts: Harvard University Press, 1958), p. 130.

3. Ibid., p. 143. This was part of a worldwide shift in Communist tactics.

4. Ibid., p. 150.

5. Fred Thompson, The I. W. W., Its First Fifty Years (1905-1955) (Chicago: Adria Printing Co., 1955), p. 163. "Job action" usually took the form of a "quickie" strike against a ship at an opportune time (such as just before sailing) to press for limited objectives.

6. Goldberg, op. cit., p. 146.

7. Ibid., p. 165.

8. William L. Standard, Merchant Seamen, A Short History of Their Struggles (New York: International Publishers, 1947), p. 140.

9. Goldberg, op. cit., p. 166.

10. Standard, op. cit., pp. 106-07.

11. Goldberg, op. cit., p. 174.

12. Ibid., p. 181.

13. U. S. Department of Commerce, Maritime Administration, "Seafaring Employment, Oceangoing Commercial Ships, 1,000 Gross Tons and Over," unpublished table dated Apr. 5, 1971.

14. C. W. Uhlinger, "The Wages of American Seamen, 1939-1952" (doctoral diss., Fordham University, 1956), p. 179.

15. Handbook of Merchant Shipping Statistics Through 1958, p. 192.

16. Goldberg, op. cit., p. 206.

17. Elmo Paul Hohman, History of American Merchant Seamen (Hamden, Connecticut: Shoestring Press, 1956), p. 83.

18. Traffic World, Mar. 6, 1965, p. 31.

19. Hohman, op. cit., p. 102.

20. Goldberg, op. cit., p. 259.

21. Elmo Paul Hohman, "Merchant Seamen in the United States, 1937-1952," International Labor Review 67, no. 1 (Jan. 1953): 29.

22. Goldberg, op. cit., pp. 259-60.

23. For an excellent discussion of the oil companies and their seamen's unions, see John J. Collins, Never off Pay, the Story of the Independent Tanker Union 1937-1962 (New York: Fordham University Press, 1964).

EXPANSION OF THE RIVALRY TO THE
OFFICERS' UNIONS

On May 12, 1949, the SIU formed the Brotherhood of Marine Engineers (BME) to challenge the jurisdiction of the Marine Engineers Beneficial Association (MEBA). The latter had long been the traditional representative of licensed marine engineers. Although a strict craft union, it affiliated with the CIO in 1937. Since the SIU was an AFL affiliate, its creation of the BME was justifiable as a raid on a CIO union. In retrospect, however, it appears more like an extension of the SIU relative to the NMU.

When chartered, the BME was little more than a filing cabinet in the SIU hall. Its first chance to move into MEBA jurisdiction came in August 1949, when the MEBA struck Isbrandtsen Lines, demanding a 40-hour week and a hiring-hall provision. The BME crossed MEBA picket lines and signed a contract without a hiring-hall provision. Isbrandtsen was a NMU-contract company, and the ships could sail only with NMU cooperation. In terms of the NMU-SIU rivalry, Curran was very short-sighted when he refused to back the MEBA because that was what his opposition was advocating.[1]

The second BME raid on the MEBA occurred in 1951. The MEBA threatened to strike all of its contract companies over the 40-hour week, a hiring-hall provision, and a uniform national agreement. Its conditions were accepted without a strike by all but one company, the U. S. Steel-owned Isthmian Lines. The MEBA struck the line in May, and the BME again rushed in to fill the jobs—without a hiring hall. With these two raids the SIU established the BME as an engineers' union. It was still vastly overshadowed by the MEBA but, given its predatory nature and the SIU's backing, the BME was a standing threat to the MEBA. The larger union was rendered practically impotent as a labor union, since any strike was sure to be met with BME strike-breakers.

The "no-raiding" agreement and the AFL-CIO merger in 1955 had little effect on the waterfront. The two rivals had been in separate federations; but once the SIU was chartered by the AFL to check the NMU's growth, this factor in the rivalry became unimportant. Both East Coast unions were industrial in form. In 1955 the SUP completed the transition begun on the tankers in the 1940s, when, in connection with the destruction of the Bridges-dominated NUMCS, it joined the Marine Cooks and Stewards, the Marine Firemen's Union, and itself into the Pacific District of the SIU. [2]

By 1955 the rivalry had no justification in terms of ideology or affiliation, yet it continued. The conflict that had been caused by these factors was more than made up for by the growing personal feud between Curran and Hall, the continued racial differences between the unions, and the complications caused by a rigid dual unionism. The last was especially troublesome in shipping, where bargaining units easily can, and often do, move across jurisdictional lines. Such a case occurred in 1957.

In that year Moore MacCormack Lines (MorMac) bought Robin Lines, probably to acquire its route and subsidy on the African run. MorMac was and is an NMU-contract company, and Robin was SIU. When the dispute reached the National Labor Relations Board (NLRB), it held that each of the Robin ships was a separate unit for representational purposes. [3] By this ruling the SIU could continue to represent the seven ships involved within the much larger NMU-represented MorMac fleet. Curran had no intention of accepting this and claimed, with some justification, that it jeopardized the company-wide structure of the NMU benefit programs. He petitioned the NLRB for a company-wide representation election, which he knew he would win with 27 NMU ships to the SIU's seven. As a result of this the AFL-CIO impartial umpire, David L. Cole, found the NMU in violation of the AFL-CIO constitution. Curran claimed Cole's decision was based on a misguided NLRB decision. In 1970, five of the ex-Robin Line ships were still in the MorMac fleet and under SIU contract. However, by 1973 the problem had finally disappeared. [4]

At about the time the MorMac dispute began, another episode unfolded that was to rearrange the union alignment. Although not in its orbit, the MEBA had long had closer ties with the NMU than the SIU, partly because of their mutual CIO affiliation. When the SIU formed the BME in 1949, the MEBA was forced into an anti-SIU, and thus into an even more pro-NMU, position. The International Organization of Masters, Mates, and Pilots (MMP), the deck officers' union, had remained generally aloof from the rivalry, with a slight tendency to favor the NMU. Thus both important officers' unions tended to favor the NMU in the mid-1950s.

There were also two radio operators' unions in the field. The American Radio Association (ARA) was a CIO affiliate and usually an ally of the NMU. The Radio Officers' Union (ROU) was affiliated with the AFL and was generally an SIU ally. The two radio unions competed until after the AFL-CIO merger. In 1956 they reached an understanding and have since cooperated. [5]

AMERICAN COAL SHIPPING

In 1956 the United Mine Workers (UMW), in conjunction with the mine operators and the coal-carrying railroads, formed a corporation known as American Coal Shipping (ACS). It was to obtain 30 Liberty ships from the government's National Defense Reserve Fleet (NDRF) and use them to promote the export of American coal to Europe. The UMW owned one-third of the $50 million venture. John L. Lewis, president of the UMW, was on the board of directors. The outlook for the company was bright, with expected volume to reach thousands of Liberty ship-size loads per year. [6] Of course, this many potential jobs was worth a fight. The company signed with the NMU and ARA, and "gave assurances" it would sign with the MEBA and MMP when the operation got under way.

The trouble began when John L. Lewis pressured ACS to disregard the pledge given the established officers' unions and to give the ships to the Brotherhood of Marine Officers (BMO). The BMO had been formed during the 1930s and had affiliated with District 50 of the UMW shortly after World War II. It represented all officers on the ships of two companies, American Export Lines and United Fruit Company. [7]

The BMO had a small membership and allowed nonmembers to sail on the ships of its contract companies. Both the MEBA and MMP allowed their members to work on BMO ships if they first obtained written permission from the union (perhaps with an eventual raid in mind). The first act of the MEBA and MMP after ACS had signed with the BMO was to order their members off these ships, to show how weak the BMO was. This was not enough.

Next the MEBA and MMP picketed the ACS building and the one ship it had in operation. They naturally expected that their picket lines would be honored by other AFL-CIO affiliates against the non-affiliated UMW and its District 50 appendage, the BMO. They were disappointed. The NMU and ARA crossed the picket lines and sailed with BMO officers. George Meany, president of the AFL-CIO, promised federation support for the picketing unions and put pressure on Washington to halt the release of the 30 Liberty ships. Six of the ships eventually were released and were picketed by the MEBA and MMP, to the delight of the press. When ACS went to court in November 1956 to get the picketing enjoined, John L. Lewis justified its (and his) position on the ground that this was a jurisdictional dispute and not a labor dispute. Ironically, Lewis could not use the machinery of the Taft-Hartley Act as a union leader, because he refused to sign a non-Communist affidavit, but could use it as a director of ACS.

The immediate and most far-reaching effect of the NMU's action was to alienate the MEBA and MMP. Another effect was to enhance the position of the SIU relative to the NMU within the AFL-CIO. Paul Hall had been head of the Maritime Trades Department, while Joseph Curran headed the CIO caucus known as the AFL-CIO Maritime Committee. The MEBA, a former CIO affiliate, withdrew from Curran's Maritime Committee, an action that, besides weakening the Committee, symbolized the MEBA shift away from the NMU and into the SIU camp. [8]

The ACS dispute then became much more complicated. The SIU filed charges with the NLRB to the effect that it had been discriminated against because ACS had signed with the NMU before the ships were released. A federal district court in New York held for the SIU, and ordered the company to set up a system of nondiscriminatory hiring among NMU and SIU seamen based solely on "seniority in sailing time." This sent both unions to scour the waterfront and their retirement lists for the oldest seamen they could find. A humorous event occurred when a group of elderly NMU members calling themselves the "Ancient Mariners" picketed the Washington office of the NLRB. They urged the Board to hold the representation election requested by the NMU promptly, so that they could return to retirement. [9]

Another front in the ACS dispute opened in September 1957, when the SIU struck A. H. Bull and Company, a small SIU-contract firm that had recently been acquired by ACS. The SIU walkout was in disregard of a no-strike clause, but the MEBA and MMP honored the picket line. The SIU demanded equalization of terms between Bull Lines and West Coast operators retroactive to July 1, 1957. According to Bull, in an attempt to have the strike enjoined, the SIU was putting pressure on it only to hurt ACS. The complicated legal battle that followed centered on specific performance of the no-strike clause and ended in the SIU's favor. The important point in terms of this discussion is that the SIU, MEBA, and MMP were on one side and the NMU and BMO on the other.

The many-faceted ACS remained in its complicated legal existence for another two years, but by the end of 1959 it was practically defunct. This was an important victory for the SIU and its allies, which by then included the MEBA. The NMU eventually received the BMO from District 50. It became a subdivision of the NMU, where it remains today.

It is impossible to know the extent to which Paul Hall planned or anticipated the outcome of the ACS dispute. The resulting polarization of the officers' unions was a strategic victory for the SIU and placed a powerful weapon in its hands. The acquisition of the BMO by the NMU was of less value. The MMP sojourn in the SIU fold was temporary. It quickly regained its traditional independence by cooperating with the NMU in an organizing drive. However, the MMP now had to remember that the BMO was a potential threat to its jurisdiction. Any expansion of BMO interests would align the MMP with the MEBA and SIU.

CO-OPTATION OF THE MEBA

Unlike the MMP, the MEBA was unable to free itself from the SIU. It remained a steady ally, if not a prisoner, of the SIU for the next several years.

The significance of the BME to the MEBA lay not in its size but in its willingness to cross MEBA picket lines. With the BME on its flank, the MEBA was greatly hampered in the use of the strike. This was thought especially important at the time because of the impending opening of the Saint Lawrence Seaway, which presented the deep-sea unions with a fourth coast. Some rigorous organizing was called for, and the ability to strike was essential. More immediately, some sort of reconciliation probably was necessary to insure SIU cooperation in the ACS dispute.

The AFL-CIO merger had removed a formal barrier to merger, as well as the SIU's logical justification for having an engineers' union in the first place. What probably began as an affair of convenience for the MEBA was almost to prove its downfall as an independent union.

In October 1957, in the midst of the ACS dispute, the MEBA leadership signed a merger agreement with the BME, which only a few years before had crossed its picket lines. In 1959 the MEBA membership voted by referendum (3,864 to 764) to approve the merger, and after a complex maneuver the BME became Local 101 of the MEBA.[10]

Throughout its long history the MEBA had remained highly decentralized. Each port held considerable autonomy and serviced ships while in that port with varying degrees of efficiency. In 1961 the MEBA reorganized itself into the National Marine Engineers' Beneficial Association (NMEBA), consisting of three semi-autonomous districts. What had been the old MEBA's Atlantic and Gulf Coast locals became "branches" of District I.* What had been the BME and then Local 101 became District II. The Pacific Coast locals of the old MEBA became the Pacific Coast District (PCD) of the NMEBA.

It was understood that District I would have jurisdiction over the East and Gulf Coasts and District II the Great Lakes. In exchange for MEBA's Great Lakes organization, District II was to relinquish its deep-sea jurisdiction. This never happened. District II acquired the

---

*In maritime parlance "district" and "branch" are considered SIU terminology.

Great Lakes but did not give up its saltwater contracts. It still represents the engineers on Isthmian Line ships and has acquired a large number of tramp companies.*

THE MEBA-BME merger was very important in terms of the NMU-SIU rivalry. For the next several years the MEBA was firmly in the SIU camp. Paul Hall's lieutenants in the BME, now MEBA District II, were members of the National Executive Committee of the NMEBA. As a result of the events that followed, they were able to direct the course of the NMEBA with considerable efficiency, at least to the extent of keeping it consistent with SIU policy.

In everyday operation, District II remained a separate union and District I and the PCD continued to be thought of as the MEBA. For all practical purposes, District II remained a part of the SIU.

THE NEW ALIGNMENT AND THE STRIKE OF 1961

The SIU soon put its new MEBA leverage to work. As mentioned, one of the benefits enjoyed by the NMU from its head start in the 1930s was that it organized the "cream" of the industry, the subsidized-liner sector. With one exception (Delta Lines), all East Coast subsidized operators in business in 1970 were organized by the NMU.† The SIU's strength lay in a few nonsubsidized lines and in the many tramp companies it had under contract. On the West Coast the SUP, MFU, and MCS had both the subsidized and the nonsubsidized operators under contract. Table 7.1 illustrates the relative importance of the subsidized sector to the NMU, SIU, and SUP as of 1970.

By the early 1960s the nonsubsidized sector was in trouble. This was before the Vietnam war and containerization gave the industry a temporary boost. All nonsubsidized dry-cargo ships were of World War II construction. At this time almost all subsidized ships also

---

*In 1970, District II had 41 companies operating 94 ships under contract. Many of the companies were interrelated, and 34 of them operated one ship each. U. S. Department of Commerce, Maritime Administration, Seafaring Guide . . . and Directory of Labor-Management Affiliations, 1969 (Washington: U. S. Government Printing Office, 1969), pp. 16-64; Vessel Inventory Report, 1970.

†The SIU had another subsidized company, Bloomfield Steamship Company, which operated four or five C-2's out of Gulf Coast ports in the early 1960s. The Maritime Subsidy Board (MSB) refused to renew Bloomfield's subsidy contract in 1964 because of a proposal by States Marine to buy its stock. In 1965, when a second one-year extension was offered by the MSB, Bloomfield rejected it and went out of business sometime thereafter. Traffic World, Dec. 25, 1965, p. 13.

TABLE 7.1

Companies and Ships Under Contract to the NMU, SIU, and SUP as of June 30, 1970

Union	Total		Dry-Cargo		Subsidized		Percent of Dry-Cargo Ships Subsidized
	Companies	Ships	Companies	Ships	Companies	Ships	
NMU	69	355	31	242	7	174	72
SIU	84	251	52	202	1	12	6
SUP (MFU) (MCS)	19	118	10	94	5	61	65

Notes: The SUP represents all three departments on West Coast tankers.

Subsidized ships do not include ships operated by subsidy-contract companies without subsidy.

Source: Derived from U.S. Department of Commerce, Maritime Administration, MARAD 1970, Year of Transition, annual report of the Maritime Administration for fiscal year 1970 (Washington: U.S. Government Printing Office, 1971), App. X, pp. 75-76.

were war-built. However, a replacement program had been started, and the prospects of the subsidized sector looked bright compared with those of the nonsubsidized. It is not an exaggeration to say that the part of the industry in which the SIU had practically all of its jobs was about to disappear.

To correct this situation, Paul Hall formed the National Committee for Maritime Bargaining (NCMB) shortly before the contracts were to expire on June 15, 1961. There were eight unions on the Committee, and it claimed to cover 90 percent of the industry. Actually the MEBA and MMP supplied most of this coverage by including the NMU-contract companies. Needless to say, the NMU and its allies were not represented.

The principal objectives of the NCMB were to force companies with foreign-flag operations to allow American unions to organize the crews on their "runaway ships" and to establish a joint labor-management committee to overhaul the subsidy program. The NMU was in sympathy on the "runaway" issue. Earlier in the year Curran and Hall announced their agreement on its importance in the 1961 negotiations. However, when it came to subsidies, Curran was pleased with the program as it was.

The strike began on June 15. Within a few days the MMP disaffiliated from the NCMB and agreed, along with the NMU, to submit the foreign-flag issue to a committee for study as part of an agreement with the employers' association, the American Merchant Marine Institute (AMMI).

The SIU group held out on the foreign-flag issue for several more days and forced agreement on 50 percent of the fleet before the strike was ended by President Kennedy with a 60-day injunction on June 23.[11] The NCMB faded out of existence soon after the strike, but it lasted long enough to demonstrate Hall's control over the MEBA and the strategic position of the MEBA in the industry. For the last three days of the dispute the MEBA was the only union on strike, and yet the whole East Coast remained "locked up."

THE EXPANDED RIVALRY

The 1961 strike cemented the SIU-MEBA alliance. The years following saw a series of clashes between the rival groups. In 1962 the NMU won a battle when Isbrandtsen, with MEBA District II (BME) engineers, sold 14 ships to American Export Lines, one of the two BMO-contract companies. The case could not go to the NLRB because it involved supervisory personnel; and Curran succeeded in defying a decision by an AFL-CIO impartial umpire, David L. Cole, that ruled the BMO in violation of the AFL-CIO Internal Disputes Plan.

An exception to the petty jurisdictional squabbles occurred in 1962. Within months of President Kennedy's Executive Order 10988, allowing federal employees to form unions, the NMU had organized the Atlantic Sea Command of the MSTS, consisting of 53 ships and 3,500 jobs.[12] The SIU was not a serious contender for these jobs, mainly because many of them were held by blacks. However, there was active rivalry on the West Coast. This revived some of the old ideological invective, which resulted in Curran and the NMU suing Hall and the SIU for $800,000 for libel. An article in the January 1963 issue of the MSTS Seafarer, the newspaper of the SIU's Military Sea Transport Union, claimed that "Curran was trying to take over the MSTS which would be a catastrophe in the event of war with Russia."[13] The NMU succeeded in organizing two out of three MSTS Pacific fleets, with 22 ships and 1,600 men, in the face of SIU competition.[14]

Meanwhile a dirtier campaign began on the Great Lakes when Upper Lakes Shipping, Ltd., a Canadian company, shifted 350 jobs from the SIU of Canada to the Canadian Maritime Union. The CMU had at one time been Communist-dominated and had been friendly with the NMU since the latter's founding. The SIU first entered Canadian shipping in the late 1940s in an anti-Communist raid, mentioned above in connection with the SUP "Trotskyite" insurgence. Relations between the two Canadian unions paralleled those of their American counterparts. The 1963 clash was accompanied by considerable violence and became a source of embarrassment to the United States when the SIU picketed and tied up several Canadian ships in American ports. When someone blew a hole in the side of a Canadian ship in Chicago, Secretary of Labor Willard Wirtz had to go to Ottawa for a peace conference.[15]

The trouble ended when the Canadian government ran Harold Banks, the head of SIU of Canada, out of the country and put the union under trusteeship.

The N. S. Savannah Incident

While the above was going on, the U. S. East Coast was the scene of several other newsworthy clashes. One effect of the rivalry was that it turned every dispute into a crusade. As in most crusades, the cost of the battle bore little relation to the value of the victory. For a few jobs the rivals spent large amounts of time and money while showing no concern for the damage done to the unions, the industry, or the public. Each side was so self-righteous in presenting its side of the argument and so condemning of the other that a graceful retreat or a sensible compromise was often impossible. One such controversy began in 1962 and concerned the N. S. Savannah.

The Savannah's MEBA (District I) engineers used the added bargaining power of their two years' extra training to get a raise from
States Marine Lines, the company operating the ship for the government. The MMP demanded a similar raise; and the issue went to
arbitration, as called for in the MMP agreement. The arbitrator ruled
that the mates should get the raise and that the traditional relationship between the mates' and engineers' wages should be maintained.
The engineers then demanded an additional raise, claiming that since
they had undergone extensive training in addition to that required for
a regular license and the mates had not, the traditional relationship
was no longer appropriate. The MEBA also resented the MMP arbitrator's tying its wage scale to that of the mates.

Maritime labor relations was plagued for years by such disputes.
Each union contract had an arbitration clause, but each union had its
own arbitrator. Unions of rival groups would not allow any overlapping
of their jurisdiction by that of a rival. The Savannah incident now
became a matter of principle, and the ship's engineers resigned while
the ship was on the West Coast. They were persuaded to sail the
ship until a settlement could be reached. When five months had passed
without a settlement, the engineers refused to sail from Galveston,
Texas, when the Savannah was to go on active duty in May 1963.
Curran then sent letters to States Marine and the government, offering
to man the ship and guarantee operation with BMO officers. On May 13
the MEBA engineers were laid off; and on May 17 the Commerce
Department announced that the contract with States Marine had been
canceled, and that the Savannah would be operated by American Export
Lines. [16] American Export ships are manned by the NMU and BMO.
The Savannah had no labor problems after that.

The S. S. Maximus Incident

Another minor dispute that grew out of all proportion to any
possible gains involved was the S. S. Maximus incident. The ship
had been owned and operated by Grace Lines as the S. S. Santa Monica.
In June 1963 she was bought by a new firm called Cambridge Carriers,
run by Piero Johnson, and renamed the S. S. Maximus. This was the
only vessel the company owned, and the sale had been made in
secret.

The new firm signed a contract with the BMO, and the original
ship's officers were discharged. The MEBA considered this a raid,
and began picketing the Maximus in Philadelphia. On June 20, at the
request of George Meany and the Secretary of Labor, the MEBA
discontinued picketing and allowed the Maximus to deliver Red Cross
supplies to Cuba in return for Bay of Pigs prisoners. When the ship
returned to New Orleans, the MEBA resumed its picketing. In

128

retaliation the NMU began picketing all ships owned by Bloomfield (now defunct) and Delta Lines. Both companies had MEBA engineers and SIU crews. Twenty ships were tied up by the time Cambridge Carriers faded out of business after selling the Maximus to an MEBA-contract company.[17]

The S. S. America Incident

Shortly afterward the more widely publicized tie-up of the S. S. America took place over what seems, on the surface, a very unimportant matter that did not result from action initiated by either union. However, the fact that the NMU and MEBA were involved, and were unable to reach a sensible solution, makes the dispute explainable only in terms of rivalry.

On September 14, 1963, several NMU crew members charged the first assistant engineer, Louis Neurohr, with committing "prejudicial and discriminatory acts."[18] On the day of sailing, with the crew on articles and 956 passengers on board, the NMU announced that its members would not sail the ship until Neurohr was removed. The company had reason to believe that if Neurohr was arbitrarily removed, the MEBA would walk off. Negotiations continued until 4:00 the next morning, with the passengers still on board. Both unions had arbitration clauses in their contracts to handle such disputes; but they were between the company and the union, not between unions. The two arbitrators separately considered the case and gave conflicting decisions.[19]

The ship's master then announced that the ship would sail at 8:30 A. M. The NMU walked off, and the company canceled the sailing. This was the beginning of a five-month strike, a blow from which American-flag passenger shipping never recovered. Besides the 956 passengers on board there were another 950 in Europe waiting to come home, and thousands of others with passage scheduled over the next five months.

This list is not complete. There have been other, less publicized disputes that either resulted from or were complicated by the rivalry. Most of the incidents were in themselves unimportant, but when added together they represent a severe burden on an already troubled industry. The impressive fact was the consistency with which the disputes have been between, and never within, rival groups.

MARITIME STRIKES

The labor problems of the U. S. shipping industry have been very costly. The 1961 strike has been discussed. In 1965, 1969, and 1972 there were other major strikes by seagoing personnel. In addition, and perhaps more important, there have been many minor disputes. Although they attract less attention, they too disrupt the service offered by the American-flag industry.

The large number of minor and unpredictable work stoppages has made U.S.-flag shipping less dependable than that of its foreign-flag competitors. Many shippers have learned that their chances of fulfilling delivery agreements on time are better when they use a foreign flag. Others have been forced to use foreign ships when U.S. carriers were strike-bound, and have found it convenient to continue doing so.

The immediate cost of a strike may be considerable, but it is a short-run cost. However, the indirect cost of shipping strikes resulting from traffic diversion continue indefinitely. It is in this way that the maritime unions have injured the U.S. merchant marine. The associated increases in wages and other direct costs that constitute the labor-cost disadvantage would have occurred anyway.

The most disturbing feature of most shipping industry strikes is that they serve no constructive industrial relations purpose. They are not tests of strength between labor and capital that force agreement and understanding. In the shipping industry the balance of power between any of the several important seagoing unions and the companies is totally in the favor of the union. Once a strike is in progress, ships are tied up as they return to U.S. ports. Thus the cost of a strike to the company is cumulative. In fact, it is compounded. The longer a strike lasts, the more ships that are strike-bound. Since there is a relatively fixed amount of dock space and longshoring and warehousing capacity, it takes that much longer to get the ships back into service. Liner companies have the additional problem of reestablishing their schedules. The longer a strike lasts, the longer it takes to get the ships "on berth" again.

A second cause of the high strike costs faced by the companies is the high capital-intensity of ocean shipping and the way it is financed. Ships, especially liners, are expensive, and are financed by mortgage rather than equity. As discussed in Chapter 1, mortgage and other debt servicing is a fixed cost to the firm that must be paid during a strike. The higher the company's debt-equity ratio, or the higher the fixed cost relative to total cost (other things being equal), the more vulnerable it is to a work stoppage and the resulting interruption of revenue.

There are no comparable effects on the union or its members. Most seamen take at least a month, and usually two or three months, off each year. A strike is as good a time as any to take a vacation (usually with vacation pay). In addition, there is often some shipping during a strike, either in a nonstruck sector or on ships carrying military or other essential cargo cleared to move.

There is also little, if any, cost imposed on the union and its leaders. Dues continue to be paid, since there is no check-off in the industry. The members, by temperament or custom, accept a high degree of strike activity on the part of their unions. Indeed, until a few years ago, too much "responsibility" would have been detrimental to the leaders of a maritime union.

The outcome of any maritime strike is obvious. It is only a matter of time before the companies are willing to settle on any reasonable terms. The key word is "reasonable." In contract negotiations it will be those additional costs that can be convincingly passed forward to the Maritime Subsidy Board or other government agencies, and thus not result in a contraction of the industry.

Few shipping industry strikes in recent years have been over simple cost issues. The multi-employer bargaining units and the fairly high level of earnings have made such disputes less difficult. The problems occur when one of two issues is introduced: loss of jobs (automation) or union rivalry.

The strike in a situation where the employer is practically impotent does not lend itself to the solution of either type of problem. Unfortunately, almost all work stoppages in recent years have involved either employment levels in some form or have been essentially inter-union disputes.

Pointing out the dysfunctional nature of most shipping industry strikes does not mean that they are irrational. The critical importance of jobs to maritime unions requires that they aggressively pursue every opportunity to acquire additional jobs. With two competing unions in the field, there is a tragic inevitability about the rivalry-caused work stoppages.

SUMMARY

An assessment of the cost of maritime union rivalry is beyond the scope of this study. It is possible, however, that it has been of greater detriment to the U.S. merchant marine than the labor-cost disadvantage per se. Perhaps a more accurate statement would be that the indirect labor costs resulting from unsuccessful labor relations, coupled with the direct labor-cost disadvantage, have greatly amplified the problem.

Access to foreign building and the adoption of new technology would have gone a long way toward offsetting the higher direct-labor costs of the U.S. flag. However, it would not compensate for the indirect labor-related costs. In fact, new high-cost, highly productive ships are especially vulnerable to the disruptions caused by work stoppages. As capital-intensity increases, each striking seaman idles that much more capital. And as that happens, the need for successful industrial relations, and the cost of unsuccessful industrial relations, grow.

The expanded interunion rivalry ended, or became less intense, about 1965. This is fortunate, for the situation was very unstable. Each crew union had the ability to raid the other via its officer-union allies. The importance of job control had not diminished, and the industry continued to contract. There is no question that the new weapons would have been used repeatedly had intersectoral rivalry not arisen.

NOTES

1. H. W. Benson, "Some MEBA History," Union Democracy in Action 15 (undated): 8.
2. J. P. Goldberg, The Maritime Story: A Study in Labor-Management Relations (Cambridge, Mass.: Harvard University Press, 1958), p. 261.
3. Bureau of National Affairs, Daily Labor Report, Oct. 24, 1962, 208: A-10.
4. Vessel Inventory Report, 1970, p. 73. Vessel Inventory Report, 1973, p. 44.
5. A. W. Warner and A. S. Eichner, "Analysis of Labor-Management Relations in the Off-Shore Operations of the East Coast Maritime Industry" (1966), p. 5.
6. Business Week, Nov. 10, 1956, p. 162.
7. Warner and Eichner, op. cit., p. 2.
8. Business Week, Dec. 1, 1956, p. 143.
9. Bureau of National Affairs, Daily Labor Report, February 7, 1958, 27: A-5.
10. American Marine Engineer (NMEBA newspaper), June 1959, p. 4.
11. Seafarer's Log (SIU newspaper), June 1961, p. 3.
12. Bureau of National Affairs, Daily Labor Report, July 18, 1962, 139: A-10.
13. Ibid., May 16, 1963, 96: A-10.
14. Ibid., Oct. 30, 1962, 212: A-10.
15. U.S. News & World Report, Sept. 23, 1963, pp. 91-92.
16. Ibid., May 37, 1963, pp. 74-75.
17. U.S. Congress, Senate, Committee on Commerce, Hearings on Settlement of Maritime Interunion Disputes, 88th Cong., 1st sess. (Washington: U.S. Government Printing Office, 1963), pp. 105-07. The record does not show the company that bought the Maximus. It was not returned to Grace Lines.
18. Ibid., p. 20.
19. Ibid., p. 50. As a result of this dispute the NMU and MEBA agreed that future problems of this nature would be jointly arbitrated by their respective arbitrators. Warner and Eichner, op. cit., p. 234.

8

**INTERSECTORAL
RIVALRY**

INTRODUCTION

The plight of the U. S. merchant marine has never been a secret to those associated with the industry. The failure of national maritime policy has long been recognized, though its cause may not have been. By about 1960, however, the problem was pressing. The war-built ships were 15 years old or more, and rapidly approaching the end of their customary economic life. The ship replacement program of the subsidized sector had hardly begun; and foreign-flag vessels, fully recovered from World War II, were forcing U. S. ships out of most competitive international trade.

Table 8.1 illustrates the experience of the industry during the 1950s and 1960s. It shows that the U. S. merchant marine was in steady decline throughout the 1950s in terms of percent of U. S. foreign trade carried. Absolute tonnage carried by U. S. ships declined irregularly from 49. 7 million tons in 1950 to 31. 0 million in 1960, despite a 127 percent increase in the volume of U. S. oceanborne foreign trade from 117. 5 million tons in 1950 to 277. 9 million in 1960.

Following the temporary expansion associated with the Korean conflict, the fleet began to decline in terms of number of ships and employment as well. The number of ships decreased from 1, 145 in 1950 to 951 in 1960, or by 20. 4 percent. Of course this does not reflect the qualitative decline due to aging.

Shipboard employment declined from 56, 629 to 49, 153, or by 13. 2 percent, during the same period. Actually, this underestimates the impact of the decline in employment in two respects. First, there was a considerable expansion of seagoing employment due to the Korean war. It peaked in 1952 at 70, 736 jobs. The increment of 14, 000 jobs swelled the ranks of the seagoing work force and reversed the decline following World War II. Industry commitment is strong in

TABLE 8.1

Experience of the U.S. Merchant Marine, 1950-70

Year	Ships June 30	Employment June 30	Total Tons	U.S. Flag Tons	Percent Commercial Tons U.S. Ships Carried
1950	1,145	56,629	117.5	49.7	42.3
1951	1,414	69,473	193.1	76.8	39.8
1952	1,432	70,736	187.9	64.4	34.3
1953	1,405	69,125	178.0	51.7	29.1
1954	1,113	55,797	177.0	48.7	27.5
1955	1,153	57,468	226.2	53.1	23.5
1956	1,091	57,192	260.1	53.9	20.7
1957	1,153	61,059	289.3	50.8	17.6
1958	941	51,515	253.3	30.9	12.2
1959	937	50,223	267.0	27.1	10.2
1960	951	49,153	277.9	31.0	11.1
1961	621	30,930	272.4	26.3	9.7
1962	915	47,346	296.8	29.6	10.0
1963	919	47,996	311.6	28.5	9.2
1964	915	47,979	332.8	30.5	9.2
1965	779	39,125	371.3	27.7	7.5
1966	1,019	51,889	392.3	26.2	6.7
1967	1,083	54,584	387.6	20.5	5.3
1968	1,080	54,150	418.6	25.0	6.0
1969	992	47,464	427.9	20.7	4.8
1970	798	37,580	472.5	26.5	5.6

Notes: Tonnages are in millions of long tons.

Work stoppages occurred in 1961, 1965, and 1969.

Sources: Ships and employment—U.S. Department of Commerce, Maritime Administration, "Seafaring Employment, Oceangoing Commercial Ships 1,000 Gross Tons and over," unpublished table dated Apr. 5, 1971. Cargo data—1950-69, MARAD 1970, Year of Transition, annual report of the Maritime Administration for fiscal year 1970 (Washington: U.S. Government Printing Office, 1971), Chart VI, p. 27; "Value and Tonnage of Commercial Cargo Carried in United States Oceanborne Foreign Trade," unpublished table dated July 21, 1971.

ocean shipping. Because of the hiring halls, a reduction in employment is spread over a large part of the work force rather than falling
on a relatively small number of workers who are then forced to seek
employment elsewhere. Few committed seamen ever leave the industry
for lack of work. There is usually enough work to live on, and a considerable amount of nonworking time each year is expected.

The relevant decline in jobs during the 1950s was from 70,736
in 1952 to 49,153 in 1960. The difference is 21,583, or 30.5 percent.
This is a drastic reduction in employment. However, it still understates the true impact on the work force and the unions because it
takes a minimum of 1.5 men to fill each shipboard job. The Korean
war expansion added more men to the work force (or prevented more
from leaving) than the increased number of jobs indicates. Consequently, the contraction that began in 1952 caused more displacement
and unemployment than the figures indicate. The real impact in terms
of unemployment and underemployment may have been in the neighbor-
hood of 30,000 man-years of employment.

This may overstate the case somewhat. During times of poor
shipping, the unions are effectively closed to most new members.
Thus, attrition from death, retirement, and other industry exit reduces
the impact to some extent. In addition, the brunt of the underemployment falls on the younger men, who have the last chance to bid on
jobs and usually must get off a ship after each trip.*

To the union as an organization, the reduction is not so mitigated.
The decrease in the number of jobs a union has under contract eventually reduces its membership, and thus its revenue, by a factor of more
than one but perhaps not as much as 1.5. The member-job ratio
increases during periods of slack shipping, although it is usually
kept higher than the minimum 1.5, in order to generate more dues
revenue. In 1962-63 the overall ratio for officers was 1.72, and for
crew 1.69.[1] There are limits, however, to how high the ratio may go
before membership dissatisfaction becomes a problem to the union
leaders.

The future of the U.S. merchant marine looked bleak in the late
1950s and early 1960s. It had experienced a long period of decline
throughout the 1950s and it looked like the decline would continue.
With the exception of 35 Mariners built during the early 1950s, a
number of tankers, and the beginning of a replacement program for
the subsidized liner fleet, little had been done to cope with the

---

*Shipping rules vary among unions. All crew unions divide their
memberships into several classes based on seniority in the union.
Men with "full books" (book men) are allowed to bid on jobs first. If
a job is not taken by a "full book," the next category is allowed to
bid, and so on. The SIU has A, B, and C "books" and a "C card."
The NMU has "groups" 1 through 4. The MEBA and MMP introduced
similar procedures during the 1960s.

impending problem of obsolescence. This was before the reprieve granted the war-built tonnage by the Vietnam conflict, the rise of containerization under the American flag, and the Ship Exchange Program.

In 1960 Public Law 86-575 established a program under which unsubsidized operators could exchange their older war-built vessels for less used and more efficient vessels from the National Defense Reserve Fleet. In 1965 the program was altered slightly by Public Law 89-254, and its life was extended through 1970. [2]

This was important legislation for the nonsubsidized sector. Although the ships traded out were of approximately the same age as those traded in, they had spent much of their life in lay-up. Once put into class, they were relatively new ships in an operational sense. Of course, they were still World War II vintage and could not effectively compete with ships built in the 1960s. They were, however, capable of operation for many years, and gave the nonsubsidized companies a second lease on life.

Table 8.2 illustrates the experience of the Ship Exchange Program. Between its inception on July 5, 1960, and June 30, 1970, a total of 125 ships were traded in and 121 traded out. Of the trade-outs 23 were T-2 tankers, which were received by both tanker and dry-cargo operators. Two of the ships were small refrigerated ships to be used in the domestic trades. [3] The remaining 96 were dry-cargo vessels built relatively late in World War II. A large number of the dry-cargo trade-outs were ex-troopships.*

A total of 49 companies had participated in the program through December 31, 1968. Six of them received a total of 64 ships. [4] All but one of them (Central Gulf, seven trade-outs) were SIU-contract companies. Of the 112 ships traded out through the end of 1968, 80 went to SIU-contract companies and 25 to NMU-contract companies. Seven ships were received by West Coast companies under contract to the SUP and other West Coast unions. [5]

The trade-out program was of far greater importance to the SIU and its companies than to the NMU and the subsidized operators. Not only was the number of SIU ships more than three times as large in absolute terms, but 80 ships represent a significant fraction of the jobs controlled by the SIU. Approximately 3,200 SIU jobs (or 4,800 man-years of employment) were on traded-out ships. In contrast, the 25 NMU ships, representing approximately 1,000 jobs, are dwarfed by the much larger subsidized liner fleet of about 250 ships (as of 1970).

The subsidized operators could not participate in the Ship Exchange Program. Thus war-built ships operated by the subsidized companies would disappear within a very few years. Ships in more

---

*The 50 C-4's traded out were "mostly troopships." MARAD 1970, Chart II, Analysis, p. 14.

TABLE 8.2

The Ship Exchange Program, 1961-70

Year	Ships Traded Out	Ships Traded in	Cash Received by MARAD	Estimated Cost of Putting Vessels to Sea
1961	4	4	276, 836	2, 871, 834
1962	4	4	115, 473	8, 241, 341
1963	11	13	920, 274	3, 902, 164
1964	16	18	1, 146, 279	30, 247, 609
1965	18	18	1, 341, 280	109, 930, 133
1966	13	13	3, 413, 653	42, 334, 486
1967	15	15	3, 695, 947	58, 046, 347
1968	22	22	7, 461, 746	89, 235, 866
1969	17	17	5, 814, 783	na
1970	1	1	235, 000	na
Total	121	125	24, 421, 231	353, 773, 780

Type of Ship	Traded Out	Traded In
Liberty		31
C-1		15
C-2	18	15
C-3	6	3
C-4	50	
AP2	8	
AP3	14	
AP7		2
Tanker		7
T-2	23	4
T-3		1
Passenger		6
Ferry		22
Bulk		19
R1	2	
Total	121	125

Source: U.S. Department of Commerce, Maritime Administration, MARAD 1970, Year of Transition, annual report of the Maritime Administration for fiscal year 1970 (Washington: U.S. Government Printing Office, 1971), Chart II, p. 14.

or less continuous operation from the 1940s to the 1960s were at the end of their economic life. In addition, ships built prior to January 1, 1946, would be ineligible for subsidy when they reached 20 years of age.[6] Thus, the NMU and the subsidized liner sector would soon be uninfluenced by the block obsolescence problem. The SIU and most of its contract companies, on the other hand, had only been granted a reprieve.

The nature of that reprieve became important when the debate over U.S. maritime policy began about 1965. The nonsubsidized dry-cargo sector, in which the SIU had its main source of jobs, could expect to operate relatively inefficient war-built tonnage for another 10 or 20 years if it could secure cargo. However, it could not successfully vie for internationally competitive cargo with foreign-flag ships. Nor could it long compete with the subsidized sector, which had a modern and more efficient fleet, for reserved government cargoes. It was imperative to the nonsubsidized liners and tramps; and the SIU, to secure a source of cargo other than the marketplace.

Given the overriding importance of the control of jobs to the shipping-industry unions and the critical relation of national maritime policy to those jobs, it was inevitable that labor relations and political activity would merge. By the late 1950s the plight of the industry in general, and the SIU and the nonsubsidized operators in particular, was obvious. The SIU had to act to prevent the disappearance of most of the jobs it had under contract and to obtain new ones.

The NMU-SIU rivalry continued throughout the 1960s. Whenever a few jobs were open to a raid, the opportunity was taken. However, this type of activity would not solve the massive problem faced by the SIU. That would require thousands of jobs, and could be achieved only by an alteration of national maritime policy and a basic restructuring of the industry.

By the mid-1960s the goal of the SIU and its allies was to capture the entire cargo preference program for the nonsubsidized operators and their inefficient war-built fleet. The NMU and the subsidized sector strongly opposed such a move. They pressed for a program that would eventually eliminate premium rates on preference cargo and allow U.S. operators to build abroad or to purchase foreign-built ships. As will be developed, this proposal would have destroyed the nonsubsidized sector—and the SIU along with it.

The stakes were high. The SIU camp faced either destruction or the control of a large number of jobs for many years to come. The NMU and the subsidized operators were threatened with losing a considerable traffic in government-generated cargoes. If successful, however, the NMU would control almost all East Coast shipping and finally vanquish its old enemy, the SIU. The subsidized companies would, in turn, be guaranteed continued government cargo. Presumably, once the nonsubsidized sector disappeared, they would enjoy all such traffic.

The struggle over national maritime policy began in earnest in 1965. It was resolved, at least temporarily, by the passage of the Merchant Marine Act of 1970. In the course of the battle and the preparations leading up to it, maritime union rivalry entered a new stage. The rival unions made alliances and entered into organizations with their respective contract companies. The unions and companies of each major sector battled the unions and companies of the other for the fruits of U.S. maritime policy. Thus labor organizations that had been formed to promote and protect the seamen's interest relative to that of the companies' now found it to their advantage to ally with those companies in opposition to other unions and their companies. Maritime labor relations had come a long way.

THE SIU-AMA CAMP

By the late 1950s the SIU leadership must have realized that the union faced disaster. The SIU had become an efficient organization in terms of defending its jurisdiction against other unions and expanding its control of jobs whenever possible. As mentioned, however, picking up a few jobs or organizing a new tramp operator every now and then was not enough to solve its main problem. That could be done only by reversing the decline of the industry or by capturing a large number of jobs from the NMU.

The SIU first attempted to reverse the decline by dealing with the runaway ship or flag-of-convenience problem. This issue was important in the strike of 1961. As was discussed in Chapter 7, the SIU orchestrated the strike through the National Committee for Maritime Bargaining. The first objective of the NCMB was to force the companies to let American unions organize their foreign-flag ships. This proved ineffective. In 1963 the Supreme Court ruled that the National Labor Relations Board could not hold representation elections on foreign-flag ships despite their American ownership. [7]

In retrospect, the plan to organize foreign-flag ships was futile. Even if the American unions succeeded in signing up the crew of a foreign ship, there would be little hope of keeping it organized. Without a citizen-crew requirement, there is nothing to prevent the owner of a convenience-flag ship from discharging its present crew and hiring another from a different country. In fact, there is nothing to prevent him from replacing the crew in the same country, in the absence of something like our unfair labor practices.

The second aim of the SIU's National Committee for Maritime Bargaining was to get the companies to join it in an attempt to revise the subsidy laws. Although a secondary objective in 1961, this proved a more sensible approach to the SIU's problem.

The NCMB faded out of the picture sometime after 1961, but the goal of changing the subsidy program remained. The alteration of U.S. maritime policy required an instrument larger and more widely acceptable than the SIU. A labor union lobbying for such a change, especially a seafaring union with small membership and little voting strength, would easily be foiled by the well-organized and prestigious subsidized companies.

The SIU's approach was to organize its contract companies into the American Maritime Association (AMA). Before 1961 the companies with SIU crews negotiated through an organization known as the "Max Harrison Group." In the course of the 1961 strike the parties formed the Joint Committee for Maritime Industry. The Joint Committee was shortly thereafter reorganized into the American Maritime Association for legal reasons[8] (probably to avoid unfair labor practice charges of company assistance to the union).

The AMA is ostensibly a management organization that negotiates on behalf of a large number of nonsubsidized companies with the SIU and various officers' unions. Max Harrison was made president of the new organization. The other officers were mostly SIU men.[9] An exception was the executive vice-president, Ed Altman. He was the elected president of the MEBA, then in the process of being eased out by the pro-SIU forces within the MEBA.

The main function of the AMA is lobbying. It also negotiates with the SIU and other unions, but this is secondary. The main collective bargaining function of the AMA is to equalize labor costs among the SIU tramp and independent tanker companies, thus allowing increases to be passed forward to the government and oil companies.

The political function of the AMA is more important. It has been an active lobby appearing at Congressional hearings since 1963. In that year the AMA comprised 118 deep-sea companies with 330 ships.[10] In 1968 it had 90 companies with 237 ships.[11] And in 1970, 68 companies with 234 ships.[12] Thus the AMA presents its views and those of the SIU on behalf of a sizable employer organization.

Since 1967 the AMA has been ably represented at Congressional hearings by Alfred Maskin, bearing various titles.* Prior to joining the AMA, Maskin had been with the SIU for 14 years.[13]

The SIU influence or control over the AMA should not be viewed out of perspective. The individual companies are powerless relative to the union. Even if they combined, they could offer little real resistance. Given the diversity of interests and weak individual positions of many of the companies, it is doubtful that the nonsubsidized sector could have effectively organized itself. Moreover, there are few real differences of interest between the SIU and most of its contract companies.

---

*Legislative Director (1967), Director of Research and Legislation (1968), Executive Director (1970).

Once it was realized that organizing foreign-flag ships was not the answer, it was clear that a major overhaul of national maritime policy along lines favorable to the SIU and the nonsubsidized sector was necessary. To achieve this, an effective lobby had to be organized. Undoubtedly the nonsubsidized operators realized this and readily joined the AMA. Practically all SIU companies are AMA members.*

By 1963 the AMA was well organized, representing 118 deep-sea companies with 330 ships. Curiously, a number of them were under NMU contract. States Marine Lines, with 25 ships, was the only important one among them. Apparently States Marine, an unsubsidized liner and tramp company, found the AMA goals more compatible than those of the American Merchant Marine Institute. It retained its AMA membership through 1969, although the NMU did not negotiate with the AMA. [14] This indicates the importance of the AMA's political function relative to collective bargaining.

The AMA became the main unsubsidized labor-management alliance in the battle to reshape national maritime policy. The picture is complicated by the appearance (and disappearance) of other management organizations, such as the American Tramp Shipowners' Association; Independent Owners of American-Flag C-Type Vessels, Victories and Liberties; and the Committee of American Tanker Owners. [15] It also is common for representatives of individual companies to appear on their own behalf.

The member companies of these organizations were almost always members of the AMA as well. Though their spokesmen sometimes presented different views on secondary issues or emphasized different points, they did not disagree with the AMA on important matters. And the AMA did not disagree with the SIU on important matters. The SIU sometimes acted and spoke through the AFL-CIO Maritime Trades Department (MTD), of which Paul Hall is president. However, the MTD never disagreed with the SIU. Accordingly an SIU-AMA position is identifiable on important questions and represents the position of the unsubsidized sector as a whole.

THE LABOR-MANAGEMENT ALLIANCE
IN THE SUBSIDIZED SECTOR

The NMU head start on the SIU in the 1930s allowed it to organize most of the subsidized companies on the East Coast. It also won

---

*The exceptions in 1970 were Cities Service (four tankers), Moore McCormack (five SIU-contract ships), and six other companies operating eight tankers and three bulk carriers.

representation in those proprietary tanker fleets that do not have independent company unions (with the exception of Cities Service). Though
the NMU had a number of other companies, notably States Marine and
Isbrandtsen, its main strength has always been among the subsidized
liners and proprietary tankers.

It is accurate to say that the NMU bargains with the "establishment," whereas the SIU-contract companies are the relative outsiders.
Thus, when the SIU set out to revise national maritime policy in the
early 1960s, it was a direct threat to the NMU. For just as the SIU's
prospects were dependent upon the nonsubsidized companies, the
fate of the NMU was tied to the subsidized liner and proprietary tanker
companies.

The proprietary tankers were not initially under attack by the SIU,
but the subsidized liners were. During the early 1960s the subsidized
companies operated over 300 ships, including a number of very labor-
intensive passenger ships. Over 15,000 NMU jobs were threatened
by the SIU. The NMU naturally was anxious to protect them. However,
the NMU did not have to organize the subsidized operators. They had
a long history of management organization, and the NMU had only to
join them.

Employer Organization

The main maritime management organization on the East Coast,
the American Merchant Marine Institute (AMMI), was organized in
1937, in response to the success of the NMU. It was actually a
reorganization of the American Steamship Owners' Association (ASOA),
which had been formed in 1919 and occasionally handled labor relations for its member companies. [16]

The AMMI dry-cargo negotiations were centered in the Maritime
Service Committee (MSC) by the 1960s. The MSC negotiated with the
NMU and the various officers' unions, although each company signed
a contract individually. [17] In 1962 a similar body, the Tanker Service
Committee (TSC), was formed to deal with the NMU and other unions
on behalf of the tanker-company members of the AMMI. The efforts
of the MSC and TSC were coordinated by a common chairman. [18]

In 1967 the AMMI consisted of 37 companies operating 450 ships.
Half of its member companies were in dry-cargo and half in tanker
operation. Its 18-member board of directors consisted of 9 dry-cargo
and 9 tanker-company representatives. [19]

The established machinery of the AMMI broke down during the
1960s. Presumably the cause was the differential impact the proposals
to modify U.S. maritime policy would have on its member companies.
Labor relations are still handled by the MSC and the TSC, but they
are now independent organizations. The AMMI ceased its labor-

relations activity about 1967. [20] It continued in formal existence until 1969. [21] By then, however, its lobbying function on behalf of the sub-sidized liner companies had also passed into other hands.

The membership of the AMMI apparently was too diverse to allow it to remain intact during the stressful period of the 1960s. In addition to the subsidized operations and proprietary tankers, it encompassed several nonsubsidized dry-cargo operators and a number of independent tanker companies. The different segments of the AMMI's membership naturally have different interests. As long as there was little chance of changing U.S. maritime policy, this presented no problem. Until the 1960s the common problems of bargaining with the NMU over-shadowed most differences. However, once the SIU initiated its campaign to modify national maritime policy, the Institute's days were numbered.

The East Coast subsidized members of the AMMI and their West Coast counterparts, who were members of the Pacific Maritime Associ-ation (PMA), were joined in an organization called the Committee of American Steamship Lines (CASL), which had been in existence since 1953. [22] However, it was either relatively dormant or its activities were in areas other than legislation. During this period the AMMI lobbied on behalf of the East Coast subsidized operators. Another organization, the Pacific American Steam Ship Association (PASSA), performed the same function for the West Coast companies.

In the mid-1960s CASL became very active as a lobby of the subsidized sector. It was a separate organization from the AMMI and PASSA. Its East Coast member companies remained AMMI members. [23] Similarly, its West Coast members retained membership in the PMA for bargaining purposes and in the PASSA for lobbying.

The CASL embraced the subsidized-liner sector on both coasts. * It marshaled the political support of the most prestigious companies in American shipping, and its spokesmen were often the presidents of the largest of these companies.

The CASL presented the position of the subsidized liner sector throughout most of the battle over national maritime policy. In January 1969 the CASL and what was left of the AMMI and PASSA merged to form a new organization, the American Institute of Merchant Shipping (AIMS). [24] By then the real battle was over. Although the Merchant Marine Act of 1970 had not yet been enacted, the fundamental ques-tions had been disposed of and a compromise reached.

---

*American Export-Isbrandtsen Lines was not a member of CASL in 1967, but it did belong to the Labor-Management Maritime Com-mittee. Senate, Hearings on U.S. Maritime Policy, 1967, p. 481.

The political role of the NMU was less active than that of the SIU. It did not have to organize its contract companies into an employer organization as the SIU did, since that had already been done most effectively by the employers themselves. However, the NMU had an important part to play in the debate over national maritime policy, and it played it well.

The traditional political instrument of the NMU and its labor allies was the AFL-CIO Maritime Committee. The Maritime Committee originated in the CIO and was carried into the merged AFL-CIO with Joseph Curran as its president. It is the counterpart of Paul Hall's Maritime Trades Department, which was originally an AFL component.

The Maritime Committee had too diverse a membership to speak forcefully for the NMU-subsidized sector position. Also, it would have been difficult to project an image of labor-management cooperation from an AFL-CIO body. The answer was a new organization, the Labor-Management Maritime Committee (LMMC)

The LMMC was formed in 1950.[25] However, it was largely inactive until resurrected in the 1960s to speak on behalf of the NMU and the subsidized liner operators.

The LMMC had two codirectors. One was Hoyt Haddock, who was also executive secretary of the AFL-CIO Maritime Committee.[26] The LMMC and the Maritime Committee were "associated organizations."[27] Haddock spoke for both. Actually, both organizations and Haddock mirrored the positions of the NMU. The other codirector was Earl W. Clark, who represented the companies.

THE WEST COAST

The debate over national maritime policy was largely an East Coast affair. This is especially so for the unions. The reasons are not hard to find.

Unions

The NMU-SIU rivalry was not important on the West Coast. The relatively autonomous affiliates of the Seafarers' International Union of North America (SIU, NA)—the SUP, MFU, and MCS—have the whole coast effectively organized. There are NMU halls in West Coast ports, but they are mainly to service MSTS and East Coast NMU ships calling there.

All West Coast companies, subsidized and unsubsidized, are under contract to the SUP and other SIU, NA affiliates. Thus the differential effects of a change in U. S. maritime policy would be largely canceled out as far as the unions were concerned.

The West Coast unions logically should have identified with the subsidized operators. Out of a total of 118 privately owned vessels under contract to the SUP, 94 were dry cargo and 24 were tankers. Of the 94 dry-cargo ships, 61 were subsidized liners operated by five West Coast companies. Another 17 were operated by Matson Navigation. (See Table 8. 3.) Although a nonsubsidized operator primarily in the domestic trade, Matson occupied a peculiar place among shipping companies. It was a prosperous and established liner company with interests similar to those of the subsidized companies. Matson also controlled an offshore affiliate, Oceanic Steamship, that was a subsidy-contract company. Thus 78 out of the 94 dry-cargo ships operated by the contract companies of the West Coast unions were "establishment" (as of 1970).

The West Coast tanker fleet was similar. Out of 24 tankships under contract to the SUP* in 1970, 15 were operated by Standard Oil of California and 2 by an affiliate of Getty (Western Hemisphere Oil Corp.). Out of the 7 others, one carried wine.

To summarize, the industry under contract to the West Coast unions was very similar to the NMU fleet. Both the West Coast unions and NMU had their main source of jobs among the subsidized liners and proprietary tankers. The SIU, on the other hand, had its strength among nonsubsidized liners, tramps, and independent tankers. A change in national maritime policy would, therefore, affect the SUP group in a manner similar to the NMU.

Logically, the West Coast unions should have supported the NMU. However, this would have pitted them against the East Coast affiliate of the SIU, NA and its president, Paul Hall. After 25 years of interunion rivalry and the strong loyalties and hostilities generated, it would have been a drastic move for the SUP group to support the NMU against the SIU. The result was that the West Coast unions remained silent.

Companies

The West Coast employers were more active. However, their activities were coordinated with their East Coast counterparts through the CASL. The established West Coast maritime employer organization

---

*The SUP represents the personnel in all three departments on West Coast tankers.

TABLE 8.3

Pacific Maritime Association Companies and Ships, 1970

Company	No. Ships
Subsidized Operators	
American Mail Line	10
American President Lines	24
Oceanic S.S. Co.	5
Pacific Far East Lines	15
States S.S. Co.	13
Total	67*
Tankers	
Standard Oil of California	15
Pico Tankers Corp.	1
Total	16
Domestic Lines	
Alaska S.S. Co.	6
Matson Navigation Co.	17
Total	23
Tramps	
Chamberlain, WR	1
Pierce, Al Co.	1
Total	2
Total PMA	108

*Includes six ships operated without subsidy.

Sources: U.S. Department of Commerce, Maritime Administration, Seafaring Guide . . . and Directory of Labor-Management Affiliations, 1969 (Washington: U.S. Government Printing Office, 1969), pp. 16-64; and Vessel Inventory Report . . . 1970, Report no. MAR-560-19 (Washington: Maritime Administration, 1971).

was and is the Pacific Maritime Association (PMA). It too remained silent throughout the dispute. Again the reasons are not hard to find.

PMA consists of over 100 American and foreign ship operators, stevedoring companies, terminal companies, and "other employers of maritime labor."[28] Table 8.3 shows that as of 1970, the PMA consisted of 11 U.S.-flag shipping companies operating 108 ships.

The five subsidized companies with 67 ships (61 of which received subsidy) presented their position through CASL. Matson Navigation, with 17 ships, did not join CASL but presented its own case, which usually was consistent with the CASL position. As on the East Coast, the proprietary tanker operators did not take a stand on the central issues under debate. Thus, the PMA had no position to take.

The handful of independent tanker companies on the West Coast bargain separately with the SUP. [29] They took no active part in the debate on national maritime policy.

SUMMARY

Maritime union rivalry began as a contest between the established NMU and the new and aggressive SIU. By the 1950s the initial causes of the dispute, such as the AFL and CIO split and ideology, had given way to an overriding concern with protecting and acquiring jobs. Beginning about 1956 the relatively simple NMU-SIU controversy expanded to include the officers' unions. This more complex period resulted in a polarization of maritime labor around the SIU and the NMU. This stage in the rivalry reached its apex during the strike of 1961.

The 1961 strike was an early effort by the SIU to improve its worsening situation. The attempt to retrieve the "runaway" ships failed. However, the other goal of the National Committee for Maritime Bargaining, restructuring the subsidy program, was pursued throughout the 1960s.

During the period following the 1961 strike, the traditional union rivalry entered a new stage. The SIU organized its employers into the AMA. The NMU allied with the members of the CASL to form the LMMC. The debate that followed was essentially between labor and management coalitions in two competing sectors.

Regardless of immediate affiliation, most advocates can be identified with one of the groups. The SIU-AMA position was championed by officials of the SIU, AMA, and the AFL-CIO Maritime Trades Department, as well as by company presidents in the unsubsidized sector. The NMU-CASL position was pressed by spokesmen from the NMU, LMMC, and Maritime Committee, as well as by officials of the AMMI, CASL, and presidents of the subsidized companies. Most of the other organizations presented positions that were either identifiable, or at least consistent, with one of the two camps.

The connection between the traditional NMU-SIU rivalry and the intersectoral debate over national maritime policy of the 1960s is not perfect. Although the positions of the two East Coast crew unions were in conflict on this, as they always had been, there were new elements that are not as easily explained. The subsidized operators reorganized themselves and were capable of pursuing their own interests with or without the NMU alliance. The officers' unions generally sided with the NMU-CASL position, but they did so in their own interest rather than as NMU allies. The SIU apparently was unable to acquire the active support of the West Coast crew unions, although it did neutralize them.

The most important exception to a clear NMU-SIU rivalry interpretation of the debate is the position of the shipbuilding industry. This important and effective lobby has long played a central role in shaping U.S. maritime policy, and it was very active during the debate of the 1960s in the form of the Shipbuilders' Council of America (SCA).

The activity of the shipbuilding industry will be understated in the pages that follow. The shipbuilders played a relatively unimportant part in the determination of the two issues most central to the shipping industry, foreign building and cargo preference. They were adamantly opposed to foreign building, which placed them in agreement with the SIU-AMA position. However, their opposition was so established and so predictable that it was not a variable in the decision. It was a part of the context within which the controversy between the SIU-AMA and NMU-CASL took place. The shipbuilders were not directly affected or concerned by the second critical issue, cargo preference.

It should not be supposed that the shipbuilding industry has lost its political clout. It has not. Its opposition to foreign building undoubtedly influenced the outcome of the debate, although it was not an important part of it. Rather, it was a constant current against which the proponents of foreign building had to work in addition to the opposition of the SIU-AMA interests.

With these qualifications in mind, it is interesting to consider the debate on national maritime policy as an expansion of the NMU-SIU rivalry. The gains to be made at the bargaining table had been overshadowed by the importance of jobs to the unions and their members. Once the industry was fully organized (and the hope of organizing foreign-flag ships was dashed), the only remaining source of jobs was to raid the other union.

It would not be unwarranted to interpret the position of the SIU-AMA in regard to cargo preference as a giant raid on the NMU. Likewise, the response of the NMU and its employer allies would have destroyed the nonsubsidized sector, and consequently the SIU, if implemented. Thus the NMU would have captured the SIU jobs involved.

The debate on U.S. maritime policy was larger than the NMU-SIU rivalry. It involved parties not usually involved in the rivalry, such as the U.S. government and the shipbuilding industry. It also excluded parties that often have been involved in the rivalry, such as the West Coast crew unions and the longshoremen. However, the debate cannot be fully comprehended without an understanding of the NMU-SIU conflict, which had grown into a larger intersector rivalry.

NOTES

1. See H. S. Ruchlin, Manpower Resources of the U. S. Maritime Industry: A Definitional and Descriptive Analysis of the Maritime Labor Force, P. B. 178, 727 (Washington: U. S. Department of Commerce, 1968), pp. 120-21.

2. LMMC, The U. S. Merchant Marine Today, p. 155; 74 Stat. 312 (1960), 46 U. S. C. A. 1160 (1971); 79 Stat. 980 (1965), 46 U. S. C. A. 1160 (1971).

3. LMCC, The U. S. Merchant Marine Today, Table 47, p. 156.

4. Ibid.

5. Ibid., Table 48, p. 160; U. S. Department of Commerce, Maritime Administration, Seafaring Guide . . . and Directory of Labor-Management Affiliations, 1969 (Washington: U. S. Government Printing Office, 1969), pp. 16-64.

6. 49 Stat. 2003 (1936) Sec. 605(b), 46 U. S. C. A. 1175 (1958). Ships built after January 1, 1946, are eligible for subsidy for 25 years.

7. McCulloch versus Sociedad National, etc., 372 U. S. 1083 S. Ct. Rep. 671 (1963). Cited in A. W. Warner and A. S. Eichner, "Analysis of Labor-Management Relations in the Off-Shore Operations of the East Coast Maritime Industry" (1966), p. 170.

8. U. S. Department of Commerce, Maritime Administration, Seafaring Guide . . . and Directory of Labor-Management Affiliations, 1969 (Washington: U. S. Government Printing Office, 1969), p. 2.

9. Warner and Eichner, op. cit., p. 69.

10. U. S. Congress, House, Committee on Merchant Marine and Fisheries, Hearings on Maritime Labor Legislation, Pt. I, 88th Cong., 1st sess. (Washington: U. S. Government Printing Office, 1963), p. 259. Cited hereafter as House, Hearings on Maritime Labor Legislation, Pt. I, 1963.

11. House, Hearings on Long-Range Maritime Program, 1968, p. 96. Examination of the record (pp. 97-105) reveals 93 companies.

12. House, Hearings on President's Maritime Program, Pt. II, 1970, pp. 525-26.

13. House, Hearings on Long-Range Maritime Program, 1968, p. 45.

14. Letter to the author from Eugene P. Spector, NMU Research Director, dated Feb. 18, 1972.

The other SIU-contract companies that did not belong to the AMA in 1963 were four tramp outfits with 14 ships apparently in bankruptcy ("in care of Earl J. Smith") and a tramp affiliate of Isbrandtsen (Sea Mist Shipping Corp.). House, Hearings on Maritime Labor

Legislation, Pt. I, 1963, pp. 266-69. All but States Marine are out of business, and it was not an AMA member in 1970.

15. Senate, Hearings on U.S. Maritime Policy, 1967, p. 393; House, Hearings on Long-Range Maritime Program, 1968, p. 480.

16. C. W. Uhlinger, "The Wages of American Seamen, 1939-1952" (Ph. D. diss., Fordham University, 1956), p. 107.

17. Joseph P. Goldberg, "The Effects of the Structure of Collective Bargaining in Selected Industries: The Maritime Industry," Labor Law Journal 21, no. 8 (Aug. 1970): 507.

18. Warner and Eichner, op. cit., p. 77.

19. Senate, Hearings on U.S. Maritime Policy, 1967, p. 345.

20. House, Hearings on Long-Range Maritime Program, 1968, p. 331.

21. Seafaring Guide . . . and Directory of Labor-Management Affiliations, p. 1.

22. Traffic World, Jan. 27, 1968, p. 25.

23. Warner and Eichner, op. cit., p. 76.

24. Seafaring Guide . . . and Directory of Labor-Management Affiliations, p. 1.

25. LMMC, The U.S. Merchant Marine Today, p. 172.

26. Senate, Hearings on U.S. Maritime Policy, 1967, p. 473.

27. House, Hearings on Long-Range Maritime Program, 1968, p. 435.

28. Traffic World, Mar. 25, 1967, p. 194.

29. Goldberg, "The Effects of the Structure of Collective Bargaining in Selected Industries: The Maritime Industry," p. 39.

INTRODUCTION

It is hard to pinpoint the beginning of the debate on national maritime policy. To some extent it is a continuing dispute that has been in progress at some level for many decades. It periodically intensifies and draws the attention of outsiders. This usually occurs before the passage of important marine legislation. It most recently occurred during 1965-70.

The most critical issue in the debate on national maritime policy was foreign building. It had been debated at length prior to World War I, and the statutory prohibition was removed in 1912. The effective prohibition that evolved after that was not widely recognized.

In 1961 the Secretary of Commerce established the Maritime Evaluation Committee (MEC) to study the industry. It reported in 1963. One of its recommendations called for the allowance of foreign-built ships in the domestic trades. [1] In 1964 a bill that would have extended the subsidy program to the domestic trades (S. 1774) contained a provision that would have allowed domestic operators to build abroad if no action was taken on their subsidy application. The bill was strongly opposed by the Commerce Department, the shipbuilding industry, and the shipbuilding unions. The AMA (Paul Hall) and the AFL-CIO Maritime Committee (Joseph Curran) also opposed the foreign-building provision. [2] The bill was effectively killed. Its main interest to this discussion is as a herald of events to come.

On March 2, 1964, Nicholas Johnson was sworn in as Maritime Administrator at the age of 29, with no previous maritime experience. [3] A year later (February 9, 1965), in a speech at New Orleans, he outlined three alternatives that could be taken in regard to U. S. merchant marine: the industry could be allowed to decline; larger sums could be spent on subsidy; or enough could be spent on CDS to support an adequate shipbuilding industry, and then the fleet could be allowed to expand to its economic limits by permitting foreign building and purchase. [4]

The New Orleans speech was probably a "trial balloon" to test industry and public response to a radical departure from traditional U. S. maritime policy. The reaction of the shipbuilding and shipping industries was immediate and negative. Another incident occurred when a Maritime Administration brochure failed to mention domestic building as a component of U. S. maritime policy. The ever-watchful Shipbuilders' Council of America was again critical. [5] The importance of these seemingly harmless events is that they occurred while this very issue was being debated by the members of the Maritime Advisory Committee (MAC).

THE MARITIME ADVISORY COMMITTEE
AND THE IMTF REPORT

The first round in the debate on national maritime policy began in a rather roundabout way. In the summer of 1963 the Russian wheat harvest failed. On October 8, 1963, President Kennedy approved the sale of American grain to the USSR. On the following day Kennedy announced that the grain would be transported in American-flag vessels. [6]

In the weeks that followed, a complex controversy arose over several waivers granted by the Department of Commerce to the licensed grain exporters, to the effect that they did not have to use 100 percent, or even 50 percent, American bottoms. On December 9, 1963, the matter came to a head when the Maritime Trades Department of the AFL-CIO began picketing a foreign-flag ship loading grain in Albany, New York. Of the 38 organizations affiliated with the Department, three are seafaring unions: the SIU, MEBA, and ARA. The International Longshoremen's Association (ILA), an occasional ally of the SIU, also is affiliated. [7] The picketing was an SIU action clothed in the respectability of the AFL-CIO unit to gain wider acceptance.

It is not surprising that the SIU was disturbed by the Department of Commerce waivers. In addition to the loss of jobs immediately involved, it saw the waivers as one more attempt to undermine cargo preference. Understandably, anything that threatened the cargo preference program would be fought by the SIU.

The picketing proved ineffective. On February 18, 1964, Thomas W. Gleason, president of the 50,000-member ILA, entered the picture. As union president and as chairman of the Joint Maritime Labor Committee, he announced that the longshoremen would refuse to handle grain destined for Eastern Europe. [8]

Ignoring possible patriotic reasons, the ILA move is best explained as a favor to the SIU. The longshoremen had nothing to gain or lose. They would have loaded the grain regardless of the flag that carried it. The ILA action is an example of the Byzantine alliances and loyalties that have resulted from interunion rivalry in the maritime industry.

President Lyndon B. Johnson asked Gleason to remove the pickets. He refused. Johnson then made a statement to the effect that 50 percent of the grain destined for Russia would be lifted by U.S.-flag ships. In addition, two committees would be established for the purpose of "answering problems" once the ships were moving. One, to deal with short-range problems associated with the Russian grain sales, was called the Grievance Committee. The other, to deal with longer-range problems, was named the Maritime Advisory Committee (MAC).

The Grievance Committee is of limited relevance to this discussion. It met between May 13 and November 23, 1964. Its decisions were all against the SIU position, and it faded out of existence when the SIU ceased using it. [9]

The 15-member MAC was of greater importance. It met from September 21, 1964, to November 30, 1965. The meetings were tripartite and chaired by the Secretary of Commerce.

The MAC was unable to reach agreement. In May 1965, Secretary of Commerce Connor (chairman of the MAC) announced that if the Committee was unable to agree on recommendations within two weeks, he would ask the Maritime Administration and his staff to put together a proposal for the Committee's consideration. On June 10, he announced the creation of the Interagency Maritime Task Force (IMTF) to work closely with the MAC. [10]

The IMTF was composed of representatives from the Bureau of the Budget, Council of Economic Advisers, Federal Maritime Commission, Maritime Administration, and Departments of State, Defense, Agriculture, Labor, and Commerce. [11] It was under the direction of the newly appointed Undersecretary of Commerce for Transportation, Alan S. Boyd.

The IMTF was initially under the control or influence of the Maritime Administrator, Nicholas Johnson. Boyd had been sworn in as Undersecretary only a few days before the IMTF was formed and, like Johnson, had had no previous maritime experience. [12] When asked whether the IMTF was still in existence in July, Boyd replied, "I have had no contact with such a force." [13] He assumed a stronger role within the IMTF sometime later, although Johnson certainly remained influential.

While the MAC was meeting, the Johnson administration apparently was pressing a position of its own, mainly through Nicholas Johnson (no relation to the President). The impression one gets is that Nicholas Johnson was most strongly resisted by the SIU. [14] The government proposal undoubtedly included foreign building.

At some point Nicholas Johnson and his supporters ceased trying to convert the industry and labor members of the MAC and began working separately. During the summer of 1965, while the MAC was meeting, its government advisors were working on their own (IMTF) report. The SIU group was unaware of this. The other members of the MAC apparently were also uninformed. [15]

Over the weekend of September 25-26, 1965, a 120-page report was "leaked" in Washington. Boyd stressed that it was only a working paper. [16] On October 7 a revised 51-page version of the report (plus 10 exhibits) was presented simultaneously to the MAC, which was meeting that day, and to the press. [17] The report was dated October 4, 1965, and entitled The Merchant Marine in National Defense and Trade: A Policy and a Program. It soon became known as the Boyd Report.

The important proposals of the IMTF report reflected those of an AMMI study of a year earlier, A New National Maritime Policy. [18] Among other things, the AMMI report called for the right of American operators to build (and repair) in foreign yards and the phasing out of cargo rate preference. [19] The IMTF report called for foreign building and the phasing out of all cargo preference. [20]

The release of the IMTF report to the press on the same day that it was presented to the MAC was a drastic move. It probably appeared to Johnson and Boyd as the best way of bringing the basic issues before the relevant public, and may have reflected their frustration with the MAC. As will be seen, they succeeded in bringing the issues into the open—where they were debated at length.

THE MAC REPORT

The IMTF report spurred the industry parties into action. The unions formed the Joint Maritime Labor Committee, which included the NMU, SIU, and everyone else. [21] For a brief period maritime labor was unified—on this issue. CASL also came out in opposition to foreign building. [22]

A majority of the Maritime Advisory Committee rejected the IMTF report and established an MAC subcommittee to draft a report of its own. [23] On November 30, 1965, a majority of the MAC adopted a report entitled "Maritime Policy and Program of the United States," prepared by three of its public members. [24] For the purpose of this discussion, the main elements of the MAC report were the following:

1. Continue CDS, but pay it directly to the yards, and allow CDS for construction of bulk carriers.

2. Continue the cost parity concept in ODS, but extend it to currently unsubsidized liner operators and to bulk carriers to be built under the program.
3. All ship construction and ship repair to be done in U. S. shipyards.
4. Continue cargo preference laws, but phase out rate differentials on government cargo as new vessels are constructed and placed in service. [25]

There was nothing earth-shaking in the MAC proposals. They essentially recommended maintaining the status quo while expanding the existing system to bulk carrier operation. Cargo (rate) preference was to be phased out. However, the requirement that ships be built in the United States insured that this would take many years, because new construction would continue to be limited by government appropriations. Since the current subsidized operators were under contract to the Maritime Administration to replace their ships as they age, the volume of bulk-carrier construction that could be expected within the next decade was modest.

The MAC report obviously was designed to generate agreement. It succeeded, temporarily, as far as the unions and most of the companies were concerned. Two company members, H. Lee White of Marine Navigation and Joseph Andreae of Humble Oil, dissented. Both of these firms have extensive foreign-flag connections. * Two public members not present at the meeting at which the MAC report was accepted, Deane W. Malott of Cornell University and Lewis A. Lapham, sided with the minority after reading White's convincing dissent. [26] Thus the MAC majority that accepted the report consisted of 11 of the 15 members on the Committee, including three public members that prepared it. Nevertheless, the MAC represented the nearest thing to a consensus that the shipping industry had known since World War II.

IMPACT OF THE IMTF REPORT

The IMTF report, if accepted, would have been a disaster to the SIU-AMA group. Though earlier proposals calling for foreign

---

*Marine Navigation is part of Marine Transport Lines, which controls extensive holdings under the flag of Liberia. Labor-Management Maritime Committee, An Analysis of Dual U. S. -Foreign Flag Shipping Interests (Non-Industrial Carriers) (Washington: LMMC, ca. 1970), pp. 13-14. Cited hereafter as LMMC, An Analysis of Dual U. S. -Foreign Flag Shipping Interests.

building and cargo preference had been under attack for years, they could be dealt with as interest-group propaganda or the work of those not familiar with the industry. The IMTF report, however, was the work of a prestigious committee reflecting a broad cross section of government thinking and was probably backed by the Johnson administration. Foreign building and the elimination of cargo preference were not major threats to the subsidized operators and the NMU group. There were features of the IMTF report that they disliked, and they probably resented the manner in which it was made public; but there was nothing in it that threatened their survival. In fact, the subsidized sector would have gained considerably.

The IMTF proposals made sense in terms of the U.S. shipping industry. The foreign-building feature would have reversed a hundred years of ineffective U.S. maritime policy and allowed the industry to adopt the new technology. This would have permitted it to immediately offset the ship-cost disadvantage that the American-flag fleet had historically suffered and largely to offset the labor-cost disadvantage. The problem was that although the IMTF proposal was appropriate for the U.S. merchant marine in the aggregate, its successful implementation would have required a profound restructuring of the shipping industry, including the elimination of the existing nonsubsidized sector.

Technically the nonsubsidized operators could qualify for subsidy or build abroad. At first glance this would seem to solve the problem of block obsolescence of the U.S.-flag merchant marine in general and of the AMA-member companies in particular. On closer inspection, however, the introduction of foreign-built or foreign-purchased ships to the protected trades would have been a disaster to the operators already in those trades.

The Vessel Exchange Program was then in the process of improving the nonsubsidized fleet. Through fiscal 1965, 57 ships had been traded in and 53 traded out, and the program was in full swing. [27] Most of the ships traded out were received by SIU-AMA companies. In addition, a respectable number of tankships had been constructed under the Trade Out and Build Program by independent tanker operators. AMA-member companies built 17 out of a total of 34 tankers contracted for by nonoil companies between 1955 and 1958. [28] These ships were delivered from the yards between 1956 and 1964. Interestingly, AMA members did not resume ordering new construction until 1968, in which year 10 tankers were ordered. [29] By then the foreign-building question had been settled as far as the industry was concerned.

The AMA fleet represented a considerable investment in 1965, much of it recent. Although the dry-cargo ships owned by its members were of World War II construction, many had been acquired only recently. The companies had spent large sums of money in payments to the Maritime Administration and in costs associated with putting the ships to sea. By 1965 all companies participating in the Vessel

Exchange Program had paid $3.8 million to MARAD and had spent $92.5 million on placing the ships in operation. By 1970, when the program ended, the totals were $24.4 million and $353.8 million, respectively. [30] Another $274.3 million had been spent by AMA companies on new tanker construction. [31]

All of the AMA ships operated in the protected or preference trades, from which foreign-built ships are excluded. As long as this continued, the AMA fleet could operate at a profit. The higher costs associated with American-flag operation could be passed forward to the government and the oil companies. The more efficient ships and companies were, naturally, more profitable than the less efficient. However, all of the dry-cargo ships were of World War II construction and had fairly high operating costs. This kept the charter rates paid by the government at a level high enough to insure a reasonable return on investment. The tankers were all built in U.S. yards, which were very costly by international standards, and thus carried commensurately high debt. The servicing of this debt placed a common floor under the rates.

U.S. maritime policy assured that things would stay this way. The supply of American-built ships in existence that could be operated at a profit was limited and quickly disappearing. New construction was effectively limited to U.S. yards with a cost approximately double that of foreign yards. The additional construction costs, and the attending costs of financing them, rendered new dry-cargo ships uncompetitive with their war-built sisters. The new tankers constructed under the Trade Out and Build Program were a one-shot deal. By 1965 the program had ended.

The IMTF proposal to allow foreign building and foreign purchase of vessels under five years of age would have destroyed this placid scene. There would suddenly be an unlimited supply of modern, efficient tonnage—especially tankers and bulk carriers well suited for the transport of the part of government cargo that moves at preferential rates.

The new bulk carriers would soon have set the rates for the movement of preference cargo. With their lower construction costs and greater efficiency, they would deliver at lower rates than the war-built ships operated by the SIU-AMA group. In a very short time the existing tramp operators would be driven from the preference trades. A similar development would have occurred in the domestic trades.

To make matters worse from an SIU-AMA point of view, there was no provision in the IMTF program to protect the existing tramp operators. The subsidies for bulk carrier operation would be available to new and existing operators now receiving subsidy in that sector. Tramp operators would "also be encouraged to participate in this program to avoid a complete turnover in this segment of the industry." (Emphasis added.) Furthermore, applicants would be considered on the basis of amount of shipping capacity provided per dollar of subsidy and "relative security of investment (e.g., charterers as contrasted with speculative operators), union agreements on manning, etc."[32]

Whether the IMTF knew it or not, its report would have meant the end of the AMA-member companies and the SIU. Though not completely spelled out, the message of its report was that the subsidized liner companies would be encouraged to enter the bulk trades with government support. The new bulk carriers would quickly eliminate the existing tramp operators. Although the latter were theoretically eligible to construct new bulk carriers abroad or apply for CDS to build them in American yards, it would be the existing subsidized operators that would be most able to take quick advantage of the new freedom. Given the criteria under which the subsidy applications would be considered, it is doubtful that much of the limited funding would find its way to SIU-AMA companies.

The impact of the IMTF report on the subsidized sector would have been quite different. Not only would the subsidized operators continue to dominate the liner trades, but they would be able to enter the bulk trades with government aid. Of course, if the IMTF report was fully implemented, there would be no cargo preference remaining. However, the new bulk carriers built abroad or with CDS and receiving an operating subsidy would not need cargo preference. Indeed, the subsidized carriers had called for the elimination of rate preference only a year before.

The AMMI proposed the elimination only of rate preference, whereas the IMTF program would have phased out both route and rate preference for liners as well as for bulk carriers. This is an important conceptual distinction, but its practical effect on the liner sector would be limited. Liner traffic usually moves at conference rates regardless of flag. No large-scale desertion of the American-flag liners by the government agencies would have occurred. There would have been no reason for it, since the rates and quality of service are the same (except during strikes). If some "establishment traffic" did find its way to foreign bottoms, the move could have been checked by informal means, as it is in other shipping countries.

The elimination of cargo (rate) preference to the tramp sector would have been a second disaster. As has been discussed, rates on U.S.-flag tramps are considerably higher than on their foreign-flag counterparts. If the government agencies involved could conserve funding by shipping all of their cargo under foreign flags, they surely would, as their grudging acceptance of the 50 percent requirement indicates.

If implemented, the proposal to end cargo preference would have presented the SIU-AMA with a major problem in itself. When compared with foreign building and the entry of the established subsidized companies into bulk carriage, it became only a secondary problem.

The immediate problem was the proposed right to build and buy foreign tonnage. This provision would have allowed an immediate and massive influx of cheaper and more efficient foreign-built ships into the cargo preference and domestic markets. This would immediately destroy a large amount of existing investment, even if the older ships could successfully compete for government cargoes. [33] For example, if an operator has a $10 million ship and comparable ships suddenly become available for $5 million, the value of his investment is automatically cut in half. That is, he could sell that ship for only $5 million, even though it cost him twice that.

In addition, a $5 million ship can operate at a profit at lower rates than a ship costing $10 million. Since the ships would be competing, rates would quickly fall to a level below which the most costly ship could operate at a profit while servicing its debt. Furthermore, if the foreign-built ship was modern and efficient, which it would be, matters would be that much worse for the war-built vessel.

Thus, if implemented, the IMTF report would have had a very different impact on the two major sectors and their unions. The subsidized operators and the NMU would not have been hurt by the main provisions of the report. The SIU-AMA group would have been destroyed.

The IMTF report caused a great debate on national maritime policy. The primary issue was foreign building. If the proponents of foreign building succeeded, the elimination of cargo preference would have remained a secondary issue. However, in the course of the debate each party took a position on cargo preference that made it as important as foreign building.

THE PUBLIC CAMPAIGN

As was described, the initial reaction to the IMTF report from most of the industry was negative. The Maritime Advisory Committee continued its work and issued its report. There was little else it could do.

The MAC had been in existence for over a year. Undoubtedly the positions of its members had been stated repeatedly. It would have been difficult for any of them suddenly to alter established positions, even if they wanted to. In addition, the way in which the IMTF report was made public must have offended many of the MAC members.

The position of the unions had been firmly established at the AFL-CIO convention in December 1965. Resolution number 217, sponsored by Joseph Curran, among others, was strongly against foreign building. It carried unanimously. [34] If any of the companies were initially in favor of the IMTF program, they did not say so.

Early support for the IMTF report was limited to its authors. It appears, however, that the report reflected the position of the Johnson administration. Although the IMTF report was released in an unusual manner and did not carry the official endorsement of the Administration, it had wide backing within the government. For the purposes of this discussion, the IMTF proposals may be considered President Johnson's maritime program.

Alan S. Boyd reportedly had been given the task of developing a workable maritime program by the Administration. [35] This required developing the program itself and then generating the support necessary for its enactment. The IMTF report was the program. It only remained to sell it to the relevant public and the industry.

There apparently was a division of labor between Boyd and Nicholas Johnson. Boyd assumed a low public profile on maritime matters. This is partly explained by his position as Undersecretary of Commerce for Transportation, which gave him many other interests. He was also to become the nation's first Secretary of Transportation a year later. It is possible that he was being kept out of the line of fire until after his confirmation. However, during this period he was active within the shipping industry, lining up support for the program.

Nicholas Johnson, in contrast, commenced an active campaign of selling the program to the public. He spoke before numerous groups across the country in favor of the IMTF report. This made him the main target of the foes of foreign building—which at that time included almost everyone.

Johnson continued his speeches throughout the winter and into the spring of 1966. His position was continuously disputed by his opponents, especially those from the shipbuilding industry. In April, while on a tour of the Far East, Johnson held a press conference in Tokyo. He told a group of Japanese reporters that a large percentage of future U. S. -flag ships would be built in Japan and that this policy had the support of the Administration. [36] They had him.

Representative Edward A. Garmatz (D-Md.), chairman of the House Merchant Marine and Fisheries Committee and a strong enemy of foreign building in any form, demanded and received a transcript of Johnson's statement. An array of protest mounted against Johnson, including the picketing of the Maritime Administration building by unions from the shipbuilding industry. In June, shortly before he was scheduled to appear before the Garmatz committee, Johnson was appointed to a position on the Federal Communications Commission. Deputy Administrator James W. Gulick was named Acting Maritime Administrator on June 29, the same day Johnson was sworn in as a member of the FCC. [37]

THE INDUSTRY CAMPAIGN

With the removal of Nicholas Johnson, the controversy over the IMTF report and foreign building died down somewhat. Much of the attention of the interested parties at this time was taken by the question of whether the Maritime Administration should be included in the new Department of Transportation. Meanwhile, Alan Boyd was quietly attempting to build a "consensus group" in support of the IMTF position within the industry.

Boyd let it be known that the Administration would not support a program that did not have foreign building as one of its elements. [38] However, it was this very element that was most objectionable to a large part of the industry. It would have been impossible to get industry consensus on any program that contained foreign building. There was nothing that could be promised the SIU-AMA group that would induce it to commit suicide.

Perhaps the Administration did not recognize the effect that foreign building would have on the nonsubsidized sector. Or perhaps it underestimated the political influence and abilities of the forces against it. The opposition of the shipbuilding industry and its unions was predictable. The IMTF report tried to convince the reader that there would be no decline in shipyard employment under the new program and that the disruptive effects of foreign building would be minimized by allowing it only when approved by the Maritime Administrator, subject to the review of the Secretary of Commerce. [39]

The shipbuilders were not comforted. To them the domestic-building requirement is an article of faith. Thus anything that questions it is heresy and automatically is rejected. No amount of assurance could have mollified them.

The SIU-AMA group also was unimpressed by the safeguards. The approval of Maritime Administrator Nicholas Johnson on a question of foreign building probably was not taken seriously. Furthermore, the nonsubsidized sector was no doubt unwilling to place its fate in the hands of a Maritime Administration that had historically identified its interests with those of the subsidized operators.

The shipbuilding industry and the SIU-AMA group stood fast in their opposition to the IMTF report. However, several other parties abandoned their earlier position and came out in favor of foreign building. By May 1967 the AMMI, CASL, NMU, MEBA (excluding District 2), and the MMP had issued statements in favor of what had become the Boyd proposal. [40]

The story of how and why these changes occurred is not fully known. It seems that considerable negotiating had taken place. The AMMI was given assurances that the subsidy program would remain unchanged as far as its members were concerned, that foreign building would be allowed, and that no action would be taken on the oil-import

quota system. The last was important to the proprietary tanker operators, who made up half of the membership of the AMMI. The members
of CASL were then still within the AMMI, and CASL also changed its
position. CASL allegedly was told that if its members went along with
the "consensus group," four additional liner companies would be
granted experimental subsidy and that the established subsidized operators would be allowed to "monitor" the new subsidized companies
for three to five years. The nonsubsidized operators were told that if
they joined the "consensus group," the cargo preference program
would be continued. [41]

The shift of the subsidized sector from the MAC position to the
Boyd position was not very difficult. After all, CASL had called for
foreign building on its own, and the proposals were probably to its
long-run advantage. The unions that changed sides undoubtedly found
the new position uncomfortable.

All of the unions had endorsed Resolution 217 at the 1965 AFL-CIO
convention. Joseph Curran qualified his endorsement of foreign building
by limiting it to situations where the demand for ships exceeded the
ability of U.S. yards to produce them or when matching funds from the
government (CDS) were unavailable. [42] This was not an important
qualification.

In March 1967, the MEBA (minus District 2) and the MMP joined
the NMU in a statement supporting the Boyd program. [43] Again there
was a qualification on the endorsement of foreign building that concerned protecting the jobs and working conditions of American shipyard workers.

The alignment of the MEBA with the NMU reflects its renewed
independence. During the 1961 strike the MEBA was firmly in the SIU
camp. The alliance was unnatural, and would not have lasted as long
as it did if it had not been for a number of disputes between the NMU
and BMO and the MEBA.

SUMMARY

In less than 18 months, support for the IMTF report had gone
from practically zero to most of the shipping industry. Supporters of
the report included the AMMI, CASL, NMU, MMP, and MEBA. This
coalition will be termed the NMU-CASL group.

Those in opposition to the Boyd program included the SIU and
MEBA District 2, along with the unsubsidized companies organized
in the AMA, the SIU-AMA group. Of course, for their own reasons
the shipbuilding industry and its unions remained adamantly opposed
to foreign building in any form.

There were other groups and organizations that took positions
on various provisions of the program. Many of these issues—such as

the extension of reserve funds to the unsubsidized operators, the nuclear ship question, and research and development—are important in their own right. However, in terms of a revision of national maritime policy and its impact on the main parties, they were incidental.

The central issues were foreign building and cargo preference. They overshadowed everything else, and the SIU-AMA and NMU-CASL groups knew it.

NOTES

1. Maritime Evaluation Committee, Maritime Resources for Security and Trade, Final Report (Washington: U.S. Department of Commerce, 1963), Recommendation 21, p. 58.

2. Traffic World, Mar. 7, 1964, p. 41; Aug. 17, 1963, p. 34; Feb. 15, 1964, p. 29.

3. Ibid., Mar. 7, 1964, p. 44.

4. Ibid., Feb. 13, 1965, p. 19.

5. Ibid., Feb. 20, 1965, p. 80; Mar. 6, 1965, p. 36; July 3, 1965, p. 23.

6. Senate, Hearings on U.S. Maritime Policy, 1967, p. 172.

7. U.S. Department of Commerce, Bureau of Labor Statistics, Directory of National and International Unions in the United States, 1967, Bulletin no. 1596 (Washington: U.S. Government Printing Office, 1968), p. 8.

8. Senate, Hearings on U.S. Maritime Policy, 1967, p. 174. The joint Maritime Labor Committee was formed (possibly resurrected) on October 5, 1965. It included the NMU, SIU, MEBA, MMP, BMO, ROU, ILA, and a number of shipyard and other labor organizations. Traffic World, Oct. 9, 1965, p. 44.

9. Senate, Hearings on U.S. Maritime Policy, 1967, p. 175.

10. Traffic World, May 22, 1965, p. 51; June 19, 1965, p. 19.

11. U.S. Interagency Maritime Task Force, The Merchant Marine in National Defense and Trade: A Policy and a Program (Washington: IMTF, 1965), p. 1. Hereafter cited as IMTF Report.

12. Senate, Hearings on U.S. Maritime Policy, 1967, p. 179.

13. Traffic World, July 17, 1965, p. 26.

14. Senate, Hearings on U.S. Maritime Policy, 1967, p. 176.

15. Ibid., pp. 180, 145.

16. Traffic World, Oct. 2, 1965, p. 23.

17. Ibid., Oct. 9, 1965, p. 15; Senate, Hearings on U.S. Maritime Policy, 1967, p. 182.

18. Senate, Hearings on U.S. Maritime Policy, 1967, p. 346. The report is reproduced as App. E of the hearings, pp. 713-52. Significantly, it was not adopted by the AMMI board of directors until Mar. 10, 1966.

19. Ibid., App. E, pp. 718, 731.

20. IMTF Report, pp. 27-28, 32.

21. Traffic World, Oct. 9, 1965, p. 44.

22. Ibid., Nov. 27, 1965, p. 38.

23. Ibid., Oct. 16, 1965, p. 19.

24. Reproduced in Senate, Hearings on U.S. Maritime Policy, 1967, pp. 217-40. The public members who prepared the report were Thomas P. Guerin, James J. Healy, and Theodore W. Kheel.

25. Ibid., pp. 169-71.

26. The dissent of White and statements in its support by members Andreae, Malott, and Lapham are reproduced in Senate, Hearings on U.S. Maritime Policy, 1967, pp. 682-711.

27. LMMC, The U.S. Merchant Marine Today, Table 47, p. 157.

28. Ibid., Table 42, p. 146.

29. Ibid., Table 54, p. 179.

30. MARAD 1970, Chart II, p. 14.

31. LMMC, The U.S. Merchant Marine Today, Table 42, p. 146.

32. IMTF Report, pp. 33-34.

33. Senate, Hearings on U.S. Maritime Policy, 1967, p. 402.

34. Ibid., pp. 464, 194.

35. House, Hearings on Long-Range Maritime Program, 1968, p. 584.

36. Traffic World, Apr. 16, 1966, p. 38.

37. Ibid., Apr. 23, 1966, p. 45; June 25, 1966, p. 106; July 2, 1966, p. 28.

38. Senate, Hearings on U.S. Maritime Policy, 1967, p. 353.

39. IMTF Report, p. 49, and Exhibit IV, p. 28.

40. Senate, Hearings on U.S. Maritime Policy, 1967, p. 122.

41. Ibid., pp. 186-87.

42. Ibid., p. 467.

43. Traffic World, Mar. 25, 1967, p. 112.

10

INTRODUCTION

In 1967 Alan Boyd was promoted from Undersecretary of Commerce for Transportation to Secretary of the newly formed Department of Transportation. The Maritime Administration had been left in the Department of Commerce. As mentioned, Nicholas Johnson had moved from the Maritime Administration to the Federal Communications Commission in 1966.

Another front in the debate on national maritime policy then developed between the Johnson administration and the Congressional committees dealing with the merchant marine. The Congressmen were impatient with the Administration for not coming forward with a formal maritime program, as it had pledged. They had traditionally opposed foreign building and continued to do so, thus supporting the shipbuilding industry and the SIU-AMA on the most critical issue.

The Administration knew that it could not get a program containing foreign building through Congress without wide agreement from the shipping industry. If the committees were faced with total acceptance of a program by the shipping industry, they would have found it difficult to sustain their opposition to foreign building merely to protect the shipbuilding industry. However, as long as the SIU-AMA coalition also opposed foreign building, the Congressmen could maintain their position in support of the domestic yards.

Technically, the Johnson administration did not have a maritime program. The IMTF, though representing all of the Executive Branch with an interest in the maritime industry, seems to have been considered independent of the Administration and its report, the work of Boyd and a group of bureaucrats. This now seems ridiculous, but the fiction served a purpose.

Had the Johnson administration put its name on a maritime program, the fight would have been out in the open. Positions, including that of the Administration, would have become fixed. No one wanted that. From an SIU-AMA point of view, as long as the Administration position was unofficial, it was flexible and subject to change. To the proponents of the IMTF report, the fiction allowed time to marshal support for the program. The Administration probably wanted to avoid an open battle on the maritime question, which might have complicated other, more politically important, legislation.

By 1967 the debate had become a standoff. The sides had been formed. The central issue was foreign building. Everyone that could be convinced of the wisdom of the IMTF report, had been. There was no chance of the SIU-AMA group or the shipbuilding industry supporting it.

The situation could not continue as it was. Most of the U.S. merchant marine was between 20 and 25 years old. When the war-induced demand for ships ended, much of the U.S. fleet would disappear. Something had to be done before that happened.

THE NEW BOYD PROPOSALS OF 1967

By 1967 there was strong pressure on the Johnson administration to formulate a maritime program before it was too late to do any good. The questionable status of the IMTF report and the lack of an official Administration position discouraged Congress from acting. But the existence of the IMTF report and the informal backing of its provisions by the Administration prevented the President from playing a more positive role.

In early 1967 Congress acted to force the issue. Senator E. L. Bartlett (D-Alaska), chairman of the Subcommittee on Merchant Marine and Fisheries of the Senate Commerce Committee, scheduled hearings for February. Shortly before then, he was informed that the Administration was about to develop a comprehensive maritime program and the hearings were postponed until April 1967.

When the hearings began on April 12, 1967, acting Secretary of Commerce, Alexander B. Trowbridge, indicated that the Administration had not yet formulated its program. [1] Secretary of Transportation Alan Boyd also was scheduled to appear that day, but did not. When he did appear on May 1, he presented a proposal to the committee. However, it was not the Administration's program. Rather, it was Boyd's new proposal, which he had not submitted to the President because of lack of industry support. [2]

The Boyd proposal of 1967 was substantially different from the IMTF report of 1965. Many of the changes had most likely been made in an effort to placate opposition and to generate support for the program. One of the more important modifications was that cargo preference was to be retained. However, foreign building remained.

Foreign Building

The retention of cargo preference probably was intended to placate the SIU-AMA group. It was not enough. A continuation of cargo preference without an effective prohibition of foreign building was meaningless to the nonsubsidized sector. Boyd knew that if he removed "foreign construction in any way shape or form," the program would be acceptable to the industry. However, he believed it essential to the program and refused to do so. [3]

Boyd's position was that the country should not expand its shipyards to take care of the immediate problem and then be faced with massive overcapacity in the shipbuilding industry. [4] The argument was sound; however, the destructive impact of foreign building on the nonsubsidized sector remained. It would be difficult to convince Congress to retract foreign building at some unspecified future date and appropriate the additional funding necessary to replace it. And if the U.S. merchant marine thrived under the freedom to build abroad, as this writer thinks it would, it would be impossible.

By the 1967 hearings, positions on foreign building had been firmly established. They may be simplified as NMU-CASL in favor, SIU-AMA against. Joseph Curran followed a list of qualifications with an endorsement. The AMMI was still in the field and favored foreign building and purchase, as did the CASL. [5]

The SIU-AMA camp remained opposed to foreign building. It was joined in its opposition by various other organizations. [6] In addition, four nonsubsidized companies that were members of the AMMI (American Trading and Production, Hudson Waterways, Maritime Overseas, and Sabine Towing and Transportation) resigned in protest against the Institute's position on the Boyd proposal. [7] Two of the companies, Hudson Waterways and Maritime Overseas, were SIU-contract companies. [8] Of course, the shipbuilders and their unions remained as adamantly opposed to foreign building as ever.

Cargo Preference

The new Boyd proposals retained cargo preference in an attempt to placate the SIU-AMA group. It did not work. Not only did the industry remain divided on the question of foreign building, but the cargo preference question now became an important and complex issue in its own right. Although Boy was prepared to compromise on foreign preference, the parties were not.

The SIU-AMA group suggested a program containing a section calling for an expansion of cargo preference and the application of the preference principle to commodities regulated by government quotas, such as oil and sugar. [9] The independent tanker owners were especially interested in a requirement that 50 percent of all quota oil be carried in U.S. ships.

The Committee of American Tanker Owners (CATO) pointed out that 2 million barrels of oil were then brought into the U.S. every day. That equaled about 300,000 tons, or 9 tankships of about 37,000 dwt each arriving per day. If the oil was transported from Venezuela to the East Coast, it would require a 14-day round trip. Thus a 50 percent requirement applied to 2 million barrels per day of quota oil would have supported a fleet of 126 tankers of 37,000 dwt each. In addition, the system would discriminate primarily against the generally unpopular flags-of-convenience ships, which then carried 55 to 60 percent of U.S. oil imports. [10]

The oil companies undoubtedly opposed the proposition. However, when a spokesman for the organization representing their foreign-flag interests, the American Committee for Flags of Necessity (ACFN), testified, there was no mention of the proposal to extend cargo preference to oil imports. CASL opposed the scheme on the ground that it would lead to retaliation from other countries.

The NMU-CASL position was that cargo rate preference should be eliminated but route preference maintained permanently. [11] It argued that all shipping countries route their government cargo on home-flag ships. Any shipper has the same right, and there are administrative advantages to using one's own flag (language, law, custom, etc.). However, when the government must pay rates higher than world rates, it is a different matter.

The NMU-CASL proposal to phase out preference rates while retaining route preference was tied in with the construction of new ships and the retirement of obsolete ones. Like many suggestions, it was attractive in the abstract but, when applied to the shipping industry, it took on added meaning.

Rate preference is applicable mainly to the carriage of bulk cargoes in full-ship lots by the vessels that compose the tramp sector and by independent tankers. Liner cargo shipped by the government supposedly moves at the same conference rates as commercial cargo. [12] As has been demonstrated, most of the tramp companies and many independent tanker companies are members of the AMA and bargain with the SIU. The NMU, on the other hand, has its strength in the subsidized liner sector and among the proprietary tanker operators. Therefore, the elimination of cargo rate preference would have been very detrimental to the SIU-AMA group while presenting no problem to the NMU and its allies.

The NMU-CASL attack on rate preference was a major threat to the SIU-AMA group. The latter, with its serviceable but uncompetitive and aging tramp fleet, looked upon protected government cargoes as a "vast, new, and permanent field."[13] Money had been invested and jobs were at stake. The SIU-AMA response was interesting.

Tax-Deferred Reserve Funds

An important but less controversial item in the debate over national maritime policy was the extension of the reserve funds to the nonsubsidized operators. No one was against this proposal. The NMU-CASL companies had benefited from the reserve funds in the past, and hoped to use them if they entered the bulk trades. CASL did not think reserve funds were called for in the domestic trades, however.[14] Significantly, subsidized operators usually may not operate in the domestic trades.

Access to reserve funds was of great importance to the SIU-AMA group. Their extension to the nonsubsidized sector had been proposed as early as 1965 by Sea-Land Service.[15] In 1967 the issue was pressed by the Committee of American Tanker Owners as a complete substitute for foreign building.[16] It later became a central element in the SIU-AMA strategy.

The importance of the reserve funds to the nonsubsidized sector as a substitute for foreign building was that they would allow a more gradual replacement of the tramp fleet. Under a proposal later advanced by the SIU-AMA group, the established subsidized operators would have been denied the use of existing reserves for bulk carrier construction.[17] Thus the subsidized and unsubsidized operators would both start from scratch in the bulk and domestic trades.

Location of the Maritime Administration

The Department of Transportation had been organized in early 1967 with Alan Boyd as its Secretary. The Johnson administration had wanted the Maritime Administration included in the new department, along with other transportation promotion agencies. However, it had been left in the Department of Commerce by a Congressional conference committee.[18]

Secretary Boyd favored locating MARAD in Transportation. In 1967 the NMU, which in the past had advocated an independent Maritime Administration, agreed. And the AMMI followed suit because Secretary Boyd and his staff had "far exceeded" their expectations in producing a new maritime program.[19] The SIU wanted an independent Maritime Administration and the AMA agreed.[20]

The subsidiary debate on the location of the Maritime Administration mirrored the positions of the parties on the main issues and their opinions of Secretary Boyd. The location of MARAD would have been of limited interest had it not been for Boyd. Given the massive growth of intermodalism (the same container moving by two or more modes of transport), the Maritime Administration should logically have entered the new Department of Transportation. But as long as Boyd, with his controversial ideas, was in command of the new department, the SIU-AMA was bound to fight such a move. Considering the gusto with which this incidental issue was debated, it must be assumed to be a part of a larger design.

FOREIGN BUILDING RECONSIDERED

By the spring of 1968, two and a half years after the publication of the IMTF and MAC reports, the Johnson administration had not come forward with a maritime proposal bearing its official stamp. The IMTF report of 1965, as revised by Alan Boyd in 1967, apparently was the position of the Administration. But because of its unofficial nature and the balance of forces for and against it, the debate on national maritime policy had remained on dead center.

Alan Boyd and the Administration apparently were willing to let the industry deteriorate indefinitely rather than withdraw foreign building. Yet the Administration was still unwilling to submit its program to Congress without substantial industry agreement for fear that this central element would be stripped from the bill prior to enactment.

In a way, the Administration position was commendable. It apparently recognized the importance of foreign building to the development of a viable merchant marine, and refused to back down in the face of pressure. It also was aware of the need of a consensus within the shipping industry if the proposal was to survive the Congressional committees that handle maritime affairs.

The SIU-AMA forces also appreciated the importance of foreign building. Moreover, they and the shipbuilding industry knew that their continued opposition would prevent the proposal from becoming law. They too were prepared to wait.

Each party thought that time was on its side. The longer Boyd waited, the more ancient the ships of the unsubsidized sector became. The World War II-built ships were then between 23 and 27 years old. Those that were not trade-outs under the Vessel Exchange Program were at the end of their economic life. When the Vietnam war slowed down, many would be scrapped. If Boyd waited long enough, much of his opposition would literally disappear. Before that, however, the desperate condition of the industry would force acceptance of some program. Administration approval was needed for passage of such a program, and it probably would be able to name its terms once the industry and its supporters in Congress became desperate enough.

The SIU-AMA forces and their shipbuilding allies no doubt had their eye on the upcoming elections. A new Administration might be more sympathetic to their position. From an SIU-AMA point of view, no one could be worse than Boyd. More immediately, the Administration might soften its foreign-building proposal in an effort to gain political support and campaign contributions.

The modest size of the shipping industry does not reflect its ability and willingness to generate funds for political purposes. The following is a partial listing of political receipts and expenditures of seagoing unions for 1968.

Union	Receipts	Expenditures
MEBA	$264,568	$261,786
NMU Fighting Fund	255,203	84,255
SIU-COPE	61,794	63,272
SIU-SPAD	557,102	883,494

Source: Congressional Quarterly Weekly Report, Dec. 5, 1969, pp. 2457-58.

Additional sums spent during 1967 include AMMI, $12,341; AFL-CIO Maritime Committee, $17,176; and Labor-Management Maritime Committee, $29,028. [21]

In the midst of this standoff, Congress again tried to take the lead and force the Administration to act. The House and Senate committees put together their own program and began holding hearings. The Garmatz-Magnuson bill (H.R. 13940 and S. 2650) was a full maritime program and contained the proposals the Congressmen thought the Administration planned to recommend. [22] Considerable effort apparently had been made behind the scenes to encourage agreement between the warring factions. There had been negotiations between Congress and the Administration on H.R. 13940. Boyd had submitted it to the President, but did not bring it forward as an Administration bill. However, in the course of the discussions Boyd indicated that foreign building was no longer at issue. [23]

The Garmatz-Magnuson bill did not call for foreign building. The main bone of contention had thus been eliminated. Yet there were enough other problems to prevent complete industry agreement. Attempts to reach an accord between the subsidized and nonsubsidized sectors failed. [24]

With foreign building removed as an issue, chances of an agreement within the industry looked better than they had since 1965. The labor supporters of the Boyd position had always had misgivings about foreign building. Their endorsements were qualified, reflecting their discomfort. The NMU, MMP, and MEBA probably were pleased to get rid of foreign building as an issue.

Although the subsidized liner operators had proposed foreign building even before the IMTF, they were no doubt also relieved to get rid of it. As long as foreign building remained an issue, no new maritime program could be enacted. And as long as the situation remained uncertain, there would be little investment in new tonnage by anyone. No one would invest large sums of money in ship construction when they might make a better deal by waiting. In fiscal 1967 only one new ship was contracted for under the subsidy program, compared with 17 in 1966 and an average of 16.6 per year for the period 1958-66.[25]

The situation was made more desperate, from the NMU-CASL point of view, by the recent introduction of container service on the North Atlantic. The subsidized operators needed new and/or converted full containership tonnage to meet the new threat posed by Sea-Land and the foreign operators that were soon to follow its example.

Even those proponents of foreign building with the most to gain from it were willing, if not delighted, to see the matter dropped. There were many issues remaining, some of which were very controversial. However, with foreign building disposed of, a compromise was possible.

By the spring of 1968 the IMTF report and foreign building had been abandoned. Almost all industry parties were in agreement that foreign building was not the answer. The shipbuilding industry applauded the wisdom of the Congressmen for leaving foreign building out of the Garmatz-Magnuson bill. The SIU-AMA group was, of course, happy with the outcome.[26] The NMU-CASL camp accepted the absence of foreign building and was directing its attention to other matters.

Apparently the parties would have preferred to forget about the issue entirely. It was somewhat embarrassing for the NMU to shift from support of the MAC report and Resolution 217 in 1965 to a position favoring foreign building in 1967. The second shift away from the Boyd position must have been uncomfortable. Joseph Curran's brief acceptance of foreign building was now justified on the basis of qualifications. That is, his endorsement applied only when U.S. yards were full. His other condition, when government matching funds were not available, was not brought up.

It was remembered that the management codirector of the LMMC had written two documents refuting the IMTF report in 1966. The subsequent endorsement of that report by the NMU-CASL group was glossed over. The popular manner of referring to the IMTF report became the "now discredited" or "now infamous" Boyd report. Boyd's support of the IMTF report was deemed "ill-advised."[27] Clearly the IMTF report and Secretary Boyd had fallen from grace in the eyes of the NMU-CASL group.

The foreign-building issue was much less discussed in 1968 than it had been a year earlier, although it occasionally came up.

Spokesmen for Matson Navigation and American Export-Isbrandtsen Lines separately urged that the door on foreign building not be closed. No one seemed overly anxious to pursue the matter. There was almost a conspiracy of silence regarding foreign building between the industry parties. Congress apparently agreed. [28]

The ghost of foreign building emerged in another guise, however. CASL proposed that U.S. operators be allowed to bare-boat charter foreign-built and -registered ships when they had their own vessels on charter to the government. This was too close to foreign building for the shipbuilders, and they opposed it vigorously. CASL also proposed doing away with the "buy American" restrictions on equipment purchased with money other than that from the tax-deferred reserve funds. The SIU-AMA group, in contrast, proposed to strengthen the "buy American" restrictions by prohibiting ships built with foreign components from the preference trades. [29]

The relevance of the dispute over the "buy American" restrictions is that building a ship with foreign components is a partial substitute for building abroad. Predictably the industry parties split on the "buy American" item as they had on foreign construction.

The industry and the Congress apparently were willing to let the foreign building issue lie. Secretary Boyd was not. While the industry was testifying to its consensus on this issue during April and May of 1968 before the Subcommittee on Merchant Marine of the House Committee on Merchant Marine and Fisheries, the Administration was preparing a new maritime program. Alan Boyd was the Administration's spokesman for transportation matters, including maritime policy, although the Maritime Administration was not part of his department. Boyd made the Administration's new plan public on May 20, 1968, before the Senate Commerce Committee. It contained a foreign-building and foreign-purchase provision. [30]

The Johnson administration had finally come forward with an official maritime proposal. It caught the parties by surprise. Even the Maritime Administration had not been informed of the new plan until a few days before it was made public. [31] The reintroduction of foreign building at this stage in the debate was as dramatic as the initial publication of the IMTF report.

The motives of Boyd and the Administration come into question at this point. Foreign building was and is essential if the United States is ever to have a viable shipping industry. However, industry agreement appears necessary for the passage of any major modification of U.S. maritime policy. The Johnson administration recognized this in its mandate to Boyd to induce consensus on a maritime program. After two and a half years of trying this proved impossible, mainly because of the foreign-building issue. To suddenly resurrect foreign building in 1968 could have served little purpose other than to prevent the passage of the Garmatz-Magnuson bill.

There was no chance of getting foreign building once the NMU-CASL group abandoned the Boyd position. The Administration would not risk submitting a proposal containing the controversial provision to Congress in 1967 without SIU-AMA agreement. Undoubtedly it had good reason. With the entire shipping industry plus the shipbuilding industry in opposition to foreign building, the new Boyd plan had no chance whatever of passage. Indeed, the manner in which the issue was thrust upon the industry (for a second time) would, by itself, have sealed its fate. Despite Boyd's last-ditch effort, foreign building was dead. The attempt at fundamental revision of U.S. maritime policy had failed. The important debate now shifted to what had been a secondary issue.

CARGO PREFERENCE

In contrast with the accord on foreign building within the industry, the debate on cargo preference intensified. The NMU-CASL group continued its attack on rate preference as opposed to route preference. CASL argued that since the entire industry was to receive direct subsidies under the new program, there would be no need for differential rates. This position was echoed by the LMMC and by the AFL-CIO Maritime Committee. [32]

The NMU-CASL attack on rate preference was a most serious threat to the SIU-AMA group. Once foreign building had been disposed of, the unsubsidized sector was assured of a supply of operational tonnage for the immediate future. However, the war-built ships, including those traded out and converted, could not long compete with the newer, more efficient ships of the subsidized sector.

The fact that the nonsubsidized liner companies and bulk carrier-tramp companies would be eligible for subsidy was of little comfort. Funding of the subsidy program had always been modest. The degree of opposition to the subsidy program was at least partly a function of the size of the appropriation requested. Even if Congress expanded subsidy appropriations from the $300 million level of the late 1960s to $400 or $500 million, it would not help the SIU-AMA group in the immediate future.

There were too many demands on future subsidy funds for an expanded subsidy program to be a substitute for cargo preference to the unsubsidized sector. The established subsidized operators had replacement contracts with the Maritime Administration that the government would have to honor before seeking out new obligations. These same operators owned a large number of recently built break-bulk liners that had been made obsolete by containerization. Large sums of money would be needed to convert these ships to container carriers. Reconstruction-differential subsidy (RDS), which had been

176

a minor item in the past, promised to become more expensive. RDS had averaged about $2 million per year throughout the 1960s. In 1970 it sprang to $21.7 million, and amount to $27.5 million in 1971 and $29.7 million in 1972. [33]

The prospect of losing rate preference was especially disturbing to the tramp operators. In addition to being the most dependent on rate preference, they would be the last in line for subsidy. The unsubsidized liner companies would most likely have preference for funds not allocated to the established liner companies. They had maintained service on established trade routes without subsidy for many years. However, they had not replaced their ships, and now faced the added competition of containerships. The Maritime Subsidy Board would no doubt do all it could to maintain established liner companies. Once driven from a trade route, it is difficult to reestablish liner service. The bulk trades, in contrast, may be entered at any time.

A few bulk carriers would have to be built with CDS, for the sake of appearance, if nothing else. However, the number would be small, and there was no reason to think that the existing tramp companies would be given preference. In fact, considering their established reserve funds and friendly relations with the Maritime Administration, there was every reason to expect the subsidized operators to build bulk carriers with CDS.

It was essential to the SIU-AMA forces that they maintain the cargo preference program as it was or, if possible, strengthen it. The problem was most severe for the tramp operators. They and the unsubsidized liner operators were threatened by a related matter.

The Department of Defense had recently instituted a practice of competitive bidding for military cargo. This replaced the Wilson-Weeks Agreement, under which all liners were given preference over tramps. Under the new system the subsidized operators were able to underbid the nonsubsidized. Military cargo moves at "free in and out" rates rather than at conference rates. [34]

It should be noted that the subsidized carriers also disapproved of competitive bidding on military cargo. Their position was that competitive bidding is ruinous in transportation and should be illegal in liner shipping, as it is in other modes of U.S. transport.

Competitive bidding was a problem for the subsidized sector. Coupled with an attack on rate preference, it was a disaster to the unsubsidized operators. The SIU-AMA response was to begin a campaign to eliminate "double subsidy." It argued that cargo reserved for American vessels should be carried only by unsubsidized ships. [35] In its more refined form, the argument was that when subsidized ships carry preference or military cargo, the companies should be required to repay a proportional amount of the CDS and ODS received. The SIU-AMA at first pursued its goals by writing letters to various government agencies. When this failed, they moved the matter into the main debate on national maritime policy.

The NMU-CASL reaction was that ODS was paid for maintaining a trade route, and had nothing to do with the cargo preference program. CDS was for the benefit of the shipyard, not the ship operator. Thus, it would be illogical to penalize the subsidized operator for something it never received.

The second thrust of the SIU-AMA program to expand the amount of cargo available to the unsubsidized sector was to continue its demand that 50 percent of those commodities brought into the United States under a quota should be carried in American ships. This campaign was pressed most strongly by the Committee of American Tanker Owners (CATO). Many of the independent tanker operators were AMA members. The head of CATO was Joseph Kahn, chairman of Seatrain Lines, an AMA member company. It is appropriate to consider the CATO as part of the SIU-AMA group. Their positions were virtually identical. However, whereas the SIU-AMA "carried the ball" on most issues and CATO agreed, in the area of extending the preference concept to quota oil, CATO led the way. The CATO had actually begun its campaign on quota oil about 1963. [36]

OTHER ISSUES

There were numerous other issues covered by the Garmatz-Magnuson bill and other proposals. Maritime policy is an extensive and complex affair. Proposals to alter the existing structure are necessarily just as extensive and complex. The critical issues were foreign building and cargo preference. If they could be resolved in a manner acceptable to both major industry parties, the other issues would fall into place.

Tax-Deferred Reserve Funds

The most important secondary issue was the extension of the tax-deferred reserve funds to the nonsubsidized operators in the foreign trades. No one within the industry challenged this. However, the SIU-AMA group maintained a steady argument in favor of its inclusion in any new maritime program. It was argued that the tax deferment alone would almost equal the cost savings of building abroad. [37] Thus the SIU-AMA group pressed tax-deferred reserve funds as an alternative to foreign building.

The existing reserve funds of the subsidized lines did not present a major problem to the SIU-AMA group. By 1970 the former had over $95 million deposited in capital and special reserve funds. [38] Of this, $27.6 million was in the accounts of West Coast companies that probably would not enter nonsubsidized liner or tramp operation. Much of the remaining $67.4 million was committed to the replacement of existing liner tonnage under subsidy contracts. The remainder would not go far in building new ships in American yards, even with Title XI mortgage insurance.

The only debate on the extension of the tax-deferred reserve funds was whether they should be granted to ships in the domestic trades. Matson naturally favored such an extension. [39] Those companies operating in both domestic and foreign trades agreed, and pressed for at least the right to deposit revenue from their domestic operations in funds for the construction of foreign-trade ships. The subsidized operators, who were barred from the domestic trades, doubted that tax deferment was necessary in those trades. [40] On this, as on other issues, the positions of the parties reflected their self-interest.

Location of the Maritime Administration

The subsidiary debate on the location of the Maritime Administration remained active. The parties did not change their positions. The NMU-CASL group still wanted MARAD in the Department of Transportation, despite Secretary Boyd. However, it was now pressing for a Maritime Administrator appointed by the President and with considerable independence within the Department of Transportation. [41]

The FIRST Plan

In the course of the debate on national maritime policy, an interesting alternative proposal was introduced by States Marine and Isthmian Lines. FIRST stands for Fleet in Ready Status Today. The plan called for the nonsubsidized companies to build ships on their own account that would be chartered to the Secretary of Commerce, who would then charter them back to the operator at a lower rate. The operators would pay the government a share of the initial profits earned by the ship. [42] Thus, the incentive for the operator to maximize profits would not be dulled, as under the recapture provision of 1936 legislation. [43]

The FIRST plan reflected an earlier proposal by the shipbuilders called the Construction Amortization Plan. [44] The shipbuilders' plan had been prepared in August 1965, but had been overwhelmed by the controversy on foreign building that began with the publication of the IMTF report in October of that year.

179

The FIRST plan was introduced by Congressman Thomas N. Downing (D-Va.) as H.R. 16401. It had little chance of passage despite its endorsement by the shipbuilders. Paul Hall thought it was worth taking a look at. However, the subsidized sector was opposed to the plan, and without substantial industry agreement no such proposal could be enacted.

The interesting feature of the FIRST plan was its sponsors. States Marine was a nonsubsidized NMU-contract liner company, and Isthmian a nonsubsidized SIU-contract liner company. In 1968, Isthmian and States Marine were "affiliated" companies. They represented a quasi-independent position between the SIU-AMA and NMU-CASL factions. With Columbia Steamship Company and Waterman Steamship Company, they made up an organization called the American Unsubsidized Lines (AUL). Isthmian, Columbia, and Waterman were all SIU-contract companies and also members of the AMA. It is not surprising, therefore, that the AUL position usually paralleled that of the SIU-AMA. However, in 1968 Isthmian refused to endorse the SIU-AMA position, and with its affiliate States Marine proposed its own plan. [45]

SUMMARY

In 1961, when the debate on national maritime policy began, the U.S.-flag shipping industry was in trouble. By 1965, when the question of foreign building was introduced, it had experienced somewhat of a reprieve. The subsidized operators had replaced a number of their ships with the aid of CDS, and many nonsubsidized companies had upgraded their fleets through the vessel exchange program. Containerization had developed in the domestic trades while not yet rendering the new tonnage of the subsidized companies obsolete. The number of ships had stabilized at a little over 900, and seagoing employment at 47,000. [46]

The Vietnam buildup had begun about 1965. By 1968 it was at its height. However, once American activities in Vietnam "wound down," a large part of the U.S. fleet would be scrapped. By 1968 public opinion in the United States had become strongly antiwar. It was only a matter of time before the United States disengaged militarily, regardless of who won the presidential election in November. Thus, the formal debate on national maritime policy had been going on for over three years while the industry rapidly approached a major crisis.

The Johnson administration had failed to generate a consensus within the shipping industry in favor of a new maritime program containing foreign building. Despite its efforts, by 1968 the industry parties were united in their opposition to foreign building, if on nothing else. The relevant Congressional committees were strongly against foreign building, and the shipbuilding industry and unions were as opposed to it as ever. The only advocate of foreign building of any importance in 1968 was the Johnson administration, as represented by Alan Boyd.

It is the position of this study that foreign building is an essential ingredient of successful U.S. maritime policy. It would have been regrettable for the Johnson administration to accept a new maritime program without foreign building. Such a program would have continued the major mistake of the past century. However, the situation that prevailed in 1968 was even worse. Not only did the shipping industry not have access to foreign-built tonnage, but the possibility that foreign building would be allowed in the future was inhibiting domestic construction. Moreover, the deadlock between the Administration and the industry prevented the passage of other needed reforms in the existing maritime program.

A new maritime program containing foreign building (with adequate safeguards for existing investment) would have been ideal. A program without foreign building, but with improvements in the existing law and calling for larger subsidy appropriations, would have been acceptable. But the deadlock that existed in 1968, which resulted in neither, was the worst thing that could have happened.

NOTES

1. Senate, Hearings on U.S. Maritime Policy, 1967, p. 24.
2. Ibid., p. 120.
3. Ibid.
4. Ibid., p. 204.
5. Ibid., pp. 466, 353, 320.
6. Ibid., Committee of American Tanker Owners, p. 244; ibid., Independent Owners of American C-Type Vessels, and American Tramp Shipowners' Association, p. 393.
7. Ibid., p. 453.
8. Seafaring Guide . . . and Directory of Labor-Management Affiliations, pp. 34, 39.
9. Senate, Hearings on U.S. Maritime Policy, 1967, p. 393.
10. Ibid., pp. 272, 406.
11. Ibid., p. 171.
12. House, Hearings on Long-Range Maritime Program, 1968, p. 164. In recent years military cargo has been subject to competitive bidding, and rates on it have been below conference rates.
13. Ibid., p. 117.
14. Senate, Hearings on U.S. Maritime Policy, 1967, p. 324.
15. House, Hearings on Long-range Maritime Program, 1968, p. 417.

16. Senate, Hearings on U.S. Maritime Policy, 1967, pp. 250-52.

17. House, Hearings on Long-Range Maritime Program, 1968, p. 534.

18. Traffic World, Oct. 22, 1966, p. 20.

19. Senate, Hearings on U.S. Maritime Policy, 1967, pp. 96, 472, 360.

20. Ibid., pp. 154, 398.

21. Congressional Quarterly Weekly Report, July 12, 1968,

22. House, Hearings on Long-Range Maritime Program, 1968, pp. 1758-60.

23. Ibid., p. 694; Traffic World, Sept. 2, 1967, p. 67.

24. House, Hearings on Long-Range Maritime Program, 1968, pp. 164, 317.

25. MARAD 1970, Chart IV, p. 23.

26. House, Hearings on Long-Range Maritime Program, 1968, pp. 262, 87.

27. Ibid., pp. 413, 459, 436, 457, 420.

28. Ibid., pp. 464, 476, 523, 537, 695.

29. Ibid., pp. 573, 223, 69.

30. Ibid., p. 691.

31. Ibid., p. 688.

32. Ibid., pp. 155, 157, 448, 419. Hoyt Haddock was co-director of the LMMC and executive secretary of the AFL-CIO Maritime Committee.

33. MARAD 1972, Chart I, p. 24.

34. House, Hearings on Long-Range Maritime Program, 1968, pp. 367, 382.

35. Ibid., pp. 113, 484, 489, 707, 714.

36. Ibid., pp. 503, 508.

37. Ibid., p. 486.

38. MARAD 1970, Appendix XI, p. 77.

39. House, Hearings on Long-Range Maritime Program, 1968, p. 669.

40. Senate, Hearings on U.S. Maritime Policy, 1967, p. 324.

41. House, Hearings on Long-Range Maritime Program, 1968, pp. 419-22.

42. Ibid., p. 349.

43. 49 Stat. 2003 (1936) Sec. 605(5), 46 U.S.C.A. 1176 (1958).

44. House, Hearings on Long-Range Maritime Program, 1968, App. C, p. 576.

45. Ibid., pp. 340, 196.

46. U.S. Department of Commerce, Maritime Administration, "Seafaring Employment, Oceangoing Commercial Ships 1,000 Gross Tons and over," unpublished table dated Apr. 5, 1971.

11

INTRODUCTION

In their 1968 nominating conventions both political parties pledged a vigorous American-built ship replacement program. [1] Platform pledges are tailored to generate votes, not shape policies. However, the foreign-building issue was such an obstacle to the passage of a maritime program that the incoming President would have been well-advised to avoid it, since its inclusion would have doomed any proposal to failure.

During his campaign Richard Nixon promised the maritime industry "remedial measures far more constructive and far more comprehensive than those of his predecessor."[2] This was not overly ambitious. Nixon was elected in November 1968 and took office in January 1969. He appointed John A. Volpe as Secretary of Transportation, Maurice H. Stans as Secretary of Commerce, and Andrew E. Gibson as Maritime Administrator.

The Johnson administration had shifted authority for maritime policy and legislative matters from the Department of Commerce and the Maritime Administration to the newly formed Department of Transportation, headed by Secretary Boyd. Perhaps it would be more accurate to say that these matters were entrusted to Alan Boyd as Undersecretary of Commerce for Transportation, and he carried them over when appointed Secretary of Transportation. This approach coincided with the Johnson administration's position that MARAD should be part of the Department of Transportation. Accordingly, the Maritime Administration was downgraded in political terms after Nicholas Johnson left by appointing James W. Gulick, a career official, as Acting Administrator.

Under the Nixon administration, maritime policy and legislative matters were transferred back to Commerce and the Maritime

Administration. The President's spokesmen for maritime affairs became Secretary of Commerce Stans and Maritime Administrator Gibson, with the latter playing the more active role in relation to the industry. Thus Gibson was Boyd's successor as far as maritime policy was concerned.

Andrew E. Gibson was the antithesis of Boyd, and an excellent choice for Maritime Administrator. He was an ex-ship's master who had served as a manager and executive with Grace Lines from 1953 to 1967 before joining an international management consulting firm. He thus had intimate knowledge of the industry while not having an immediate connection with any organization or sector.

Gibson's background and abilities gave him an understanding of the subtleties of the industry while insuring wide acceptance. There was little chance that he would run into many of the problems faced by Alan Boyd and Nicholas Johnson. Nor was there much chance that he would resort to their discomforting tactics.

THE NIXON MARITIME PROPOSAL

Shortly after assuming office, President Nixon came under pressure to make good his campaign promise. Little time was lost. On October 23, 1969, the President's maritime program was presented to Congress and outlined by Secretary of Commerce Stans. [3] It was introduced as legislation by Rep. Edward Garmatz (D-Md.), chairman of the House Committee on Merchant Marine and Fisheries, and others as H.R. 15424 on December 23, 1969. [4] Hearings were scheduled for February 1970. Its companion bill in the Senate was S. 3287. Hearings were scheduled on it for March by the Merchant Marine Subcommittee of the Senate Commerce Committee. [5]

The Nixon proposal was well-designed to gain the acceptance needed for passage, although it was drafted without consulting the industry. [6] This is not surprising. After years of consultation, Congressional hearings, and public debate, there was little question where the major parties stood on important issues. Additional consultation would have served little purpose and would have taken time.

H.R. 15424 was a long and complex piece of legislation that amended the Merchant Act of 1936. [7] It contained many measures not pertinent to the present discussion. The salient features for our purposes were the following:

1. A commitment to build 300 ships over the next 10 years.
2. Extension of CDS and ODS to bulk carriers.*

---

*Bulk carriers include both dry and liquid bulk carriers (tankers) under the new program. House, Hearings on President's Maritime Program, Pt. II, 1970, p. 220.

3. CDS contracts to be made with the yards rather than the shipowner.
4. The CDS ceiling was technically to remain at 50 percent.* The actual ceiling was to drop to 45 percent in fiscal 1971 and thereafter by 2 percent per year until it reached 35 percent in 1976. If this goal was not met, a Shipbuilding Commission was to study the problem and make recommendations.
5. The "buy American" requirement would be limited to major components of the hull and superstructure, and all items covered by CDS.
6. The cargo preference program was to remain unchanged. However, a goal of extending subsidies to bulk carriers was the eventual elimination of rate preference.
7. ODS was to be discontinued for subsistence of officers and crew on cargo ships and for maintenance and repairs for ships built after January 1, 1970.
8. ODS for labor costs would be based on collective bargaining costs, as computed by the Secretary of Commerce at intervals of two to four years, adjusted by an index of annual changes in wage and benefit costs in other industries.

Between October 1969 and February 1970, Gibson consulted with the shipping and shipbuilding industry groups. [8] His efforts were highly successful. By early 1970 there was almost universal acceptance of the program as proposed. [9] The groundwork had been done well, and the chances of the bill's enactment were high. However, the proposal left many questions unanswered or only partly answered. Before a law could be passed, the debate would have to continue. As will be seen, the Merchant Marine Act of 1970 reflects a skillful compromise that protects the interests of the SIU-AMA forces while placating the NMU-CASL group.

FOREIGN BUILDING

The most critical question facing the disputants remained foreign building. As the fleet continued to age and as foreign flags adopted containerization, the need for access to large amounts of new tonnage grew. As long as the U.S. flag was tied to the American yards, there was little chance of overcoming the worsening problem of block obsolescence. Even if American shipbuilding costs improved greatly relative to those of foreign yards and/or there was a large increase in the funding of the subsidy program, the picture would remain bleak. Since shipbuilding capacity is fixed over a rather lengthy short run,

---

*The temporary legislation allowing a 55 percent ceiling would be allowed to expire on June 30, 1970. House, Hearings on President's Maritime Program, Pt. II, 197.

additional orders resulting from lower ship prices or increased subsidy would only translate into more backlog for the yards.

The Nixon proposal avoided the touchy issue of foreign building. However, it was ever-present between the lines and behind the scenes. Joseph Curran reemerged as an advocate of foreign building for nonsubsidized operators in the foreign trades. [10] This shift from his position of 1968 was caused partly by the placing into service of Central Gulf's Japanese-built and Norwegian-manned LASH-type ship, MV Arcadia Forest. Prudential Lines had developed the design in 1967, but could not get delivery from a U.S. yard until 1971. Central Gulf's Norwegian subsidiary got delivery from Japan in 15 months, and the ship was then in operation from the U.S. Gulf to Northern Europe under the Norwegian flag. [11]

The subsidized operators, now organized in the American Institute of Merchant Shipping (AIMS), were also having second thoughts about foreign building. [12] However, it was too late. The SIU-AMA group had repeatedly demonstrated its ability to stop any program it did not favor. Although Paul Hall hinted that he might consider foreign building at some future date, [13] its time had not yet come. Needless to say, the shipbuilding industry remained opposed to foreign building.

The NMU-CASL group did not need foreign building for its own sake. It needed cheaper ships. If American shipyards could produce ships at internationally competitive prices, half of the problem would be solved. There remained the problem of getting enough tonnage within the next few years to successfully participate in the technological revolution. However, either the problems associated with limited shipyard capacity were not foreseen, or it was assumed that there was considerable unused capacity available.

If the ship-cost disadvantage of the United States could be reduced significantly, the available CDS funds would go that much further. And if the need for operating subsidy could also be reduced, there presumably would be additional funds available for ship construction. The Nixon administration's maritime program is best understood as an attempt to offset the ship-cost disadvantage of U.S. maritime policy, given the impossibility of getting foreign building or greatly increased subsidy appropriations.

The cost of U.S.-built ships was attacked in two ways. First, the shipbuilding industry was given a challenge to reduce costs enough to allow the CDS ceiling to drop from the 55 percent effective in 1970 to 35 percent in 1976. This was not an unreasonable goal. Although it represents a 57 percent reduction in subsidy payments, it calls for only a 20 percent reduction in shipbuilding costs.

The scheduled reduction from 55 to 35 percent ceiling was based on past studies made by the shipbuilding industry and on speeches and articles by shipbuilding executives. [14] Presumably there was some "fat" in the industry resulting from the operation of the 1936 legislation. A shipowner who received subsidy paid foreign cost for

186

the vessel, and thus was under little pressure to hold costs down. Also, the fact that the subsidy was awarded to the shipping company, and not the shipyard, meant that ships were constructed one at a time, or a few at a time at best. This precluded serial construction of standard-design ships or other "mass production" improvements.

The problem of the single-ship contract was compounded by the spotty nature of the subsidy program. With no long-range commitment and the threat of foreign building hanging over the industry, investment in shipbuilding was restricted.

The Nixon proposal attacked this part of the ship-cost disadvantage by making the shipyard, rather than the ship owner, the recipient of the subsidy and by pledging a 10-year commitment to build 30 ships per year. The combined effect would, it was hoped, be to allow the yards to develop standard-design (or use CMX-design) ships, which they could market to the industry in sizable "flights" at lower costs. The per-ship cost of each vessel in a "flight" decreases, up to about seven or eight ships. [15] The commitment to build 30 ships a year presumably would induce increased investment in shipbuilding, thus pushing ship costs down even further. In addition, the elimination of the three-party contract used under the 1936 legislation would result in considerable savings in administration and design change. The shipping industry complained of hundreds of design changes required by the Maritime Administration after a construction contract had been awarded. *

The second attack on the ship-cost disadvantage contained in the Nixon program was to weaken the "buy American" requirement of the existing legislation. The requirement found its way into the 1936 legislation because of the depression and nationalism of the 1930s. By the 1960s it served only to make the cost disadvantage of building ships in the United States complete. To the extent that the "buy American" requirement could be weakened, the ship-cost disadvantage of the U. S. merchant marine would be lessened.

The Nixon proposal limited the "buy American" requirement to major components of the hull and superstructure, plus all subsidizable items. At first glance this would appear to benefit only nonsubsidized construction mainly for the domestic trades. However, it could have been a built-in way of reducing the cost of the subsidy program. If the Maritime Subsidy Board (MSB) wanted to spread its funds over the construction of a greater number of ships, it could disallow subsidy on certain equipment obtainable in foreign shipbuilding centers at lower costs. For example, if refrigeration

---

*It was not uncommon for the Maritime Administration to propose 1, 200 or 1, 300 design changes. House, Hearings on Long-Range Maritime Program, 1968, p. 185.

equipment for liquefied natural gas tankers can be obtained cheaper in France, it would not be subsidized.

The combination of a long-run commitment to construct 30 ships a year, the direct subsidy to the yards, and the weakening of the "buy American" requirement could have allowed the shipbuilders to reduce costs by the 20 percent needed to meet the Nixon administration's challenge. In fact, if the built-in "escape valve" was used by the MSB, there would have been no reason for not meeting it. All that MSB would have had to do was to generally disallow subsidy payment on more items, such as electrical equipment, piping, and paint. Since the domestic market of the United States insures that such equipment and supplies will always be available to the shipbuilding industry, there is no reason to subsidize them when they are used in ships. The CDS program was meant to sustain a domestic shipbuilding capacity, not its refrigeration, electrical equipment, or other "uptown" suppliers. [16]

Whether it would have been politically possible to use the weakened "buy American" provision in this way is not known. The Shipbuilders' Council of America strongly opposed the change, as did shipyard labor. [17] With SIU-AMA support it was able to thwart Administration efforts to weaken the "buy American" provision. H. R. 15424 contained the Administration language, but the Senate bill left the requirement unchanged. A compromise was reached in conference committee: the Secretary of Commerce may waive the requirement only "with respect to certain items when the scheduled delivery date of the ship was threatened. "[18] Thus the "escape valve," which could have insured the success of the new program, was eliminated at the final stage in the legislative process. This was most unfortunate. However, while it lasted, the attack on the "buy American" requirement gave the program a credibility that allowed NMU-CASL support for a program without foreign building.

The Nixon proposal effectively defused the foreign building issue as far as the shipping industry was concerned. The advocates of foreign building were given the promise of a reduced ship-cost disadvantage and access to more domestic-built tonnage. They had the added assurance that if ship costs, as reflected in the CDS ceiling, did not come down significantly, a Shipbuilding Commission would study the matter and recommend changes. AIMS recommended instructing the Commission to consider the impact of domestic building on the operators. With the NMU advocating foreign building and the SIU hinting that it would reconsider it if the shipbuilders did not meet the challenge, the promise of lower ship costs was very credible. [19]

The SIU-AMA won its battle on foreign building. Though it remained a future possibility, it would not become a major hazard until the traded-out and converted ships of the SIU-AMA fleet were ready for replacement or, at least, fully depreciated. The Shipbuilding Commission could not be called into action until 1972. Allowing for the usual administrative delays, foreign building would not present a threat to the SIU-AMA group until the mid- or late 1970s. By then the nonsubsidized operators would have accumulated sizable tax-deferred reserve funds, providing they could keep carrying government cargoes at preferred rates.

CARGO PREFERENCE

With foreign building effectively compromised, cargo preference became paramount. A major goal of the Nixon proposal was to reduce and eventually eliminate cargo rate preference. This was to be done by subsidizing the construction and operation of bulk carriers and requiring such ships to spend some portion of their life in the preference trades.

The subsidized-liner operators were interested in entering the bulk trades if subsidies were available. [20] From an SIU-AMA perspective, the entry of the subsidized-liner companies into bulk-carrier operation would be almost as disastrous as foreign building. It would not take many real bulk carriers to drop the bottom out of the cargo preference market.

In addition to their impact on rates, the new bulks would replace existing bulk carriers of the "stretched-out" T-2 variety at a rate of two or more to one. The remaining war-built, nonconverted freighters operating in the preference trades would be displaced at a rate of four or more to one. The latter group would be the first to go, but the existing bulk carriers would also be hard-hit. Most of them carried mortgages based on their value at established rates supported by the cargo preference program. If rates fell or if the added bulk-carrier capacity reduced charter possibilities, the burden of servicing mortgages would place many of the existing bulk and tramp operators in a difficult position.

The SIU-AMA response was to demand that nonsubsidized companies operating in the bulk trades be given preference for bulk-carrier subsidies. [21] The group also wanted assurances that bulk carriers afforded CDS and ODS would not compete with nonsubsidized ships for preference cargoes.

Gibson placated the SIU-AMA fears with a pledge that presently nonsubsidized bulk-trade operators would be given preference for subsidized bulk-carrier operation. [22] Moreover, he proposed a transition period of two years during which nonsubsidized ships would be protected from competition with the new subsidized bulks. [23] Since it would take at least three years from the passage of the new legislation until any of the new bulks were in the water, the older ships would be spared until after 1975. This apparently was acceptable to the SIU-AMA group.

Industry acceptance of the Nixon proposal insured that it would become law. This presented the SIU-AMA group with a new problem. The Merchant Marine Act of 1936 prohibited subsidized operators from having foreign-flag operations. [24] However, many SIU-AMA tramp companies had foreign-flag affiliations. An LMMC study reported that as of the end of 1969, 73 SIU-contract companies and 57 AMA members had foreign-flag shipping interests. [25] Many of these companies were interrelated. Five parent organizations controlled 39 of the nominal companies. [26] It was these large tramp operators that were most anxious to get into subsidized bulk-carrier operation. They were also the companies with the financial resources and stability necessary to meet the Maritime Administration's standards for obtaining subsidy.

In addition to the five large tramp operators and many smaller ones, two SIU-AMA liner companies had foreign-flag affiliations. Isthmian Lines was controlled by States Marine, which had foreign-flag operations. Waterman Steamship Co. was connected with Gatx/Boothe, which also had foreign-flag interests.

All told, 56 SIU-AMA companies operating 130 U.S.-flag ships were connected with foreign-flag operations. [27] Not only was a significant part of the SIU-AMA fleet ineligible for bulk-carrier subsidies, including those most likely to be otherwise eligible, but the strongest companies within the AMA were among them. Gibson's commitment to give preference to the presently unsubsidized tramp operators was of little value if none would be eligible because of their foreign-flag interests.

One solution would have been to require the operators to divest themselves of their foreign-flag ships before receiving subsidies. This would either force them to accept considerable losses as they dumped their foreign-flag tonnage on a depressed market or delay their entry into subsidized bulk-carrier operation until the preference to be granted them was worthless. This clearly would have been unacceptable to the SIU-AMA group.

A better approach was to allow operators with foreign-flag tonnage to continue such operations long enough to phase them out profitably. Undoubtedly the matter of "grandfather rights" had been discussed privately; but when Gibson accepted the idea publicly on February 25, 1970, the matter was out in the open. [28]

The SIU-AMA group hailed the idea with relief. [29] Understandably the NMU-CASL interests opposed the "grandfather" provision. [30] The industry again split along predictable lines on an issue that was remote from the central provisions under discussion.

Although superficially of limited interest, the "grandfather clause" was central to the passage of the Merchant Marine Act of 1970. It could not have been passed without SIU-AMA support. That support would have been impossible without protecting the operators then in the bulk trades from being forced out of business by the established subsidized operators entering those trades. This was accomplished by giving the unsubsidized operators preference in obtaining subsidies for bulk-carrier operation. However, if such subsidies were to be denied because of foreign-flag interests, or made prohibitively expensive, the scheme would not work. Naturally the "grandfather clause" passed and was incorporated into the new legislation. [31]

The "grandfather clause" was a new issue in the fight over cargo preference. Its resolution removed an obstacle to the passage of the 1970 legislation. However, it did not settle the larger contest over which sector would benefit from the cargo-preference program in the long run.

The Nixon proposal left the cargo-preference program unchanged except for its goal of eventually eliminating rate preference. Even if the subsidization of bulk carriers succeeded in eliminating rate preference, it would take several, if not many, years. In the meantime, the future of the SIU-AMA and the profitability of the NMU-CASL groups were, and would remain, dependent upon the cargo preference program.

The SIU-AMA group continued its attack on the "double subsidy" enjoyed by the subsidized operators when they carried preference cargo. [32] The NMU-CASL continued its position in favor of phasing out rate preference. [33] As has been explained, the fight for the spoils of the cargo-preference program was as important as the foreign-building controversy once the latter was compromised.

Once the question of eligibility for bulk-carrier subsidy was cleared up for companies with foreign-flag affiliations, that part of the program was acceptable to all. However, the intersector conflict over "double subsidies" and rate preference continued unabated. If the Administration's program was to become law, it would be necessary to remove this issue from the debate long enough to build the industry consensus necessary for passage.

The cargo-preference debate was effectively removed as a problem by referring it to a Maritime Subsidy Board hearing. Docket number S-244, generally know as the "double subsidy hearings," allowed the parties an excuse to discontinue the debate on "double subsidies" while awaiting the outcome of the case.

No doubt the subsidized operators felt that there was little chance the MSB would rule in a way that would jeopardize the profitability or existence of the companies it was to support. The hearings allowed the disruptive "double subsidy" issue to be effectively sidetracked while the Nixon program was legislated. [34] The rate-preference issue had been similarly withdrawn from the debate by the bulk-carrier subsidy provision of the program itself.

The Nixon administration had skillfully neutralized the two most explosive issues in the debate over national maritime policy. Although there were many other features and problems associated with the new program, the two critical ones had been dealt with. The remaining issues were less difficult.

The tax-deferred reserve funds remained central to much of the debate on national maritime policy. The SIU-AMA group considered them more important than the expansion of the subsidy program. [35] This is understandable. A realistic appraisal of the future must conclude that the number of additional companies and ships that would be brought under the subsidy program would be small. Indeed, some companies did not want to participate in the program.

Sea-Land was the most outspoken in not wanting subsidies. [36] The reason is obvious and has wider application. Sea-Land has a large operation in the domestic trades, with which it would be reluctant to part. Domestic trade is especially important to a container operation. Sea-Land can route boxes anywhere in its system without a break in the bill of lading. For instance, it can offer service from Japan to Puerto Rico although it may not have direct service on that route. It simply routes the container from Japan to a U. S. port, where it is transferred to a Sea-Land ship that calls at Puerto Rico. A subsidized company may not operate in the domestic trades, and consequently is prohibited from offering such foreign-domestic routings. Presumably, any company with large domestic operations (or ambitions) would have some reluctance about accepting a subsidy contract.

All nonsubsidized operators agreed on the importance of tax-deferred reserve funds. The subsidized companies had long favored their extension to nonsubsidized foreign trade operations as well. The only dispute was whether earnings from the domestic trades should be deposited in the funds and whether such funds should be used to construct vessels for the domestic trades.

The earlier position of the NMU-CASL group was that the funds should be limited to the foreign trades. This was predictable, since they are not allowed in the domestic trades. In 1970 the subsidized operators appeared unconcerned with the issue. This may have been a gesture to remove what could have been a problem to the enactment of a new maritime program. In addition, tax deferment was important to Matson Navigation, which had been a quasi-ally of the subsidized sector. Also, at least one subsidized company, United States Lines, was at this time in the process of withdrawing from the subsidy program.* It is possible that it and others were considering entering the domestic trades at some future date.

Any attempt to grant tax deferment to ships operating in the coastal and intercoastal trades was sure to draw the opposition of the railroads and truckers. Both are politically powerful, and it

---

*U. S. Lines ceased to be a subsidized operator on Nov. 6, 1970. MARAD 1972, App. X, p. 89.

would have been difficult to get such a proposal through Congress. The solution was to allow such ships to be withdrawn only for the construction of vessels in the foreign and noncontiguous trades. This was another sensible compromise. It gave everyone what they needed without generating additional opposition.

It should be noted that capital construction funds, as they are now called, may be used for the construction of vessels only in the United States. This was also to everyone's liking.

SUMMARY

On October 21, 1970, one year after transmitting his maritime message to Congress and 10 months after the introduction of H. R. 15424, President Nixon signed the Merchant Marine Act of 1970. In contrast with the efforts of the Johnson administration, the matter had been handled with political skill from beginning to end. The extent of the success is reflected in the fact that when the Act came up for vote in the House and Senate, only two negative votes were cast.[37] All segments of the industry supported the new program. Considering the diversity of interests, conflicting positions, and the ability of either major industry group to stop a program it disliked, this must be hailed as a victory for the Nixon administration.

It has been argued that the underlying flaw in U. S. maritime policy from the 19th century to the present has been the effective requirement that the shipping industry build its vessels in domestic yards. The 1970 legislation did not alter this requirement. In fact, it reinforced it by limiting the use of capital construction fund withdrawals to ships built in the United States.

In the opinion of this observer, the retention of the foreign-building prohibition will plague the efforts to build a viable U. S. merchant marine for as long as it exists. In that respect the 1970 legislation is less than it should be. However, given the peculiarities of the shipping industry, it was impossible to get industry acceptance of any program that allowed foreign building. And given the central importance of the Congressional merchant marine committees and the realities of the American political system, it would have been impossible to obtain passage of such a program without substantial industry agreement.

Foreign building was wisely omitted from the Nixon proposal. However, its place was taken by a convincing scheme to reduce CDS and ODS expenses, which would increase the effectiveness of the subsidy appropriations. If successful, and especially if the proposed weakening of the "buy American" requirement was fully utilized, the new program could have been a reasonable substitute for foreign building to the NMU-CASL group. Yet the absence of foreign building per se and other features of the proposal, such as the extension of the capital construction funds and the proposed arrangements made to protect the present tramp and bulk-carrier operators, made it acceptable to the SIU-AMA group.

The second critical issue also was handled well. The dispute over who would dominate the preference trades could not have been resolved by the new legislation, so it was left unchanged except for the praiseworthy goal of eventually eliminating rate preference. The debate over "double subsidies" and rate preference was successfully sidetracked long enough to allow the brief consensus necessary for the passage of H.R. 15424.

NOTES

1. Traffic World, Feb. 1, 1969, p. 23.
2. Ibid., p. 24.
3. President Nixon's message to Congress, Document no. 91-183, dated Oct. 23, 1970, is reproduced in U.S. Congress, House, Committee on Merchant Marine and Fisheries, Subcommittee on Merchant Marine, Hearings on President's Maritime Program, Pt. I, 91st Cong., 1st sess. (Washington: U.S. Government Printing Office, 1969), pp. 2-6.
4. House, Hearings on President's Maritime Program, Pt. II, 1970, p. 83.
5. Traffic World, Feb. 14, 1970, p. 79.
6. House, Hearings on President's Maritime Program, Pt. II, 1970, pp. 344, 395.
7. The proposal consisted of H.R. 15424, H.R. 15425, and H.R. 15640, and is reproduced in House, Hearings on President's Maritime Program, Pt. II, 1970, pp. 84-122. It will be referred to as H.R. 15424 in this study.
8. Ibid., p. 328. This consultation took place after the proposal was introduced.
9. Ibid., p. 171.
10. House, Hearings on President's Maritime Program, Pt. II, 1970, pp. 680, 690, 694.
11. Ibid., p. 689. The LASH concept was first presented to MARAD by Prudential-Grace Lines in March 1967. Prudential-Grace's first LASH was delivered in late 1970 and, after labor disputes with the ILA and MMP, went into service in 1971. Traffic World, Dec. 7, 1970, p. 74; Feb. 1, 1971, p. 63; Oct. 8, 1973, p. 67.
12. House, Hearings on President's Maritime Program, Pt. II, 1970, p. 341.
13. Ibid., p. 751.
14. Ibid., p. 213.

15. Senate, Hearings on U.S. Maritime Policy, 1967, p. 129.

16. House, Hearings on President's Maritime Program, 1970, p. 337.

17. Ibid., pp. 283, 408.

18. U.S. Congress, House Merchant Marine Program Conference Report (to accompany H.R. 15424), 91st Cong., 2nd sess., Report no. 91-1555, dated Oct. 2, 1970, p. 5.

19. House, Hearings on President's Maritime Program, 1970, pp. 341, 752.

20. Ibid., pp. 167, 272, 535, 653.

21. Ibid., pp. 535, 744.

22. Ibid., p. 635.

23. Ibid., p. 201.

24. 49 Stat. 2012 (1936) Sec. 804, 46 U.S.C.A. 1222 (1958).

25. LMMC, An Analysis of Dual U.S.-Foreign Flag Shipping Interests, pp. 9-22.

26. Ibid. Maritime Overseas, 10 companies; Ocean Shipping & Trading, 5; Ogden Marine, 15; Penn Shipping, 4; and Victory Carriers, 5.

27. Ibid. A number of SIU-non-AMA companies and one "NMU-AMA" company are not included. The LMMC emphasizes that its listing is partial (p. 6).

28. House, Hearings on President's Maritime Program, 1970, p. 635.

29. Ibid., p. 745.

30. LMMC, An Analysis of Dual U.S.-Foreign Flag Shipping Interests, p. 3.

31. 84 Stat. 1021 (1970) Sec. 804 (c), 46 U.S.C.A. 1153 (1972).

32. House, Hearings on President's Maritime Program, 1970, p. 377.

33. LMMC, The U.S. Merchant Marine Today, p. 127.

34. House, Hearings on President's Maritime Program, 1970, p. 669. The agreement to shift the double-subsidy argument to the MSB apparently was reached about August 1969. A petition filed with the Secretary of Commerce by the AMA on July 1, 1969, was referred to the MARAD on December 1, 1969. The MSB ordered a hearing (S-244) that began in January 1970. On January 12, 1972, the MSB issued its "final opinion and order," which rejected most of the findings of its own chief examiner (Paul Pfeiffer) and established a rule whereby ODS would be proportionately reduced when the carriage of preference cargo exceeded 50 percent of revenue. For our purposes, the ruling agreed with the SIU-AMA in principle while it protected the subsidized sector in practice. On August 7, 1972, the AMA asked the U.S. District Court in Washington to review and revise the MSB judgment. In February 1973 the AMA asked the court to expedite its handling of the matter. Traffic World, Aug. 9, 1969, p. 68; Dec. 6,

1969, p. 66; Feb. 28, 1970, p. 10; Apr. 4, 1970, p. 72; July 27, 1970, p. 67; Nov. 2, 1970, p. 83; Nov. 16, 1970, p. 72; Jan. 18, 1971, p. 55; May 3, 1971, p. 87; Dec. 20, 1971, p. 59; June 19, 1972, p. 67; Aug. 14, 1972, p. 62; Feb. 19, 1973, p. 86.

35. House, Hearings on President's Maritime Program, 1970, pp. 535, 538, 591.

36. Ibid., p. 418.

37. MARAD 1970, p. 1.

12

**THE U.S.
MERCHANT MARINE
IN THE 1970s**

THE MERCHANT MARINE ACT OF 1970

The Merchant Marine Act of 1970 is now law. Clearly any new program would have been an improvement on the situation that existed before its passage. In that respect at least, the new program was a victory for the Nixon administration and for the U.S. shipping industry.

Many of the features of the new law are improvements on the 1936 legislation. The extension of tax-exempt reserve funds to the unsubsidized operators is an example. Others, such as the direct CDS contracts with the yards rather than with the shipowner, the extension of subsidies to bulk carriers, the elimination of ODS for subsistence, maintenance, and repairs, and a number of other changes should make the Act more workable. To the extent that the industry suffered from red tape and excessive regulation under the 1936 legislation, there have been improvements.

The main problems faced by the U.S. shipping industry are a product of the fundamentals of U.S. maritime policy. Nothing has been done to change these fundamentals, and the problems they cause remain. In that respect, the Merchant Marine Act of 1970 is a failure.

The critical flaw in U.S. maritime policy has historically been the ship-cost disadvantage resulting from a statutory or effective requirement that American-flag ships be built in U.S. shipyards. The attempt, beginning in 1965, to alter this fundamental policy element failed; and the major mistake of the past maritime policy has been carried forward into the post-1970 period.

The Nixon proposal contained provisions designed to reduce the effective CDS from the 55 percent level in operation in the 1960s to 35 percent by 1976. This represents a 20 percent reduction in domestic shipbuilding costs. Considering the statements of spokesmen for the shipbuilding industry, the apparent economies available from serial construction and standard design, plus the recent international currency realignments, make this objective not unreasonable. Indeed, considerable progress has already been made. The average CDS rate for 1973 was 41 percent (down from an average of 53.6 percent in 1969).[1] Moreover, there will be little trouble staying within the 39 percent limit (which became effective on July 1, 1973) for tankers, bulk carriers, and LNG ships. Contracts for a number of tankers were let in 1973 with CDS rates ranging from 33.40 to 36.47 percent.[2] Even more impressive is the 24 percent rate that applies to a number of LNG ships.[3] It should be noted that there are now only a few yards in the world that build LNG vessels and that demand for them is high. Their price in foreign yards no doubt reflects this seller's market, and is higher than can be explained by cost considerations alone. This, in turn, narrows the differential (ship-cost disadvantage) between American and foreign shipbuilding centers.

Assuming that the projected reduction in shipbuilding costs are fully available to nonsubsidized operators, the latter will still face about a 54 percent ship-cost disadvantage. This was a severe enough handicap during the pre-World War II period to inhibit ship construction. Since modern ocean shipping is more capital-intensive than it was then, a 54 percent ship-cost disadvantage will no doubt be sufficient to discourage nonsubsidized ship construction for the foreign trades. A 20 percent reduction in the cost of ships is not a substitute for foreign building. The main importance of the reduced construction and other subsidy costs is that they allow a given level of funding to be spread over the construction and operation of a larger number of ships.

If it is assumed that funding available to new ship construction will not increase enormously in the near future, and that access to foreign building without penalty will continue to be effectively unavailable, it follows that the number of ships that will be built each year is a function of the cost of ships. Thus the only hope of attaining the goal of 300 ships in 10 years without greatly increasing subsidy appropriations is to reduce construction costs.

The goal of reducing the CDS ceiling to 35 percent by 1976 should be attainable. In fact, devaluation of the dollar and revaluation of the Japanese yen should make it a rather easy goal. How much lower the ceiling will go without a weakened "buy American" requirement is an open question. In the opinion of this writer, ship costs will not fall more than the 20 percent now planned. There undoubtedly are economies available below the 20 percent reduction. However, there will be no incentive for the shipbuilders to reach for them. If past experience is of any help, the CDS ceiling will be the effective construction subsidy.

The second fundamental problem resulting from U.S. maritime policy is the labor-cost disadvantage. As the CDS offsets the ship-cost disadvantage, the ODS offsets the labor-cost disadvantage. The

TABLE 12.1

Operating-Differential Subsidy, 1960-71

Year	No. of Subsidized Companies	No. of Subsidized Ships	Total ODS Expenditure	ODS per Ship
1960	15	313	$152,756,000	$ 488,000
1961	15	300	150,143,000	500,000
1962	15	314	181,919,000	579,000
1963	15	316	220,677,000	698,000
1964	15	318	203,037,000	638,000
1965	15	311	213,334,000	686,000
1966	14	309	186,628,000	604,000
1967	14	311	175,632,000	565,000
1968	14	307	200,130,000	651,000
1969	14	293	194,703,000	665,000
1970	13	247	205,732,000	833,000
1971	12	206	268,021,000	1,301,000

Source: U.S. Department of Commerce, Annual Report of the Secretary of Commerce (Washington: U.S. Government Printing Office, 1964-71), pagination varies.

current decline of the U.S. shipping industry will not be reversed by the 20 percent reduction in the cost of American-built ships. Nor will it be greatly affected by the planned savings in ODS costs.

It will be noted in Table 12.1 that ODS expenditure has been at roughly the $200 million level each year since 1962, with considerable variation from year to year. However, the number of ships covered by ODS decreased significantly beginning in 1968. The per-vessel operating subsidy consequently rose from $651,000 in fiscal 1968 to $833,000 in 1970 and to a whopping $1,301,000 in 1971. This 100 percent rise in ODS expenditure per ship occurred even though a number of costly and heavily subsidized passenger ships were laid up during this period. It should be noted that some of this increase reflects inflation.

The Wage-Subsidy Index

The main thrust of the Nixon administration's efforts to reduce ODS costs was the establishment of a procedure designed to place the operators under some cost pressure during labor negotiations. This was to be done by basing subsidy payments for labor costs on "collective bargaining costs," as determined by the Secretary of Commerce at intervals of two to four years. Between these periodic determinations the payments are to be based on the most recently determined "collective bargaining cost," adjusted by an index of increases in wage costs in other transportation and nonagricultural industries. A safeguard was built into the procedure whereby a shipowner cannot lose or gain more than 5 percent over a four-year period and proportionately lesser percentages for shorter periods. [4]

The implication of this feature of the 1970 Act is that subsidized operators have been too soft during contract negotiations. By placing the negotiators under a degree of cost pressure, it was hoped that they would be more resistant to union demands.

It was necessary to do something about seagoing labor costs. They represent 85 percent of the operating-subsidy dollar. [5] An attempt to get ODS costs under control must begin with labor costs. It is doubtful, however, that the new system will have much impact. Its main effect will be to force the negotiators to time the more important increases in labor costs to the periodic determinations of "collective bargaining costs."

The wages of American seamen have gone up, and their hours down, in response to more fundamental forces than collective bargaining. Once seagoing wages were tied to the shoreside economy, they caught up with, and then paralleled, those in other American industries. Wages in manufacturing and other transportation industries also have gone up markedly during the postwar period.

This is a difficult problem, and there are no ready answers. If the unions have the preponderance of strength in a maritime strike, then the cause of such strikes not explainable by interunion rivalry or job control must be sought beyond the usual collective bargaining arena.

It was argued that the extreme imbalance of bargaining power existing in ocean shipping requires the companies to settle on any reasonable terms. In the subsidized sector this was reinforced by the fact that the government paid 100 percent of all additional wage costs under the parity concept of the 1936 legislation. Thus the subsidized operators logically should never have taken a strike over economic matters.

No important shipping industry strike has been over truly wage-related or economic matters since the 1950s. There often were economic considerations present, but they were never the pivotal issues in the disputes. The 1961 strike was largely an expression of interunion rivalry and a vain attempt to reverse the plight of the SIU.

The 1965 strike was greatly aggravated by the tougher stand taken by the Maritime Subsidy Board and Maritime Administrator Nicholas Johnson in 1964 and 1965 regarding manning levels and pension and welfare costs. [6] The strike involved the officers' unions and the AMMI. The key issues were pensions and manning. The AMMI-member companies resented supporting a pension fund for MEBA members that also covered the employees of the AMA companies, many of which they thought were about to go out of business. [7] Their resentment was no doubt inflamed by the possibility of not having those pension costs subsidized. Agreement was reached only after Secretary of Commerce John T. Connor reversed an MSB ruling disallowing subsidy on a portion of an earlier settlement. [8]

In 1969, the next year that major seagoing contracts were open, all unions but the MMP signed without a strike. In June the mates struck dry-cargo operators for two days and companies belonging to the Tanker Service Committee for two weeks. [9] The main issue was parity with the MEBA. Again in 1972 the MMP struck Sea-Land over the manning of new ships (SL-7s), and the West Coast operators (PMA) over whether captains' and first mates' jobs would rotate through the hall and whether certain shoreside personnel (port captains) would be covered by the contract. The latter strike lasted 41 days and idled 40 ships. [10]

The tragedy of maritime industrial relations in recent years is that strikes have been directed at companies that often cannot cope with the problems presented. Therefore, placing the companies under more cost pressure at negotiations will be of little help.

Subsistence Subsidy

Another attack on the rising cost of ODS was to discontinue subsidy on subsistence of officers and crew on nonpassenger ships. This provision was justified by the modest cost involved. In calendar 1968 it amounted to only $1,733,000, or 1.02 percent of total ODS expenditure. [11] One suspects that the cost of administering the account was more than the amount paid out. Regardless, it was a minor expense and will be a small saving.

Maintenance and Repair

Another effort to reduce ODS expenditure was the elimination of subsidy on maintenance and repairs on ships built after 1970. It was expected that ships built after that would be designed to minimize maintenance and repair costs. [12] Undoubtedly they will be.

There are many materials that are initially more expensive but cut maintenance costs. For instance, the use of nonferrous metals or stainless steel eliminates the considerable corrosion problem associated with the use of steel around salt water. With construction costs subsidized and maintenance and repair costs not covered, operators will build better and more costly ships, thus reducing their maintenance and repair expenses.

It should be noted that many of the technical advances of the postwar period reduce maintenance and repair costs without adding significantly to the price of the ship: better paints, plastic piping, and alternating current. With the exception of the T-2 tanker, all World War II-built ships employed DC electrical systems.

The savings associated with the elimination of maintenance and repair subsidy will be modest. Much of the reduction will result in higher construction subsidies or would have occurred anyway. Furthermore, the elimination applies only to ships built after 1970. It will take many years before the change applies to the whole fleet.

Summary

Passage of the Merchant Marine Act of 1970 was a victory of sorts. It ended the deadlock that existed from 1965 through 1968. The cost of that success, however, was a program without the controversial element of foreign building. Thus the 1970 legislation dealt with the superstructure of secondary elements of national maritime policy. The fundamental problem of the effective domestic-building requirement was left untouched.

The Nixon proposal, if enacted in its entirety, could have eased the ship-cost disadvantage considerably. The key was the weakened "buy American" provision. It would have immediately reduced ship costs to nonsubsidized operators in the domestic and preference trades. In addition, it would have allowed the Maritime Subsidy Board to spread its funding further by disallowing subsidy on items that could be obtained cheaper abroad (excluding major elements of hull and superstructure).

It is impossible to know to what extent a weakened "buy American" provision would have been used. It would depend on the strength and stature of the Maritime Administrator, Secretary of Commerce, and, ultimately, the man in the White House. Regardless, the provision was not carried into the final legislation. The other elements of the new Act designed to reduce subsidy expenditure will be of limited effect.

The other fundamental problem resulting from U.S. maritime policy, the labor-cost disadvantage, also was left intact. No one even suggested weakening the citizen-crew requirement. It would be a difficult position to maintain in an industry premised on national defense. In addition, the demonstrated importance of the maritime unions in legislative matters precluded such a position.

202

The labor-cost disadvantage associated with paying American wages would have been a severe handicap in itself. When that high-cost labor is employed on obsolete tonnage, the resulting cost disadvantage is greatly amplified.

MARITIME INDUSTRIAL RELATIONS

Industrial relations in the shipping industry have improved in recent years. Perhaps it would be more accurate to say that the arena of conflict has shifted. The interunion rivalry that plagued the industry for so long was replaced by intersectoral rivalry during the 1960s, when the conflict was carried out via the political process, rather than on the docks and in the courts. Since 1970 efforts have been made to project an image of labor-management cooperation and responsibility. This has been mainly directed at American shippers, many of whom have shifted to foreign-flag ships because of the chronic labor unrest in the American shipping industry. Unfortunately, the success of the campaign to restore their faith has been greatly weakened by the manning-related strikes of the MMP.

Of course, interunion disputes also still occur. A recent example began on August 3, 1971, when a new company manned a ship (the S. S. Floridian) with deck officers belonging to the Associated Maritime Officers (AMO), an affiliate of the MEBA District 2 and the SIU. The MMP threw a picket line around the ship that was respected by the longshoremen (ILA).* In retaliation, District 2 began picketing other companies with contracts with the MMP (Sea-Land and Seatrain).

By the time a court order ended the dispute on September 16, it had caused considerable disruption. Again the employers were caught in the middle of an interunion conflict and had no means of solving it.

Although the Floridian incident is similar to the interunion disputes of the early 1960s, it should not be viewed out of context. This type of incident is rare now. Two events have occurred that operate in the direction of stability in maritime industrial relations.

First, the MEBA (minus District 2) has reasserted its independence of the SIU. This is most encouraging. When the MEBA was under the influence of the SIU, maritime industrial relations were very unstable. Having an important union operating against its own interests would have been bad enough. To have the SIU in control of the policies of a union representing the engineering officers on most

---

*The MMP was then in the process of becoming an autonomous affiliate of the ILA. The merger was completed in January 1972, when the MMP became the International Marine Division of the ILA. Traffic World, Jan. 10, 1972, p. 24.

NMU-contract ships was worse. It presented too many opportunities for SIU raids on NMU jobs in addition to the day-to-day problems that occur in any work situation (such as the S. S. America incident).

It is difficult to say just when and how the MEBA reasserted its independence. It probably reflects an internal shift within the union. In any event, the MEBA was free of the SIU by 1965 and has remained so ever since.

The second stabilizing event in maritime industrial relations was the debate on national maritime policy. It was made obvious to all involved that the companies and unions within each major sector had more in common than in conflict. Undoubtedly the knowledge was present long before. However, the impending debate forced a restructuring of the industry along lines demanded by the upcoming legislative battle.

Five or more years of cooperation and communication by the major parties within each camp have softened their relationships. Of course, there remain vital differences in the interests of the two main industry factions. Intersectoral rivalry will be with us for some time to come, despite calls for cooperation and efforts to improve the industry's image.

Despite occasional interunion raids and other manning-related disputes, industrial relations in ocean shipping today are more stable and less destructive than ten or fifteen years ago. The crew unions no longer strike over economic issues. The SIU and NMU have not struck over contract terms since 1961, and even that strike was over noneconomic matters.

The MEBA and MMP struck in 1965, and the MMP in 1969 on the East Coast and in 1972 on the West Coast. The MEBA and MMP are now more militant (or less "responsible") than the crew unions. This may be a short-lived condition. The NMU's BMO and the SIU's MEBA (District 2) and AMO stand ready to raid the two main officers' unions. Companies struck by the MEBA and/or the MMP are vulnerable to a raid from one of the small officers' unions, backed by its parent crew union. Although the position of the MMP has been strengthened on the East Coast by its merger with the ILA, the threat is made credible by the large numbers of unemployed licensed personnel "on the beach" as a result of upgrading schools run by the SIU and NMU and the staggering decline of the industry since 1968.

THE DECLINE

The crisis resulting from the war-induced block obsolescence and a dysfunctional national maritime policy has arrived. The American merchant marine was in trouble in the early 1960s. It was saved temporarily by a number of events, including the ship replacement program of the subsidized sector, the vessel exchange program of the nonsubsidized sector, containerization, and the expanded shipping needs associated with the Vietnam conflict. None granted a permanent solution.

As was discussed in Chapter 5, 182 ships had been contracted for by the subsidized operators as of 1970. Only 156 had been delivered, and only 9 of them had been built as full containerships. Of course, many of the ships built with subsidy have been, or are being, converted to containerships.

The American lead in containerization is now threatened because of its forced reliance on trade-outs and other war-built tonnage. As the Europeans and Japanese enter the container trades, the old ships are unable to compete successfully. Although a converted trade-out may be expected to last for many years, a ship built in the 1940s cannot compete with one built in the 1970s.

The Vietnam buildup was the most important factor in postponing the collapse of the U.S.-flag shipping industry. Table 12.2 illustrates the experience of the U.S. flag for the period 1960-71.

The apparent stability of the fleet from 1960 to 1965 is misleading. Although the military buildup in Vietnam began in earnest in 1965, the United States had been supporting the Saigon regime for several years before then. No doubt the level of supply increased throughout the period. To the extent that military shipments to Southeast Asia on U.S.-flag ships grew, they masked the decline of American-flag commercial shipping.

The number of U.S.-flag ships began to rise in 1965 and remained above 1,000 through the end of 1968. However, to meet the inflated demand resulting from the war, the government chartered a large number of ships from the National Defense Reserve Fleet (NDRF) to private operators. The expansion of the U.S. fleet associated with the war was entirely made up of these General Agency Agreement (GAA) ships. The number of non-GAA ships declined throughout the Vietnam war despite the increased availability of military cargo. The recent decline of the U.S. flag really began about 1966, but was masked by the Vietnam buildup and the GAA program.

The Vietnam war began "winding down" about 1969, and so did the active U.S. merchant marine. As of May 1, 1972, it reached 598 oceangoing vessels of 1,000 gross tons and over supplying only 27,114 shipboard jobs. [13] This was down from 1,113 ships and 54,150 jobs as recently as June 30, 1968. [14]

The U.S. merchant marine has undergone the worst contraction in its history. In less than four years (1968-72), 515 ships and 27,000 shipboard jobs (at least 40,000 man-years of employment) disappeared. Shipboard employment was literally cut in half.

The collapse of the U.S. shipping industry has been a disaster. The only consolation that may be taken is that the decline probably is over. The 598 ships in operation on May 1, 1972, consisted of

TABLE 12.2

The Impact of General Agency Agreement Ships
on the U.S. Merchant Marine, 1960-71

Year	Number of Ships September 30	GAA Ships (calendar year)	Non-GAA Ships
1960	945		945
1961	903		903
1962	885		885
1963	911		911
1964	919	3	916
1965	948	2	946
1966	1,066	109	957
1967	1,084	166	918
1968	1,053	144	909
1969	955	144	811
1970	770	2	768
1971	699	1	698

Sources: U.S. Department of Commerce, Maritime Administration, "Seafaring Employment, Oceangoing Commercial Ships 1,000 Gross Tons and Over," unpublished table dated April 5, 1971; U.S. Department of Commerce, Annual Report of the Secretary of Commerce (Washington: U.S. Government Printing Office, 1968, 1971), pp. 91 and 63, respectively.

4 combination passenger/freight vessels, 378 dry-cargo ships, and 216 tankers. Ignoring the four combination ships, it is arguable that the number of dry-cargo ships will not fall much further. There are about 180 fairly new ships that are a result of the ship replacement program and about 30 Mariners that are still serviceable. Another 50 ships in the dry-cargo domestic trades are insulated from foreign competition and the "wind-down" of the war. Also, the 40 or so rebuilt containerships probably will remain competitive for the next few years. Thus there are approximately 300 dry-cargo ships, not counting the tramps supported by the cargo preference program.

There were 216 tankers in operation on May 1, 1972 (down from 247 a year before). Much of the decrease probably took place among tankers engaged in the Southeast Asia trade. There is a given amount of tanker capacity required in the domestic trades. Although the number of U.S.-flag tankers may decrease further as larger vessels enter the market, it is doubtful that their number will fall much more within the next few years. In fact, increased demand for petroleum products and the eventual development of Alaska's North Slope oil fields may increase the number of tankships flying the U.S. flag.

An educated guess is that the total number of U.S.-flag ships will fall to 550 by 1975. After that it will go down to perhaps 500 ships as the rebuilt World War II ships and Mariners reach obsolescence.

EVALUATION

The debate on national maritime policy has not ended. The Merchant Marine Act of 1970 will fail to build and maintain a viable merchant marine. As the industry continues to decline during the 1970s, the debate will have to be resumed.

The Merchant Marine Act of 1970 cannot, and will not, revitalize the U.S. shipping industry. As long as it stands unchanged, it will limit the flag to the new tonnage allowed by Congressional appropriations and the wisdom of the administrators of those funds. In this age of rapid development of marine technology, that will not be enough. When the current condition of the U.S. fleet is considered, the folly of such a limitation is obvious.

CDS has increased markedly since the passage of the 1970 legislation. CDS expenditure ranged between $73 million and $97 million from fiscal 1963 to 1970.[15] During fiscal 1971 the Maritime Administration committed over $169 million toward the construction of 12 new ships and reconstruction of 11 others. It had $69 million left out of a total CDS appropriation of $238 million at the end of the year.[16] The entire subsidy appropriation for fiscal 1971 under Public Law 91-247 was an impressive $425 million.[17] In fiscal 1972, under Public Law 92-53, it jumped to over $500 million, $230 million of which was earmarked for the construction of 22 new ships.[18] For fiscal 1973, appropriations amounted to $556 million, $250 million of which was earmarked for the construction of 17 new ships.[19] For fiscal 1974 the amounts were $531 million total and $275 million for CDS.[20]

The mood of Congress has clearly changed in regard to funding the maritime subsidy program. Even after discounting for inflation, the magnitude of shipping industry support has doubled. No doubt the plight of the industry and the moral commitment of a Congress that voted so overwhelmingly in favor of the 1970 legislation have played their part.

As of October 1973, the Maritime Administration could boast that contracts for 50 new ships and 16 conversions of break-bulk freighters into containerships had been let.[21] Of course, this is only part of the story. A number of other ships are built and ordered without subsidy (usually for the domestic trades). As of September 1,

1973, there were 79 ships (5.5 million dwt) under construction or on order. Thus, in addition to the 50 ships being built with subsidy, there were 29 not receiving government support (other than Title XI ship mortgage insurance in three cases). Of the 79 vessels, 32 were actually under construction.[22]

About five new ships had been built and delivered under the provisions of the 1970 legislation.* Of the 79 vessels under construction or on order, the keel had been laid on 32. Delivery dates ranged from 1973 through 1977.[23]

How encouraging is this picture? Without question the Merchant Marine Act of 1970 has been a great success for the shipbuilding industry. It now boasts a backlog of over 80 orders. There also is little question that the part of the shipping industry that fought to maintain the effective domestic building requirement (the SIU-AMA group) can take comfort in the protection afforded its investment in older ships and the jobs they provide. However, what about the shipping industry as a whole?

The debate on national maritime policy must be resumed. On September 1, 1973, the U.S. privately owned active fleet stood at 568 ships (13 million dwt).[24] The merchant marine has reached a level at which it no longer serves as an effective military auxiliary. In addition, the National Defense Reserve Fleet can no longer fill the gap, as it did in the Korean and Vietnam conflicts. As a result of a program of scrapping, the NDRF went from 2,000 ships in 1960 to 1,027 in 1970, and only 350 were considered suitable for reactivation.[25] By April 1972, the latter number had fallen to 140 ships, all of which were built during World War II and were of questionable value as military auxiliaries.[26]

When the extent of the present decline of the U.S. merchant marine and the inevitable failure of the Merchant Marine Act of 1970 become fully known, there will be a clamor for change by everyone familiar with the situation. That will signal the reopening of the debate on national maritime policy.

CONCLUSION

The need for a major overhaul of the U.S. maritime policy is obvious. It remains only to choose a course. Assuming the United States will not withdraw from world shipping (under its own flag), it

---

*This is an estimate based on the lower subsidy rate allowed by the 1970 Act. "Merchant Marine Data Sheet," July 1, 1973 and Sept. 1, 1973.

may follow one or more of three available approaches to rebuild the U.S.-flag shipping industry.

First, it may continue under the present program. As the remaining war-built ships in the U.S. fleet become inoperative, the flag will come to be totally dependent on the subsidy program for its foreign-trade tonnage. If this course is followed, it will require a massive increase in subsidy expenditure even to maintain the industry at its present reduced size.

Continued reliance on an increasingly expensive subsidy program is possible. As argued in Chapter 1, it is feasible to support a national-flag merchant marine with subsidies if, among other things, unlimited funding is available. Congress has become more openhanded with maritime appropriations since 1970. However, it is doubtful that its generosity will be sufficient to offset the staggering contraction now under way.

Second, the United States may become more protectionist in shipping matters. The campaign to require that a percentage of all oil imports be carried in U.S. bottoms has been discussed. There is strong pressure from the industry and interest in Congress in expanding preference and protection in this and other areas, even to the extent of bilateral shipping agreements. [27]

A U.S. fleet supported by increased preference and protection also is possible. Actually, this is an indirect subsidy program, with the taxpayer-consumer paying the bill in another form. Like the direct subsidy program, the cost of cargo preference and protection will increase greatly if the U.S. flag is to be maintained in this way.

Given the crisis now facing the merchant marine, the end of the reserve fleet and the appeal of the arguments in favor of expanding preference and protection, it is very likely that the United States will become more protectionist in maritime matters in the near future. This would be most regrettable. It probably would be as expensive as supporting the fleet with direct subsidies, and less efficient in the long run.

Third, the United States may allow foreign building. This too is a possibility for the reasons developed above. It would be the best approach and is the obvious recommendation of this study.

If a maritime program based on foreign building is to be effective, it must be adopted quickly. An expansion of the subsidy and preference programs would be especially regrettable at this time, as it would have the unfortunate effect of masking the need for more fundamental change for some time to come. Furthermore, such an approach would rebuild the constituent labor-management interest group dependent upon these programs in the nonsubsidized sector.

A rebuilt nonsubsidized sector supported by an expanded preference program and increased protection would no doubt be based on the continued operation of the war-built fleet and new domestic construction. The companies and unions in that sector would continue to

oppose foreign building, since it would threaten their expanded investment in American-built ships and the jobs they provide. Thus, increased
preference and protection at this time would probably deny the industry
the more basic reform of foreign building for a long time to come. In
addition, to the extent that a viable merchant marine is the goal, a
fleet dependent upon subsidy, preference, and protection is its
antithesis.

A viable U. S. merchant marine is the goal. Foreign building is
the key.

NOTES

1. Traffic World, Mar. 19, 1973, p. 79.

2. Ibid., July 2, 1973, p. 62; Oct. 15, 1973, p. 63; Dec. 24,
1973, p. 62.

3. Ibid., Nov. 19, 1973, p. 63; Dec. 10, 1973, p. 24.

4. House, Hearings on President's Maritime Program, Pt. II,
1970, pp. 627-28; 647-49.

5. U. S. Department of Commerce, Maritime Administration,
"Operating Differential Subsidy (from Inception of 1936 Merchant
Marine Act)," unpublished table and chart (311.61), prepared
Nov. 17, 1970.

6. Traffic World, Jan. 23, 1965, p. 66; Jan. 30, 1965, p. 25;
July 3, 1965, p. 83; July 17, 1965, p. 78.

7. Ibid., June 26, 1965, p. 178.

8. Ibid., June 30, 1965, p. 23; July 17, 1965, p. 90; Sept. 4,
1965, p. 29.

9. Ibid., June 21, 1969, pp. 19, 87; July 5, 1969, pp. 10, 24.

10. Ibid., Oct. 2, 1972, p. 67; Oct. 9, 1972, p. 68; Oct. 30,
1972, p. 7; Dec. 11, 1972, p. 114.

11. House, Hearings on President's Maritime Program, Pt. II,
1970, p. 215.

12. Ibid.

13. U. S. Department of Commerce, Maritime Administration,
"Maritime Manpower Report, May 1, 1972." Includes privately-
owned ships and those chartered for private operation.

14. U. S. Department of Commerce, Maritime Administration,
"Seafaring Employment, Oceangoing Commercial Ships 1, 000 Gross
Tons and Over," unpublished table dated Apr. 5, 1971.

15. MARAD 1970, Chart III, p. 22. This includes both construction and reconstruction subsidy expenditure.

16. Traffic World, July 12, 1971, pp. 56-57.

17. Ibid., May 23, 1970, p. 80.

18. Ibid., Apr. 26, 1971, p. 23; July 19, 1971, p. 66; Aug. 9,
1971, p. 78.

19. Ibid., Sept. 4, 1972, p. 9.

20. Ibid., July 30, 1973, p. 63.

21. U.S. Department of Commerce, Maritime Administration, news release (MA NR 73-38), Oct. 17, 1973, p. 2.

22. U.S. Department of Commerce, Maritime Administration, "Merchant Marine Data Sheet" (MA NR 73-37), Sept. 1, 1973. Hereafter cited as "Merchant Marine Data Sheet." On December 1, 1973, there were 88 ships (6.2 million dwt) under construction or on order.

23. Ibid., Sept. 1, 1973.

24. Ibid.

25. MARAD 1970, p. 15; App. VII, p. 71.

26. Traffic World, Apr. 24, 1972, p. 78.

27. Ibid., Apr. 26, 1971, p. 72; Sept. 13, 1971, p. 65; Oct. 11, 1971, p. 84.

BOOKS

Maritime Economics and Policy

Barker, James R., and Brandwein, Robert. The United States Merchant Marine in National Perspective. Lexington, Massachusetts: D. C. Heath and Co., 1970.

Bennathan, Esra, and Walters, A. A. The Economics of Ocean Freight Rates. New York: Frederick A. Praeger, 1969.

Eversheim, Franz. The Effects of Shipping Subsidies. Bremen: Institut fur Schiffahrtsforschung, 1958.

Ferguson, Allen R., et al. The Economic Value of the United States Merchant Marine. Evanston, Illinois: Transportation Center, Northwestern University, 1961.

Fisser, Frank M. Tramp Shipping, Development—Significance—Market Elements. Bremen: Carl Schunemann Verlag, 1957.

Gorter, Wytze. United States Shipping Policy. New York: Harper Brothers, 1956.

_____, and Hildebrandt, George H. The Pacific Coast Maritime Shipping Industry, 1930-1948. Volume II: An Analysis of Performance. Berkeley and Los Angeles: University of California Press, 1954.

Griparios, Hector. Tramp Shipping. London and New York: Thomas Nelson and Sons, 1959.

Hutchins, John G. B. The American Maritime Industries and Public Policy 1789-1914. New York: Russell & Russell, 1941.

Koopmans, Tjalling. Tanker Freight Rates and Tankship Building: An Analysis of Cyclical Fluctuations. London: P. S. King & Son, 1939.

Labor-Management Maritime Committee. The U. S. Merchant Marine Today, Sunrise or Sunset? Washington: Labor-Management Maritime Committee, 1970.

Lawrence, Samuel A. United States Merchant Shipping Policies and Politics. Washington: Brookings Institution, 1966.

Locklin, Philip D. Economics of Transportation, 6th ed. Homewood, Illinois: Richard D. Irwin, 1966.

McDowell, Carl E., and Gibbs, Helen M. Ocean Transportation. New York: McGraw-Hill, 1954.

O'Loughlin, Carleen. The Economics of Sea Transport. Oxford and New York: Pergamon Press, 1967.

Svendsen, Arnljot Stromme. Sea Transport and Shipping Economics. Bremen: Institute of Shipping Research, 1958.

Zannetos, Zenon S. The Theory of Oil Tankship Rates, An Economic Analysis of Tankship Operation. Cambridge, Massachusetts and London: Massachusetts Institute of Technology Press, 1966.

Maritime Industrial Relations

Ball, Joseph H. The Government Subsidized Union Monopoly: A Study of Labor Practices in the Shipping Industry. Washington: Labor Policy Association, 1966.

Bonwick, George J., ed. Automation on Shipboard. New York: St. Martins Press, 1967.

Collins, John J. Never Off Pay, The Story of the Independent Tanker Union, 1937-1962. New York: Fordham University Press, 1964.

Goldberg, Joseph P. The Maritime Story: A Study in Labor-Management Relations. Cambridge, Massachusetts: Harvard University Press, 1958.

Hohman, Elmo Paul. History of American Merchant Seamen. Hamdem, Connecticut: Shoestring Press, 1956.

Industrial Relations Counselors, Inc. Industrial Relations in the Ocean Shipping Industry; Bargaining Mechanisms, Experience and Results. New York: Industrial Relations Counselors, 1953.

Levinson, Harold M. Determining Forces in Collective Wage Bargaining. New York: John Wiley & Sons, 1966. Chapter 4.

216

Standard, William L. Merchant Seamen, A Short History of Their Struggles. New York: International Publishers, 1947.

Thompson, Fred. The I. W. W., Its First Fifty Years, 1905-1955. Chicago: Adria Printing Co., 1955.

ARTICLES

Maritime Economics and Policy

Arnold, Bruno. "Shipping Policies of Young Nations." Intereconomics (Hamburg), August 1967, pp. 215-19.

Borsheim, Ingebrigt. "Financing Problems in Shipping." Norwegian Shipping News 23, no. 21 (November 10, 1967): 1049-54.

Charlton, George C. "Merchant Marine Subsidies." Marine News 46 (June 1960): 16-17.

Clark, John J., and Norton, Margaret T. "The Merchant Marine: Subsidies and Competition." U. S. Naval Institute Proceedings, 93 (January 1967): 70-80.

"Container Revolution." German International (Bonn) 14 (February 1970): 34-38.

Dickinson, William B., Jr. "National Maritime Policy." Editorial Research Reports (September 29, 1965): 701-20.

"Establishment or Expansion of Merchant Marines in Developing Countries." Norwegian Shipping News 24, no. 2 (January 26, 1968): 48-54.

Franco, G. Robert. "The Operating Differential Subsidy in the 1970 Merchant Marine Act." Transportation Journal, Winter 1973, pp. 38-43.

_____. "The Wage Subsidy Index in the Merchant Marine Act of 1970." Journal of Transport Economics and Policy 7, no. 4 (September 1973): 283-90.

"Government May Revamp Its Ship Subsidies Program." Congressional Quarterly Weekly Reports 23 (March 19, 1965): 439-40.

Hutchins, John G. B. "The American Shipping Industry Since 1914." Business History Review 28, no. 2 (June 1954): 105-27.

Kohler, Hettmar R. "Structural Changes in International Shipping; Revolution in Sea Transport Through Container Use?" Inter- economics, May 1966, pp. 11-13.

Krause, Gerhard. "International Shipping, the Freight-Rate Studies of UNCTAD." Intereconomics, April 1967, pp. 97-100.

_____. "Freight Rates and Liner Conferences." Intereconomics, August 1969, pp. 249-52.

Petersen, Kaare. "Trends in Shipping—1945-1970, the Most Momen- tous Quarter Century in the History of Shipping." Norwegian Shipping News 26, no. 10C (June 1970): 25-46.

Rapping, Leonard A. "Overhauling the Nation's Maritime Policy." Challenge 14, no. 4 (March/April 1966): 12-15.

"Ship Subsidies: Persistence and Unity Bring Results." Congressional Quarterly Weekly Reports 29 (March 19, 1971): 623-30.

Stodter, Rolf. "The Future of Shipping." Norwegian Shipping News 25, no. 10C (June 6, 1969): 45-46+.

Sturmey, S. C. "National Shipping Policies." Journal of Industrial Economics 14, no. 1 (November 1965): 14-29.

_____. "Economics and International Liner Services." Journal of Transport Economics and Policy 1, no. 2 (May 1967): 190-203.

Tresselt, Dag. "Shipping and Shipping Policy in Latin America." Norwegian Shipping News 23, no. 22 (November 25, 1967): 1099-1105.

Vambery, Robert G. "The Effects of Subsidies in the United States Shipbuilding Industry." Journal of Transport Economics and Policy 2, no. 1 (January 1968): 79-93.

Zubiaga, Ramon. "Development in Marine Transport in the 20th Century." Norwegian Shipping News 22, no. 4 (February 25, 1966): 137-42.

Maritime Industrial Relations

Buck, P. B. "Technological Change and the Merchant Seaman." International Labor Review 92, no. 4 (October 1965): 298-313.

Goldberg, Joseph P. "Maritime Subsidies and Maritime Labor Relations." Industrial Relations Research Association Proceedings, 1955, pp. 328-41.

_____. "The Effects of the Structure of Collective Bargaining in Selected Industries: The Maritime Industry." Labor Law Journal 21, no. 8 (August 1970): 505-13.

Hohman, Elmo Paul. "Merchant Seamen in the United States, 1937-1952." International Labor Review 67, no. 1 (January 1953): 1-43.

_____. "Maritime Labor Economics as a Determinant of the Structure and Policy of Seamen's Unions." Industrial Relations Research Association Proceedings, 1957, pp. 163-70.

_____. "Labor Problems in the Merchant Marine." Industrial Relations Research Association Proceedings, 1961, pp. 346-53.

_____. "Work and Wages of American Merchant Seamen." Industrial and Labor Relations Review 15, no. 2 (January 1962): 221-29.

Rapping, Leonard A. "The Impact of Atlantic-Gulf Unionism on the Relative Earnings of Unlicensed Merchant Seamen." Industrial and Labor Relations Review 17, no. 1 (October 1963): 75-95.

Raskin, A. H. "Labor's Mutinous Mariners." Atlantic Monthly 214 (November 1964): 72-78.

Taft, Philip. "The Unlicensed Seafaring Unions." Industrial and Labor Relations Review 3, no. 2 (January 1950): 187-212.

Warner, Aaron W. "Technology and the Labor Force in the Offshore Maritime Industry." Industrial Relations Research Association Proceedings, 1965, pp. 139-50.

Marine Technology and General

Benford, Harry. "Engineering Economy in Tanker Design." Society of
Naval Architects and Marine Engineers Transactions 65 (1957):
775-832.

Black, Stanley W., and Russel, R. Robert. "An Alternative Estimate
of Potential GNP." Review of Economics and Statistics 51, no. 1
(February 1969): 70-76.

Datz, I. M. "A Description of the Maritime Administration Mathemat-
ical Simulation of Ship Operation." Society of Naval Architects
and Marine Engineers Transactions 72 (1964): 493-513.

Lewis, Edward V. "Research Toward More Efficient Transportation by
Sea." Society of Naval Architects and Marine Engineers Transactions 69 (1961): 129-76.

GOVERNMENT SOURCES

Booz-Allen Applied Research. Forecast of U. S. Oceanborne Foreign
Trade in Dry Bulk Commodities. P. B. 183, 250. Washington:
U. S. Department of Commerce, National Bureau of Standards,
March 1969.

_____. The National Need for a Dry Bulk Fleet. P. B. 185, 762.
Washington: U. S. Department of Commerce, National Bureau
of Standards, July 1969.

_____. Bulk Carrier Program Technical Requirements. P. B. 185, 763.
Washington: U. S. Department of Commerce, National Bureau of
Standards, Aug. 29, 1969.

Maritime Evaluation Committee. Maritime Resources for Security and
Trade, Final Report. Washington: U. S. Department of Commerce, 1963.

Ruchlin, Hirsch Samuel. Manpower Resources of the U. S. Maritime
Industry: A Definitional and Descriptive Analysis of the Maritime Labor Force. P. B. 178, 727. Washington: U. S. Department of Commerce, 1968.

U. S. Congress. House. Subcommittee on Merchant Marine and Fisheries. Hearings on Maritime Labor Legislation. Part I, 88th Cong.,
1st Sess. Washington: U. S. Government Printing Office, 1963.

U.S. Congress. House. Subcommittee on Merchant Marine and Fisheries. Hearings on Long-Range Maritime Program. 90th Cong., 2nd Sess. Washington: U.S. Government Printing Office, 1968.

_____. Hearings on President's Maritime Program. Part I, 91st Cong., 1st Sess., 1969. Part II, 91st Cong., 2nd Sess., 1970. Washington: U.S. Government Printing Office, 1969, 1970.

U.S. Congress. Senate. Committee on Commerce. Hearings on Settlement of Maritime Interunion Disputes. 88th Cong., 1st Sess. Washington: U.S. Government Printing Office, 1963.

_____. Subcommittee on Merchant Marine and Fisheries. Hearings on U.S. Maritime Policy. 90th Cong., 1st Sess. Washington: U.S. Government Printing Office, 1967.

U.S. Department of Commerce. Annual Report of the Secretary of Commerce. Washington: U.S. Government Printing Office, 1950-71.

_____. Maritime Administration. The Handbook of Merchant Shipping Statistics Through 1958. Washington: U.S. Government Printing Office, 1959.

_____. Seafaring Wage Rates, Atlantic, Gulf, and Pacific Districts for 1960, 1964, 1967, and 1968. Washington: U.S. Government Printing Office, 1961, 1965, 1968, 1969.

_____. Seafaring Guide . . . and Directory of Labor-Management Affiliations, 1969. Washington: U.S. Government Printing Office, 1969.

_____. Bulk Carriers in the World Fleet, Oceangoing Merchant Type Ships of 1000 Gross Tons and over as of December 31, 1968. Report no. MAR-560-38. Washington: U.S. Department of Commerce, 1970.

_____. Merchant Fleets of the World, Oceangoing Steam and Motor Ships of 1000 Gross Tons and over as of December 31, 1969. Report no. MAR-560-20. Washington: U.S. Government Printing Office, 1970.

_____. A Statistical Analysis of the World's Merchant Fleets Showing Age, Size, Speed & Draft by Frequency Groupings as of December 31, 1968. Washington: U.S. Government Printing Office, 1970.

U.S. Department of Commerce. Maritime Administration. Container-ships, as of June 30, 1970. Washington: Maritime Adminis-tration, ca. 1970.

_____. Ships Registered Under the Liberian, Panamanian, and Hon-duran Flags Deemed by the Navy Department to be Under Effec-tive U.S. Control as of December 31, 1969. Washington: Maritime Administration, ca. 1970.

_____. MARAD 1970, Year of Transition. Annual report of the Mari-time Administration for fiscal year 1970. Washington: U.S. Government Printing Office, 1971.

_____. Vessel Inventory Report, United States Flag Dry Cargo and Tanker Fleets 1000 Gross Tons and over as of June 30, 1970. Report no. MAR-560-19. Washington: Maritime Administration, 1971.

U.S. Department of Labor. Bureau of Labor Statistics. Employment Outlook in the Merchant Marine. Bulletin no. 1054. Washing-ton: U.S. Government Printing Office, 1951.

_____. The Earnings and Employment of Seamen on U.S. Flagships. Bulletin no. 1238. Washington: U.S. Government Printing Office, 1958.

_____. Directory of National and International Labor Unions in the United States, 1967. Bulletin no. 1596. Washington: U.S. Government Printing Office, 1968.

U.S. Government Printing Office. U.S. Laws, Statutes, Etc. — The Merchant Marine Act, 1936. Printed for the use of the Senate Commerce Committee, 86th Cong., 2nd Sess. Washington: U.S. Government Printing Office, 1961.

_____. The Merchant Marine Act of 1936, the Shipping Act of 1916, and Related Acts. Printed for the use of the House Committee on Merchant Marine and Fisheries. 91st Cong., 2nd Sess. Washington: U.S. Government Printing Office, 1970.

U.S. Interagency Maritime Task Force. The Merchant Marine in National Defense and Trade: A Policy and a Program. Wash-ington: IMTF, 1965.

222

MISCELLANEOUS SOURCES

American Merchant Marine Institute. Annual Report of the American
Merchant Marine Institute for 1967. New York (?), ca. 1968.

Bureau of National Affairs. Daily Labor Report. 1950-67. Various
issues.

Business Week

February 2, 1952	March 28, 1964
April 18, 1953	May 15, 1965
May 19, 1956	October 2, 1965
December 1, 1956	October 16, 1965
April 20, 1957	November 13, 1965
July 9, 1960	April 29, 1972
November 18, 1961	September 29, 1973
October 5, 1963	November 10, 1973

Congressional Quarterly Weekly Report
   October 31, 1969, pp. 2140, 2164
   November 7, 1969, p. 2205
   February 20, 1970, p. 561
   March 6, 1970, p. 687
   March 31, 1970, p. 735

Labor-Management Maritime Committee. An Analysis of Dual U. S. -
Foreign Flag Shipping Interests (Non-Industrial Carriers), a
Comparison of Vessels, Their Registration and Utilization.
Washington: Labor-Management Maritime Committee, ca. 1970.

National Marine Engineers' Beneficial Association, AFL-CIO. American Marine Engineer. Various issues.

Pacific Maritime Association. Pacific Maritime Association Annual
Report 1970. San Francisco, ca. 1971.

Seafarers' International Union of North America, AFL-CIO. Seafarers'
Log. Various issues.

Union Democracy in Action. Nos. 6, 15, 17, 21, 23, 24.

Traffic World. 1962-72.

Todd Daily Maritime. 1970-72.

UNPUBLISHED SOURCES

Spritzer, Allan David. "Trade Union Sponsored Training in the U.S. Maritime Industry: The Upgrading and Retraining Program of the National Maritime Union." Ph.D. dissertation, Cornell University, 1971.

Uhlinger, Charles William. "The Wages of American Seamen, 1939-1952." Ph.D. dissertation, Fordham University, 1956.

U.S. Department of Commerce, Maritime Administration. Unpublished data on oceanborne foreign trade, manpower, and various other aspects of the shipping industry. 1968-70.

U.S. Department of the Navy, Military Sea Transportation Service. "Financial and Statistical Report, Part 2, Fiscal Year 1969." Washington, 1969.

Warner, Aaron W., and Eichner, Alfred S. "Analysis of Labor-Management Relations in the Off-Shore Operations of the East Coast Maritime Industry." A study prepared for the Maritime Administration of the United States Department of Commerce. 1966. Available at the Columbia University Law Library.

Agency for International Development, 46, 93
Agriculture, Department of, 46, 93, 155
Alcoa, 112
Altman, Ed, 140
America, 129, 204
American Coal Shipping, 121-23
American Committee for Flags of Necessity, 170
American Export-Isbrandtsen Lines, 81, 85, 121, 126, 128, 143, 175
American Federation of Labor (AFL), 107-08, 108-09, 110, 113, 119, 120, 121, 144, 147
AFL-CIO, 120, 121-22, 123, 126, 144, 154, 161; Maritime Committee, 122, 144, 147, 153, 173, 176; Maritime Trades Department, 122, 141, 147, 156; Resolution 217 (1965 convention), 161, 164, 174
AFL Seamen's Union, 109
American Institute of Merchant Shipping, 143, 186, 188
American Maritime Association, 140-41, 147, 153, 158-59, 160, 164, 170, 171-72, 178, 180, 190, 201 (see also, SIU-AMA)
American Merchant Marine Institute, 126, 141, 142-43, 147, 156, 160, 163-64, 169, 171, 173, 201
American Racer, 60
American Radio Association, 121, 154
American Steamship Owners' Association, 142
American Trading and Production, 169

American Tramp Shipowners' Association, 141
American Unsubsidized Lines, 180
Andreae, Joseph, 157
Arcadia Forest, 58-59, 186
Argentina, 72
Associated Maritime Officers, 203, 204
Atlantic Container Lines, 57
Atlantic Forest, 58-59
automation, 55, 64-65

Banks, Harold, 127
Bartlett, E. L., 168
Bath Iron Works, 60
Bermuda, 70
Bloomfield Steamship Co., 129
bonus (war), 111, 113
Boyd, Alan S., 155-56, 162, 163-64, 167, 168-69, 171-73, 174, 175-76, 179, 181, 183-84
Boyd report (see, IMTF report)
Brazil, 72
Bridges, Harry, 105, 107, 108, 110, 115-16
Brotherhood of Marine Engineers, 119-20, 123 (see also, MEBA, District 2)
Brotherhood of Marine Officers, 121-23, 126, 128, 164, 204
Bull Lines, 122
Bureau of the Budget, 155
"buy American" (principle), 41, 187-88, 193, 198, 202

cabotage, 2, 9, 14, 15, 19, 21, 49, 56, 77, 94, 95, 96, 97-98
California, 106

Cambridge Carriers, 128-29
Canada, 116, 127
Canadian Maritime Union, 116,
  127
capital construction funds, 193-94
capital reserve funds, 42, 45,
  178-79 (see also, reserve funds)
cargo preference, 2, 7-8, 14, 18,
  19, 21, 46, 47, 77, 89, 91-92,
  93, 96, 97, 98, 138, 148, 154,
  156-57, 158, 159, 160-61, 164,
  165, 169, 170, 176-77, 178,
  185, 189, 191, 206, 209
Cefor Cargo Ships, 79
Central Gulf, 136, 186
Cities Service (Tanker Corp.), 117,
  141, 142
Clark, Earl W., 144
Cole, David L., 120, 126
collective bargaining costs, 185,
  200
Columbia S. S. Co., 180
Commerce, Department of, 153,
  154, 155, 167, 171, 183-84
Commission on American Shipbuilding, 185, 188-89
Committee of American Steamship
  Lines (CASL), 10, 143, 145,
  147, 156, 163-64, 169, 170,
  175, 176 (see also, NMU-
  CASL)
Committee of American Tanker
  Owners, 141, 170, 171, 178
Committee for Maritime Unity, 115
communist, 105-07, 108, 109,
  111, 114, 115-16, 122, 127
Competitive Merchant Ship, Project
  (CMX), 57, 60, 63-64, 187
conference (shipping), 12-13, 29,
  46; rates, 160, 170, 177
Congress of Industrial Organiza-
  tions (CIO), 108, 109, 110,
  113, 115, 116, 119, 120-21,
  122, 144, 147 (see also,
  AFL-CIO)
Connor, John T., 201
construction amortization plan, 179

construction-differential subsidy,
  37, 41-42, 43, 78, 85, 87-88,
  89, 90-91, 153-54, 156,
  159-60, 164, 177, 178, 180,
  186, 188, 189, 193, 197-98,
  202, 207
containerization, 12, 28, 54,
  56-60, 61, 63-64, 71, 79,
  81, 83, 84, 90, 95, 98, 124,
  136, 174, 176-77, 180, 185,
  205
Council of Economic Advisers,
  155
Cuba, 128
Cuban missile crisis, 71
Cunard Line, 57
Curran, Joseph, 106, 108, 115,
  119-20, 122, 126-27, 128,
  144, 153, 161, 169, 174,
  186

declaration of policy, 78
Defense, Department of, 47,
  155, 177
Delta Lines, 124, 129
"double subsidy," 91, 177, 191,
  194
Downing, Thomas N., 180
Eastern and Gulf Sailors'
  Association, 108
effective United States control,
  16, 70
Executive Order 10988, 127
Export-Import Bank, 47, 89

Federal Communications Com-
  mission, 162, 167
Federal Maritime Commission,
  85, 155
Federal Ship Mortgage and Loan
  Insurance, 42, 43, 179, 208
FIRST Plan, 179-80
flags of convenience, 10, 55,
  69-70, 139, 170
Floridian, 203
France, 188
French Line, 57

Garmatz, Edward A., 162, 173-74, 175, 178, 184
Gatx/Boothe Corp., 190
General Agency Agreement, 205
general strike (1934), 105
Germany, 53, 84, 111; East, 71; West, 64
Gibson, Andrew E., 183-84, 189, 190
Gleason, Thomas W., 154-55
Grace Lines, 128, 184
"grandfather rights," 190-191
Great Lakes, 3, 123-24, 127
Greece, 55
Green, William, 109
grievance committee, 155
Gulick, James W., 162, 183

Haddock, Hoyt, 144
Hall, Paul, 116, 120, 122, 124, 126, 127, 141, 144, 145, 153, 154, 180, 186
Harrison, Max, 277
hiring hall, 3, 38, 103-04, 105, 112, 117, 119, 135, 201
Holland, 84
Holland America Line, 57
Honduras, 70
"hot cargo," 107
House Subcommittee on Merchant Marine and Fisheries, 31, 162, 175, 184
Hudson Waterways, 79, 169
Humble Oil Co., 157

Independent Owners of American-Flag C-type Vessels, Victories and Liberties, 141
Interagency Maritime Task Force (IMTF report), 22, 67-68, 155-63, 167-68, 172, 174, 175, 179
Intercoastal Shipping Act, 49
International Longshoremen's Association (ILA), 109, 110, 154-55, 203, 204

International Longshoremen's and Warehousemen's Union (ILWU), 106, 107, 110-11, 115, 116
International Seamen's Union (ISU), 105, 107, 108-09, 110
ISU Pilot, 106
Industrial Workers of the World, 105, 106, 113
Interstate Commerce Act, 49
Interstate Commerce Commission, 49
Isbrandtsen Lines, 119, 126, 142
Isthmian Line, 115, 116-17, 119, 124, 179-80, 190

Japan, 7, 10, 53, 55, 60, 70-71, 79, 84, 85, 97, 162, 186, 192
"job action," 105, 106-07, 109
Johnson, Lyndon B., 2, 98, 155, 162, 168, 173; administration, 155, 158, 162, 167-68, 171, 172-73, 175-76, 180-81, 183, 193
Johnson, Nicholas, 153, 155-56, 162-63, 167, 183-84, 200
Johnson, Piero, 128
Joint Committee for Maritime Industry, 140
Joint Maritime Labor Committee, 154, 156

Kahn, Joseph, 178
Kennedy, John F., 126-27, 154
King, Jerome, 108
Korean conflict, 104, 133, 208
Kuwait, 62

Labor, Department of, 112, 155
Labor-Management Maritime Committee, 143-44, 147, 157, 158, 173, 174, 176
Lapham, Lewis A., 157

Latin America, 72
Latin American Free Trade Area, 72-73
Lewis, John L., 121-22
Liberia, 6-7, 10-11, 16, 69-70, 157
Lighter Aboard Ship (LASH), 58-59, 65, 186
Lloyd Brasiliero and Netumar, 72
Lundeberg, Harry, 105, 106-07, 109, 110, 116
Lykes Bros., 12

McLean, Malcolm, 56
Magnuson, Warren G., 173-74, 175, 178
Malone, Vincent J., 110
Malott, Deane W., 157
Manhattan, 96
Manhattan Tankers (Seatrain), 79
Marine Cooks and Stewards, 116, 120, 124, 144
Marine Engineers' Beneficial Association (MEBA), 119-20, 121-26, 128-29, 135, 140, 154, 163, 164, 173-74, 201, 203-04
MEBA, District 2, 123-24, 126, 163, 164, 203, 204 (see also, Brotherhood of Marine Engineers)
Marine Firemen, Oilers, Watertenders and Wipers, 107, 110
Marine Firemen's Union, 108, 120, 124, 144
Marine Navigation Co., 157
Marine Transport Workers, 106
Marine Workers' International Union, 105-06
Mariner (Program), 81, 87, 136, 206-07
Maritime Administration, 41-42, 45-46, 47, 60, 63, 64, 70, 78, 81, 96-97, 154, 155-56, 157, 158, 162-63, 167, 171-72, 175, 176-77, 179, 183-84, 186, 187, 190, 207
Maritime Advisory Committee, 154, 155-57, 161-62, 164, 172, 174

Maritime Commission, 41-42, 49, 111-12
Maritime Committee (see AFL-CIO)
Maritime Evaluation Committee, 153
Maritime Federation of the Pacific, 105, 107
Maritime Labor Council, 109
Maritime Labor Relations Organization (of the WSA), 112
Maritime Overseas, 169
Maritime Service Committee, 142
Maritime Subsidy Board, 124, 131, 177, 187-88, 191, 200, 202; Docket no. S-244, 191
Maritime Trades Department (see AFL-CIO)
Maritime War Emergency Board, 113
Maskin, Alfred, 140
Masters, Mates and Pilots, International Organization of, 120, 121-23, 126, 128, 135, 163, 164, 174, 201, 203, 204
Matson Navigation, 15, 56, 79, 84, 85, 89, 95, 145, 147, 175, 179, 192
Max Harrison Group, 140
Maximus, 128-29
Meany, George, 121, 128
Merchant Marine Act of 1920, 33, 35, 49
Merchant Marine Act of 1928, 33, 35
Merchant Marine Act of 1936, 8, 18, 22, 33, 35, 37, 38, 39, 41, 42, 43, 46, 78, 84, 87, 89, 92, 184, 190
Merchant Marine Act of 1970, 1, 3, 4, 14, 21, 139, 143, 185, 190, 193, 197, 200, 202, 207, 208
Military Sea Transport Service, 14, 47, 96, 117, 127, 144
Military Sea Transport Union (SIU), 127

Military Sealift Command (see
    Military Sea Transport Service)
Moore MacCormack Lines, 120,
    141

National Committee for Maritime
    Bargaining, 126, 139-40, 147
National Defense Mediation Board,
    112
National Defense Reserve Fleet,
    7, 50, 136, 205, 208
National Industrial Recovery Act,
    105
National Labor Relations Board,
    108, 120, 122, 126, 139
National Marine Engineers' Bene-
    ficial Association (see Marine
    Engineers' Beneficial Associ-
    ation)
National Maritime Union (NMU),
    106, 108-29, 135-39, 141-45,
    147-49, 158, 161, 163, 164,
    170-71, 173-74, 180, 188,
    204
NMU-CASL, 147-48, 164-65, 170-
    71, 174, 176, 178, 179, 180,
    185, 186, 188, 190, 192, 193
NMU Pilot, 108
National Union of Marine Cooks
    and Stewards, 107, 111, 116,
    120
National War Labor Board, 113
Nazi-Soviet nonaggression pact,
    111
Neurohr, Louis, 129
Neutrality Laws, 35
Nixon, Richard M., 183-84, 193;
    administration, 183-84, 186,
    188, 191, 193-197, 199-200;
    proposal, 184, 186-87, 188-89,
    190, 191, 193, 197, 202
Norway, 6, 7, 10, 55, 106

Oceanic Steamship Co., 145
operating differential subsidy, 37,
    41, 42, 45-46, 78, 87-88, 89,
    90-91, 157, 177, 184-85, 189,
    193, 197, 198-99, 200, 201

Otto Hahn, 64

Pacific American Steam Ship
    Association, 143
Pacific Far East Lines, 75
Pacific Maritime Association,
    143-44, 146, 201
Pan Atlantic Steamship Co., 56
Panama, 6, 10, 16, 70; Canal,
    61; Canal Act, 31
Panlibhon, 70
Perkins, Frances, 106
preference cargo (see cargo
    preference)
Prudential Lines, 186
Public Law no. 480, 46, 89
Public Law no. 664, 46, 89
Public Resolution no. 17, 46, 50

Radio Officers' Union, 121
Rank and File NMU Pilot, 108
R. J. Reynolds Industries, 84
reconstruction-differential sub-
    sidy, 84, 89-90, 176-77
Reconstruction Finance Corpora-
    tion, 46
Recruitment and Manning Organi-
    zation (of the WSA), 112-13
replacement program (see ship
    replacement program)
reserve funds, 171, 175, 178-79,
    189, 192, 197 (see also,
    capital reserve funds, capital
    construction funds, and
    special reserve funds)
Resolution 217 (AFL-CIO con-
    vention, 1965), 161, 164,
    174
Robin Lines, 120
Ryan, Joseph, 109

Sabine Towing and Transpor-
    tation, 169
Sailors' Union of the Pacific,
    105, 106-07, 109, 110-11,
    112, 113, 116, 124, 140-45,
    147
Saint Lawrence Seaway, 123

Santa Monica, 128
Savannah, 64, 127-28
Sea-Bee, 58
Seafarers' International Union (SIU),
    109-11, 113-14, 115-20, 122-
    124, 126-27, 129, 135, 136-
    42, 143-44, 145, 147-49, 154-
    56, 159-60, 164, 170, 171,
    173, 180, 188-89, 190, 200,
    203-04; SIU, A & G, 109, 113,
    116; SIU of Canada, 115, 127;
    SIU, NA, 109, 113, 116,
    144-45 (see also, SIU-AMA)
SIU-AMA, 141, 147-48, 158, 159-
    61, 163, 164, 167-74, 176-78,
    180, 185, 186, 188-91, 192,
    194, 208
Sea-Land Service, 12, 56, 81, 83,
    84-85, 91, 94, 171, 174, 192,
    201, 203
Seatrain Lines, 79-80, 89, 94-95,
    178, 203
Senate Commerce Committee, 131,
    168, 175, 184
Shipbuilders' Council of America,
    148, 154, 188
Shipbuilding Commission, 185,
    188-89
Ship Exchange Act (see Vessel
    Exchange Act)
Ship Registry Act of 1914, 31
ship replacement program, 81, 126,
    133, 183, 204-05, 206
Ship Sales Act of 1946, 53, 81
Shipping Act of 1916, 97
Shipping Board, 33, 49
special reserve funds, 42, 45, 178
    (see also, reserve funds)
Standard Oil of California, 145
Stans, Maurice H., 184
State, Department of, 155
Statement of Principles, 112
States Marine Lines, 128, 141,
    142, 180, 190
Suez Canal, 62-63, 69, 71
Swedish America Line, 57
Swedish Transatlantic Line, 57

Taft-Hartley Act, 122
Tamara Guilden, 93
Tanker Service Committee, 142,
    201
Trade-In and Build Program, 97
Trade-Out and Build Program, 97,
    158, 159
Transeastern (Seatrain), 79
Transportation Act of 1940, 49
Transportation, Department of,
    163, 167, 171-72, 179, 183
Treasury Department, 42
Trowbridge, Alexander B., 168

USSR, 7, 71, 111, 114, 127,
    154-55
United Fruit Co., 121
United Mine Workers, 121;
    District 50, 121, 122
United Nations Conference on
    Trade and Development, 72
United States, 66
United States Lines, 12, 57, 81,
    84, 192
United States Navy, 70, 112,
    117
Upper Lakes Shipping, 127
Uruguay, 72

Venezuela, 170
Vessel Exchange Act, 98, 136,
    158-59, 172, 180, 205
Vietnam (war), 98, 104, 124,
    136, 172, 180, 205, 208
Volpe, John A., 183

wage-subsidy index, 200
Wallenius Line, 57
Walter Kidde Co., 84
War Labor Board, 112
War Shipping Administration,
    112-13, 114
Waterman Steamship Co., 180,
    190
Western Hemisphere Oil Corp.,
    145
White, H. Lee, 157

Wilson-Weeks Agreement, 177
Wirtz, Willard, 127
Wobblies, 106, 109
World War I, 1, 2, 31-32, 33, 36,
    53, 153

World War II, 1, 28, 32, 33, 35,
    47, 53, 59, 60, 62, 64, 66,
    71, 81, 83, 87, 92, 94, 98,
    104, 111, 112, 113, 114, 121,
    124, 133, 136, 157, 158-59,
    172, 198, 202, 207, 208

JOHN G. KILGOUR is assistant professor of management sciences at California State University, Hayward. He teaches mainly in the area of labor-management relations.

After serving three years in the U.S. Navy, Dr. Kilgour began shipping out of East and Gulf Coast ports in 1959 as a member of the Seafarers' International Union of North America. In 1960 he earned a marine engineer's license and joined the Marine Engineers' Beneficial Association. He sailed full-time for various companies until 1962 and part-time thereafter through 1968.

The author has published articles in Industrial and Labor Relations Review and Journal of Maritime Law and Commerce.

Dr. Kilgour received the B.A. in economics from the University of Connecticut in 1966 and the Master of Industrial and Labor Relations degree from Cornell University in 1968. Following a year as assistant industrial relations manager with Container Corporation of America, he returned to Cornell for the Ph.D., which he received in 1972.

RELATED TITLES

Published by

Praeger Special Studies

THE FUTURE OF THE U. S. SPACE PROGRAM
Arthur L. Levine

MANAGEMENT OF TRANSPORTATION CARRIERS
Grant M. Davis, Martin T. Farris,
and Jack J. Holder, Jr.

MASS TRANSIT AND THE POLITICS OF
TECHNOLOGY: A Study of BART and the
San Francisco Bay Area
Stephen Zwerling

RATE BUREAUS AND ANTI-TRUST CONFLICTS IN
TRANSPORTATION: Public Policy Issues
Grant M. Davis and Charles S. Sherwood